Workplace Abuse, Incivility and Bullying

This book bridges an existing gap in the literature relating to the study of workplace abuse, incivility and bullying. It provides broad perspectives to capture some of the diversity associated with the study of (negative) human behaviours using different methodological approaches and in different cultural contexts. Studies in the area have grown leaps and bounds in the last few decades. As we come to know more about the nature of these adverse behaviours, the reasons they happen, and the impact they have on individuals and beyond, new gaps in knowledge emerge. On one hand the growing body of research is assisting in better understanding and managing these negative behaviours, on another, generalised information without an appreciation of the context in which the behaviours unfold may be detrimental to the cause, especially given a globalised and multicultural world.

Workplace Abuse, Incivility and Bullying presents findings from under-researched methodological and unique cultural perspectives. Such an approach will allow us to gain deep insights into the diversity and complexities associated with perceiving, being subjected to and experiencing negative behaviours at work. The book has applicability across a broad range of audience, from academics through to practitioners, and even victims and suspected perpetrators.

Maryam Omari is Associate Professor in the School of Business in the Faculty of Business and Law, Edith Cowan University. Her research interests lie in dignity and respect at work, cross-cultural management, quality of work-life issues and parallels between behaviours of animals in the natural world and those of humans at work.

Megan Paull is a co-director of the Centre for Responsible Citizenship and Sustainability, Director of Postgraduate Research and a Senior Lecturer in the School of Management and Governance at Murdoch University. Her research interests are in the areas of volunteering and nonprofit organisations, bullying and organisational behaviour and learning and teaching in higher education.

Workplace Abuse, Incivility and Bullying

Methodological and cultural perspectives

Edited by Maryam Omari
and Megan Paull

LONDON AND NEW YORK

First published 2016 by Routledge

2 Park Square, Milton Park, Abingdon, Oxfordshire OX14 4RN
711 Third Avenue, New York, NY 10017

*Routledge is an imprint of the Taylor & Francis Group,
an informa business*

First issued in paperback 2018

British Library Cataloguing in Publication Data
A catalogue record for this book is available from the British Library

Library of Congress Cataloging-in-Publication Data
Workplace abuse, incivility and bullying : methodological and
   cultural perspectives / edited by Maryam Omari and Megan
Paull. — 1 Edition.
      pages cm
 1. Bullying in the workplace.   I. Omari, Maryam, editor.
II. Paull, Megan, editor.
   HF5549.5.E43W666 2015
   650—dc23
   2015019522

ISBN: 978-1-138-82580-2 (hbk)
ISBN: 978-1-138-31695-9 (pbk)

Typeset in Galliard
by Apex CoVantage, LLC

I would like to acknowledge my wonderful parents, family and brother for their unrelenting support and love; I could not have done this without you. Thanks also goes to Tasha for keeping me company and herself warm on the modem while I worked, and Misha who has an inquisitive mind and is always busy.

Maryam Omari

My thanks go to my family, friends and colleagues who always offer love and support. I would like to acknowledge those who willingly share their experiences with researchers, even when it is difficult to do so, and to the chapter authors without whom there would be no book. Thanks also to Maryam for nearly twenty-five years of friendship – something to be treasured.

Megan Paull

Contents

Notes on contributors

Kate Blackwood is a doctoral candidate and member of the Healthy Work Group in the School of Management (Albany) at Massey University, New Zealand. Kate's PhD explores workplace bullying in the New Zealand nursing industry, with the aim of contributing to the understanding of the impact of the work environment on the efficacy of secondary intervention in bullying experiences.

Nikos Bozionelos (PhD Strathyclyde) is Professor of Organizational Behaviour and Human Resource Management at Audencia School of Management in France. His research interests lie in careers, interpersonal interaction in the workplace, high-performance work systems, organizational politics, and international mobility of workers.

Bevan Catley is Associate Professor and member of the Healthy Work Group located within the School of Management (Albany) at Massey University, New Zealand. Bevan's primary research focus has been on workplace bullying and workplace violence, and he has been involved in some of the first large scale research projects to investigate these problems in the New Zealand context.

Premilla D'Cruz, PhD, is a Professor in the Organisational Behaviour Area at the Indian Institute of Management Ahmedabad, India. Her research interests include workplace bullying, emotions in organisations, self and identity at work, information and communication technologies (ICTs), and organisations and collectivisation. She is currently Secretary of the International Association on Workplace Bullying and Harassment (IAWBH).

Darryl Forsyth is a Senior Lecturer and member of the Healthy Work Group located within the School of Management (Albany) at Massey University, New Zealand. Darryl's research foci include workplace bullying, workplace violence, information overload, and more general industrial psychology topics.

Antonia Girardi is an Associate Professor in the School of Management and Governance at Murdoch University in Western Australia. Her research interests are in the areas of management education and people management. She teaches introductory research methods for undergraduate and postgraduate students. Antonia is a past competitive ballroom dancer and has represented her state in national competition.

Burcu Guneri-Cangarli is an Associate Professor in Management at the Faculty of Business, Izmir University of Economics. She received her PhD in 2009 with a thesis entitled "Bullying Behaviours as Organisational Politics". Her research interests lie in workplace bullying, cross-cultural management, power, organisational politics, and leadership. On these topics, she has published many book chapters and articles in reputable international journals.

Petr Květon is a Researcher at the Institute of Psychology of the Czech Academy of Sciences in Brno, Czech Republic. His research interests lie in the area of quantitative research methodology, psychological testing, and methods of statistical analysis.

Jennifer (M.I.) Loh is a Senior Lecturer at the School of Psychology and Social Science at Edith Cowan University. She is a fully registered psychologist with the Australian Health Practitioner Regulation Agency (AHPRA). Her research interests lie in Organisational Psychology, especially in the dark side of organisational behaviour. She is also interested in Health Psychology (Resilience) and Cross Cultural Management.

Efrat Salton Meyer is a lecturer at the School of Behavioral sciences at the College of Management in Israel. Her research interests lie in leadership, power and motivation in organisations as well as heuristics and information processing styles. Her work as an organisational consultant focuses on growth, change, and development in workplaces at the individual, team, and corporate levels.

Mario Mikulincer is a Professor of Psychology at the School of Psychology at Interdisciplinary Center (IDC) Herzliya in Israel. His research interests lie in attachment theory and research and ways of coping with trauma and stress.

Maryam Omari is an Associate Professor at the School of Business at Edith Cowan University in Western Australia. Her research interests lie in: dignity and respect at work, human resource management, cross-cultural management, quality of work-life issues, and parallels between behaviours of animals in the natural world and those of humans at work.

Megan Paull is a senior lecturer and Director of Graduate Research in the School of Management and Governance at Murdoch University in Western Australia. Her research interests include organisational misbehaviour, bullying, and nonprofit organisations. She teaches qualitative research methods to postgraduate students and is a Director of the Centre for Responsible Citizenship and Sustainability.

Irena Pilch is an Associate Professor of Psychology at the University of Silesia, Poland. Her main research interests focus on unethical and socially aversive personality traits and behaviours. She has published a book, a number of journal articles, book chapters, and presented at conferences in the fields of organisational, political, and personality psychology.

Al-Karim Samnani is an Assistant Professor at the Odette School of Business at the University of Windsor in Canada. His research interests lie in victimization and bullying in the workplace, human resource practices, and diversity in the workplace. His research has been published in leading management journals including *Organizational Psychology Review, The Leadership Quarterly, Human Resource Management,* among others.

Manish Sharma is a PhD scholar at the School of Business, Faculty of Business and Law at the Edith Cowan University, Australia. His research interests lie in workplace bullying, workplace and cross-cultural issues, and working environments in Australian academia.

David Tappin is a Senior Lecturer and member of the Healthy Work Group located within the School of Management (Albany) at Massey University, New Zealand. His research interests include: work health and safety culture, contextual factors for musculoskeletal disorders, workplace bullying, and other influences on the design of healthy work.

Elżbieta Turska is an Associate Professor of Psychology at the University of Silesia, Poland. Her research interests are related to humans' professional activity, changes in the career model, and the adverse effects of work. She has authored a number of books and articles concerning industrial and organisational psychology. She is a founding member of the Polish Association of Organisational Psychology.

Kateřina Zábrodská is a Researcher at the Institute of Psychology of the Czech Academy of Sciences in Prague, Czech Republic. Her research interests lie in the intersection of workplace bullying and organizational behaviour, qualitative methodology, and discourse studies.

Abbreviations

BRIC	Brazil, Russia, India and China
CEE	Central and Eastern European
CIA	Central Intelligence Agency
EE	Eastern European
EU	European Union
GDP	Gross Domestic Product
GLOBE	Global Leadership and Organizational Behavior Effectiveness
IT	Information Technology
ITES-BPO	Information Technology Enabled Services-Business Process Outsourcing
MNC	Multinational Corporation
NAQ	Negative Acts Questionnaire
NAQ-R	Negative Acts Questionnaire-Revised
NATO	North Atlantic Treaty Organization
OECD	Organisation for Economic Co-operation and Development
SME	Small and Medium Sized Enterprises
US$	United States Dollar
USA	United States of America
WWI/II	World War I/II

1 Setting the scene

Workplace abuse, incivility and bullying – methodological and cultural perspectives

Maryam Omari and Megan Paull

Introduction

The main aim of this book is to bridge a gap in the literature relating to workplace abuse, incivility and bullying. The number of studies relating to inappropriate and negative workplace behaviours has grown in leaps and bounds over the last decade. As the knowledge base relating to the nature of these adverse behaviours, the reasons they happen, and the impact they have on individuals, organisations and society grows, new gaps in knowledge are exposed. On one hand, growth in research is assisting in better understanding and management of these behaviours; on the other, generalised information without an understanding of context may be detrimental to the cause, especially given a globalised and multicultural world.

It is well recognised that the genesis of research on workplace bullying is attributed to Leymann and his work in Scandinavia/Northern Europe during late last century. In the years since his seminal works were published, researchers from different disciplinary bases (see D'Cruz this volume), paradigmatic and methodological perspectives (see Samnani this volume), and cultural backgrounds (see Meyer and Mikulincer this volume) have made valuable contributions to the field. This has further enriched the literature, and has been able to, and continues to, identify new perspectives on research and practice.

This book takes a unique perspective in that it has a focus on negative workplace behaviours by many names: abuse, incivility, bullying, mobbing, victimisation, unkind behaviours (see Pilch and Turska this volume), "forcing" (see Bozionelos this volume), and others. The reason this approach was adopted was to broaden the scope of the work, to be more inclusive, and to lay the groundwork for wider discussion and debate.

The aim is not to provide a definitive stance, but rather, to provide broad perspectives to capture some of the diversity associated with the study of (negative) human behaviour using different methodological approaches, in different cultural and professional (see Zábrodská and Květon this volume) contexts. The authors of each of the chapters have chosen a focus area and methodological approach based on what is accepted and prevalent in the cultural contexts of their home nations. Many of the chapters focus on under researched, seemingly homogenous (see Guneri-Cangarli this volume) or multicultural (see Loh this volume) settings. This allows deeper insights into the diversity and complexities associated with perceiving, experiencing and addressing negative behaviours at work in different contexts.

Contextual issues

Definitions of workplace abuse, incivility and bullying abound. Some share common elements including the notions of power imbalance, persistent behaviour and threats to health and safety. Power, for example, is not static and has different meanings in different cultural settings (see Omari and Sharma this volume). In Hofstede's well-known cultural framework, different countries are positioned on a continuum between high and low on the power distance dimension, therefore expectations of appropriate behaviours in different global and multicultural settings may not be the same. The same behaviour may be perceived, construed, experienced, measured and interpreted in different ways.

Methodological issues have also been the subject of debate and discussion in the relevant literature. Much of the existing knowledge on the area has been derived from experimental designs in line with the positivist paradigm, and therefore quantitative in nature (see Paull and Girardi this volume). It is, however, well accepted that negative behaviours are subjective and interpreted through an 'eye of the beholder' perspective (see Omari and Sharma this volume). Different methodological approaches to the study of these negative behaviours can therefore only add richness and depth to the body of knowledge.

Negative behaviours, and the tolerance thereof, are also influenced by a context wider than just national or ethnic culture. In a globalised workplace, organisations not only compete within national boundaries but also internationally. Significant developments in the global arena, such as the Global Financial Crisis (GFC), have wide reaching implications, not only in a financial sense, but also with respect to staffing levels and work intensification. As economies struggle and competition intensifies, more and more organisations are asking their staff to 'do more with less'. In this context, processes are streamlined and jobs become scarce. This in turn creates environments where staff are placed under significant pressure to perform. These settings can, and do, result in a recalibration of what may be considered appropriate workplace behaviours. That is, in a competitive globalised world (see Samnani this volume), as external job opportunities remain static or decline, and the ability to leave and quickly find alternative employment is reduced, the threshold for negative workplace behaviours rises, in turn imprinting new norms into the very fabric and culture of an organisation or profession (Omari and Paull 2013). This can create situations where negative behaviours, including abuse, incivility and bullying become ingrained and tacitly accepted in workplace interactions.

The layout of this book

The main aim of this book was to bring different perspectives, methodological and cultural, to the study of workplace abuse, incivility and bullying. Influenced by Gannon and Pillai (2013), and their approach using metaphors to capture the essence of different countries and clusters of countries, the authors of each of the chapters in this book also used unique and culture specific descriptors (see Catley, Blackwood, Forsyth and Tappin this volume). The book is divided into two main sections: methodology and context, and country specific chapters, bookended by this chapter to set the scene and provide a preamble, and the final chapter bringing together implications for research and practice.

The following is a summary of each chapter:

Paradigmatic and methodological approaches

This chapter discusses the value of multiple perspectives and approaches to the study of negative behaviours at work. It provides detailed and relevant information on different paradigmatic approaches, and provides examples of how alternate methodological perspectives can be useful, and at times necessary, in understanding workplace abuse, incivility, bullying or similar behaviours.

Floorcraft: researching subjective phenomena

Practical considerations in researching the subjective phenomena of workplace abuse, incivility and bullying are the focus of this chapter. Within a context that considers organisational and cross-cultural perspectives, the discussion encourages the researcher to engage in 'floorcraft' to choreograph and perform quality research.

In the eye of the beholder: ethnic culture as a lens

Culture can be described as a lens through which different behaviours are observed, interpreted and experienced. The same behaviour may not have the same meaning in different cultural settings; interpreted through the 'eye of the beholder'. This chapter discusses culture, diversity and ethnocentrism, and brings together, compares, and contrasts, various frameworks for classifying culture to set a frame of reference for the country specific chapters.

India: a paradoxical context for workplace bullying

India's geography, history and sociocultural dynamics are complex and diverse. This chapter brings together the extant literature on workplace bullying in India, reporting on the perspectives of victim and bystander, and discussing organisational responses and legal provisions. It considers the tensions associated with recognising and addressing workplace bullying, while at the same time overlooking and denying what transpires.

Turkey: east of West, west of East

Studies report that the prevalence of workplace bullying in Turkey is higher than many other European countries at 40 per cent, with the country's culture and behavioural norms all thought to be contributing. This chapter examines workplace bullying in Turkey in relation to its legal, cultural and socio-economic characteristics. It provides insights to support the development and application of country specific prevention, and intervention strategies.

Greece: incivility, bullying and forcing in the land of bullying gods and lesser mortals

The only known study of workplace bullying in Greece reports rates similar to those of other European countries. The discussion of the context and culture of Greece, however, provides unique insights and points to the possibility of a higher prevalence of the behaviour. This chapter also introduces the notion of 'forcing' – signifying situations where individuals are forced by others to perform tasks and activities that are contained in others' work roles.

Poland: one nation, one religion – tradition and change

Research on workplace bullying/mobbing in Poland is relatively new with mixed results and findings. This chapter provides a snapshot of the small amount of existing research, the legislative frameworks, and preventative measures applied in Poland in the context of Polish history and national culture. The chapter calls for country specific research on organisational causes and consequences of bullying in Poland as a prelude to introducing policies and procedures to manage *mobbing*.

Czech Republic: workplace abuse in a post-transitional country

This chapter discusses workplace abuse in the Czech Republic: a nation in transition. The work environment in the country is described as being shaped by the legacy of the communist era, as well as the recent expansion of neoliberalism. Using their own research into workplace bullying in Czech academia as a case study, the authors explore how these forces intersect with the country's cultural profile.

Merlion: the influence of Singapore's cosmopolitan culture on workplace incivility

The focus of this chapter is on workplace incivility, identifying a dearth of research on this topic in Eastern countries such as Singapore. It considers the relationship of culture to workplace incivility through exploration of the country's profile and cultural features. Findings to date suggest that workplace incivility is accepted in Singapore, in part due to cultural influences.

Israel: a land of contrasts – the contribution of attachment orientations, gender and ethical climate in the workplace to abusive supervision

This chapter focuses on abusive supervision in Israel. It depicts characteristics of Israeli life and culture, focusing on values and norms relevant to the workplace. Reference is made to the contribution of attachment orientations, gender and ethical climate to abusive supervision in a mental healthcare organisation. Specific discussions relate to intrapersonal, interpersonal and organisational level interactions in the context of the country's culture and values.

Workplace bullying in New Zealand: 'she'll be right?'

The poor performance of New Zealand's health and safety system has been directly attributed to cultural values. This chapter explores the dynamics of workplace bullying and suggests the ways in which aspects of national cultural values may be contributing to the prevalence of the problem. It argues that a positive slant on the 'she'll be right' attitude has served New Zealanders well in a number of contexts, but not necessarily for health and safety.

Australia: the 'fair go' multicultural continent nation

Workplaces in Australia are multicultural, characterised by diverse value systems, providing different lenses through which interpersonal interactions are experienced, perceived and interpreted. Australians pride themselves on a 'fair go' for all, while at the same time not necessarily always welcoming diversity or new migrants. This chapter discusses inherent abuse, incivility and bullying issues in Australian workplaces.

Workplace abuse, incivility and bullying: the challenge of translational research

The challenges of translational research are never more evident than when a sensitive topic is the focus, such as in this book. This concluding chapter reviews and identifies key common themes examined by the contributors such as lack of consensus on definitions, the influence of history and the role of difference, and considers both future research and the challenge of translation into practice.

Towards dignity and respect at work

Many, and varied, labels have been used to describe negative and inappropriate workplace behaviours, with power, persistence and harm to the victim central to most. Some of these labels are used interchangeably in different countries as can be seen from the chapters in this book, while others provide insights into the level of the behaviour, much of which can be considered to be on a continuum ranging from being 'unkind' and low level 'bad' behaviour, or incivility, through to victimisation, abuse, 'psychological warfare' (Omari 2007), and ultimately violence. On one hand it is necessary to have clarity in labels and for definitions; on the other, this can be somewhat limiting, especially where policies and legislation are in place which result in definitional tests not being strictly met. In such situations, targets and victims may nevertheless experience adverse consequences and suffer but with no procedural or legal recourse.

The purpose of this book is not to polarise opinions or establish what is 'good or bad', rather to unearth how deep rooted beliefs and traditions shape behaviours in particular settings. There is subjectivity associated with the interpretation of negative behaviours, varying thresholds for the behaviours, and different notions of what is deemed as 'appropriate' or 'inappropriate' in a particular context. Multi-disciplinary approaches, the use of different methods, cross-cultural studies, multi-source data, and researcher and practitioner perspectives, therefore, only serve to add richness and depth to the study of negative behaviours such as abuse, incivility and bullying at work.

In the search for the ways and means of unearthing knowledge about negative behaviours at work, the parties involved should not lose sight of the end game. That is, striving towards a better society by ensuring harmonious workplace relations, and ultimately maintaining the dignity and respect of employees who spend a considerable amount of their life at work.

References

Gannon, M. J. and Pillai, R., 2013. *Understanding global cultures: Metaphorical journeys through 31 nationals, clusters of nations, continents, and diversity.* 5th ed. Thousand Oaks: Sage.

Omari, M., 2007. *Towards dignity and respect: An exploration of the nature, causes and consequences of workplace bullying.* Saarbrücken: VDM Verlag Dr. Müller.

Omari, M. and Paull, M., 2013. "Shut up and bill": Workplace bullying challenges for the legal profession. *International Journal of the Legal Profession,* 20(2), 141–60.

2 Paradigmatic and methodological approaches

Al-Karim Samnani

Introduction

Various forms of workplace victimisation have been gaining increased attention in recent years. This chapter uses the term 'workplace victimisation' as an umbrella term that encompasses negative social acts in the workplace such as incivility, bullying, abuse, and violence, among others (see Aquino and Thau 2009). Workplace abuse tends to refer to overt forms of aggression, while workplace incivility refers to more subtle acts, and workplace bullying entails repeated negative social acts over some prolonged period (Hershcovis 2011). The term 'workplace victimisation' facilitates a discussion that incorporates these various constructs while avoiding construct proliferation.

While scholars have attempted to research and understand workplace victimisation in its many forms, the epistemological and methodological approaches taken have predominantly been positivist and quantitative. While this has allowed researchers to make inferences about causal relations between workplace victimisation and its potential antecedents and/or outcomes, as well as identifying prevalence rates in various organisations, industries, and countries, these predominant approaches appear to have sacrificed – to some degree – attention devoted to the 'voices' of targets, perpetrators, and witnesses. The following section will discuss and outline methodology, epistemology, and paradigms. The next section outlines how these approaches and perspectives would seek to research and understand workplace victimisation in its many forms. The final section draws upon studies in the literature that can be categorised under each paradigmatic approach to provide examples of application.

Methodology, epistemology, and paradigms

Burrell and Morgan's (1979) framework of paradigms and the associated epistemology and methodology is discussed below. While this typology of paradigms is now over 35 years old, it has nonetheless been referred to as the "dominant paradigm model in organizational analysis" (Brand 2009, p. 434). Moreover, certain revisions have been made to the typology in this chapter, such as the collapsing of 'radical humanism' and 'radical structuralism' into a paradigm referred to as 'critical management theory'. This section begins by discussing methodological approaches to research.

Methodology

Scholars may use one of two dominant approaches, or an approach that combines the two (i.e., mixed methods research), to investigate a phenomenon: quantitative or qualitative. Quantitative research involves the use of statistical analysis to address the research question. For example, the researcher may be interested in identifying which factors lead to workplace victimisation. Alternatively, the researcher may be interested in identifying the consequences associated with workplace victimisation. In other cases, the researcher may simply be interested in identifying the prevalence of victimisation in a particular organisation, industry, or country.

Researchers typically use quantitative research methods when they are focused on generalising the results of a study to a broader population. Often, when researchers find that a certain outcome is associated with workplace victimisation in their study sample, their findings tend to suggest, even if implicitly, that employees who are victimised will tend to experience this outcome. Quantitative research also computes and reveals its findings in aggregate terms: quantitative research uses statistics that incorporates the data associated with each 'respondent' and attempts to identify commonalities across variables (i.e., factors) and the relationship among these variables.

While identifying commonalities among employees who experience a certain phenomenon is certainly a strength of this methodological approach, it also suggests a limitation. Quantitative research can consequently remove the context in which the victimisation occurred. For example, research that reports its data in aggregate values sacrifices description about how the victimisation occurred, why it occurred, when it occurred, where it occurred, and so on within each case. This information tends to be much more difficult to capture with quantitative methods. Moreover, quantitative research may find that, for example, negative affect (i.e., an individual's tendency to experience negative emotions such as sadness, anger, tension, and so on) may be associated with workplace victimisation (Robinson *et al.* 2014). However, it becomes more difficult for quantitative research to identify how and why one's tendency to experience negative emotions can make him/her more susceptible to victimising behaviour from others. While theory is often used to fill these gaps, qualitative research can provide rich detail about the events and context under which victimisation occurred.

Research using a qualitative methodology can take a number of forms such as case studies, ethnographies, and content analyses, but is most commonly conducted using interviews. One of the key goals of qualitative research is to gain rich description of the phenomenon and the context under which it occurred (Gill 2014). Through the use of interviews, researchers ask questions to gather pertinent information about the negative social acts and the events surrounding them. To gain further information, researchers will typically use probing questions to delve deeper into the comments of the interviewee/participant. Research studies using a qualitative methodology will then use interview quotes highlighting the precise words used by the participant, who may be a target, perpetrator, or witness.

Just as quantitative methods use causal relationships to better understand workplace victimisation, qualitative methods through rich descriptions allow the researcher to better understand the phenomenon. A strength of qualitative research when using interviews is that the researcher has the ability to ask questions of the participant that relate to the data provided. In other words, when a researcher gathers quantitative data, he/she is not typically able to immediately ask questions based on specific responses given by participants. When using interviews, however, the researcher has the ability to gain clarification about participant responses and ask further questions that provide further context to the events. Qualitative research also provides the participant with the ability to provide a response that he/she feels is best suited to the question asked, relative to quantitative research in which the respondent must select a point on the scale that he/she feels best describes their experience. Nevertheless, since qualitative research focuses in-depth on the experiences of employees and may often understand each participant as a separate case study with a unique context, the findings for one employee may not be very applicable to others in a broader population who experience similar behaviours.

Ultimately, the discussion above is intended to highlight the strengths of each approach. One way to perhaps maximise the strengths of each approach is to use mixed methods research (Creswell 2013), which combines quantitative and qualitative research. To illustrate, a mixed methods approach might involve quantitative data being gathered, and then qualitative interviews being used to delve deeper into participant responses. Conversely, qualitative data could be gathered first, and then used to construct a survey employing a quantitative approach. Most importantly, both approaches can be used to help better understand the phenomenon of workplace victimisation. To date, there has been far more quantitative research on workplace victimisation than qualitative research (see Aquino and Thau 2009; Samnani and Singh 2012; Schilpzand *et al.* 2014), and thus it is important to further add to this literature with direct accounts from the relevant actors in workplace victimisation to provide a more holistic understanding of the phenomenon.

Epistemology

There are two dominant epistemologies that will be discussed in this sub-section: positivism and anti-positivism. In short, a positivist epistemology suggests that knowledge can be acquired and discovered (Burrell and Morgan 1979). Furthermore, a positivist perspective believes that regularities can be discovered that will help explain phenomena of interest. Given the aims of quantitative research to identify and determine causal relationships between variables, researchers with a positivist epistemology have typically found a strong fit between epistemology and methodological approach.

Nevertheless, qualitative research can also be aligned with a positivist epistemology when researchers seek to discover regularities and seek to generalise their findings to a larger population. Researchers with a positivist epistemology who use qualitative research are more likely to identify commonalities among their participants and report these findings as potential causal relationships. Researchers may also seek to interview a large number of participants to provide a larger dataset from which certain occurrences may be tallied. In such cases, the research question(s) would be phrased in a manner consistent with a positivist epistemology.

Researchers with an anti-positivist epistemology, which suggests that 'truths' and regularities cannot be discovered (Burrell and Morgan 1979), have looked solely towards qualitative methods to address their research questions. An anti-positivist epistemology assumes a subjectivist approach towards events, in which the context is given most significance. An anti-positivist epistemology views the social world as being comprised of meanings, symbols, and social processes (Burrell and Morgan 1979). As such, researchers with an anti-positivist epistemology seek to understand the meanings and values attributed to events by the actors involved in the relevant social processes. Qualitative research is thus better positioned to provide the researcher with rich detail about the social processes involved and description about the meanings that actors attribute to the events of interest. Since *understanding* the events is of most importance to researchers with an anti-positivist epistemology, a method that provides *description* rather than prescription would represent the most consistent approach. Sociological paradigms allow researchers to categorise approaches that contain consistency between epistemology, research question(s), and methodology.

Paradigms

The discussion in this section on paradigms sets up the remainder of the chapter, which provides examples of how each paradigm could be applied to various forms of workplace victimisation. It is important to note that this chapter does not advance any single paradigm to be more 'valuable' or 'correct' than another; rather, it is believed that each paradigm offers certain strengths, and a literature that contains studies from a variety of paradigms can provide a more comprehensive and holistic understanding of a phenomenon. Consistent with Samnani (2013), this chapter discusses four paradigmatic approaches: functionalism, interpretivism, critical management, and postmodernism.

Functionalism represents the pervading paradigmatic approach in the workplace victimisation literature. Functionalism posits an objective approach towards understanding phenomena and is rooted in a positivist epistemology. Functionalism is primarily focused on identifying order and regularity and strives to offer prescriptive and pragmatic details (Burrell and Morgan 1979). Another aspect of functionalism is its fairly deterministic nature (Burrell and Morgan 1979).

Functionalist researchers believe that constructs can be measured, and that the presence of one construct can determine the extent of another construct.

Crucial to interpretivism is its central focus on individual experience and meaning (Burrell and Morgan 1979). The interpretivist paradigm is focused on eliciting rich descriptions of events and understanding the meanings that individuals attribute to their experiences. Moreover, interpretivist research strives to understand participants' interpretations, meanings, and sense-making processes. Hence, it is critical for interpretivist researchers to collect data (in the form of participant quotes and descriptions) from the frame of reference of the individuals directly involved in the event. As such, the interpretivist approach seeks to provide accounts of the ways in which the individuals involved understood the events, made sense of the events, and the meanings they attached to these events.

The critical management theory perspective proposes that the root causes of negative social events such as workplace victimisation go beyond interpersonal relations and issues, and are rather due to broader systemic aspects such as organisational bureaucracy and/or capitalism (Burrell and Morgan 1979). Central to the critical management theory is the notion of power; in particular, issues of power that may stem from notions of authority and bureaucracy result in the dominance of employees and alienate employees from realising their authentic or true self (Vannini and Franzese 2008). Hence, the critical management theory paradigm holds an anti-positivist epistemology and draws upon qualitative research methodologies.

Finally, the postmodernist paradigm believes that there is no single 'truth' that can be discovered; rather, there are multiple 'truths' involved in social processes (Cooper and Burrell 1988). Similar to the interpretivist and critical management theory paradigms, the postmodernist paradigm draws upon an anti-positivist epistemology and qualitative research methodologies. Since there is no single 'truth' (or regularities) that can be discovered according to the postmodernist paradigm, the role of context is given great importance. As discussed earlier, qualitative research methodologies allow researchers to gain rich descriptions of the context surrounding the social processes of interest. Postmodernism is also particularly interested in notions of control, and the ways in which social processes may reflect broader notions of control (Foucault 1977). In the next section, each paradigm will be more closely applied to the broad umbrella term of workplace victimisation.

Paradigms and workplace victimisation

Functionalism and workplace victimisation

There have been a large number of studies stemming from the functionalist paradigm that have investigated various forms of victimisation in the workplace. These studies may be divided into three broad categories: prevalence, antecedents, and outcomes. First, researchers have attempted to determine the rate of prevalence of victimisation in the workplace (e.g., Fox and Stallworth 2005; Lutgen-Sandvik *et al.* 2007; Schat *et al.* 2006). In these studies, researchers have used surveys to identify whether each respondent has experienced one or more negative social acts in their workplace, and tally the number of employees who have experienced these acts. Such estimates, of course, only provide information about the number of employees who report experiencing a negative social act, but do not provide detail on other events or factors surrounding the acts.

Studies that approach workplace victimisation from a functionalist paradigm have also reported that a number of factors may explain the presence of workplace victimisation. To illustrate, researchers have reported that individual personality factors (e.g., Persson *et al.* 2009), leadership types such as laissez-faire leadership (e.g., Skogstad *et al.* 2007), and work role characteristics such as role ambiguity and role conflict (e.g., Agervold and Mikkelsen 2004) can predict an employee's likelihood of experiencing victimisation. Finally, functionalist research has also reported a number of consequences associated with being a target of workplace victimisation. These consequences include both physical and psychological outcomes (e.g., Escartin *et al.* 2009) along with personal and work-related outcomes (e.g., Lutgen-Sandvik *et al.* 2007). State of the science reviews have been done to summarise the findings in the literature (e.g., Aquino and Thau 2009; Samnani and Singh 2012).

These functionalist approaches are important as they can provide some degree of understanding of the factors that lead to workplace victimisation, as well as the consequences it can have for targets. Such research has led to greater attention devoted to the topic of workplace victimisation (Samnani and Singh 2012), which can have positive implications for potential targets when it leads to stricter organisational policies and increased legislation protecting employees at work (Yamada 2004). Moreover, this research has arguably led to further investigations that focus on capturing the voices of targets, which interpretivist and other non-functionalist paradigmatic approaches seek to understand (e.g. Harrington *et al.* 2013; Mavin *et al.* 2014; Vickers 2014; Zábrodská *et al.* 2014).

Interpretivism and workplace victimisation

As mentioned earlier, interpretivism focuses on the meanings that individuals attach to their experiences. Hence, researchers approaching workplace victimisation from an interpretivist paradigm would seek to understand the meanings that targets or perpetrators attached to their experiences of victimisation. For example, targets may be asked about how they made sense of their experiences of being victimised, how they interpreted and understood the negative social acts that they were exposed to, and what these experiences meant to them. Likewise, perpetrators may be asked about how they interpreted the negative social acts directed toward the target, how they made sense of their own 'victimising' behaviours, and the meanings that they attached to these acts. While there has been research investigating targets' accounts, there has been scant attention toward perpetrators (and also witness/observer accounts).

Along with understanding the meanings and interpretations that targets, perpetrators, and/or witnesses attach to their experiences of workplace victimisation, interpretivist approaches are also particularly interested in gaining rich descriptions of the context surrounding the events. A number of qualitative research methods can be useful in identifying these contextual elements. For example, researchers may use diary studies. Through diary studies, participants note their feelings, interpretations, and experiences on a daily basis and provide descriptions about the events that occurred. Diary studies offer very fresh thoughts from employees about their experiences, and may also offer insight into how the employee's feelings evolved over time. For example, employees may begin by describing their interpretations of the negative social acts that they experience and – over time as they experience these behaviours more frequently – may come to identify them as bullying. Nevertheless, it is important to note that diary studies do not typically allow for probing questions, and the data is largely driven by the thoughts that the participant chooses to highlight (Jones and Woolley 2014).

Another qualitative approach that researchers with an interpretivist perspective may draw upon is focus groups. Focus groups involve discussions with multiple participants in a single session. Focus groups can shed light on how participants make sense of their experiences in a setting in which multiple participants share their thoughts. However, since the interpretivist paradigm seeks to understand individual meanings and experiences, researchers should be cognisant of the potential for a participant's views and thoughts to be influenced by the statements and/or presence of others. Of course, one-on-one interviews are perhaps the most common qualitative method for interpretivist researchers (Creswell 2013).

A methodological technique that researchers from an interpretivist paradigm may use is narratives. Narratives can be used alongside a wide variety of qualitative research methods and represent stories about the participant's experiences. For example, researchers can ask participants to describe their experiences in the form of a story during the interview. When using diary studies, researchers may ask participants to write their diary entries in the form of stories. Researchers may also ask participants to simply write a single narrative about their victimisation experiences and subsequently analyse the participant's narrative. Narratives can be a very valuable tool since stories can provide rich description of the context surrounding the events and experiences.

The use of metaphors may also be particularly useful. Metaphors offer insight into the ways in which the participant viewed his/her experiences. Moreover, metaphors are often insightful because they provide examples of the participant's experiences using words that may have more meaning for those that have not experienced the events themselves. For example, Tracy *et al.* (2006) found that targets used metaphors such as 'slaves', 'animals', and 'prisoners' to describe how they felt when they were bullied by another employee. They also used metaphors such as 'devil figures' and 'two-faced actors' to describe how they viewed the bully. This provides important insights into the meanings that targets attached to their experiences and helped the researcher describe the target's feelings.

While archives, documents, and other content are common in qualitative research, they may not be particularly suitable for interpretivist research. This is because interpretivist research is focused on understanding the individual meanings that participants attach to their experiences. Thus, as mentioned earlier, it is important that interpretivist research is conducted from the frame of references of the actor(s) directly involved in the events. Archives and other historical documents may offer insights about events but may not offer first-person quotes, with the exception of emails or other documentation that contains first-person speech.

There is a significant need for more interpretivist research in the workplace victimisation literature. While there has been some, although not enough, research to understand the meanings that targets attach to their experiences, there has been little interpretivist research focusing on the perpetrators of workplace victimisation (for one exception, see Omari 2007). Similarly, there has been little to no interpretivist research focusing on witnesses or observers. Moreover, the literature is limited in studies that explore the sense-making processes of targets, the ways in which targets understand their experiences over time, and the social processes surrounding workplace victimisation events. Therefore, future research is needed to understand these aspects better as well as understanding the experiences of other important actors such as perpetrators and witnesses.

Critical management theory and workplace victimisation

The critical management theory paradigm focuses on notions of power and alienation in the workplace (Burrell and Morgan 1979). When applied to workplace victimisation, critical management theory would suggest that the root causes of workplace victimisation stem from the organisation and more broadly the capitalist forces present. The critical management theory paradigm may view management practices and organisational structures of bureaucracy as promoting dehumanising and impersonal relations between employees. Furthermore, organisations create environments in which employees are in competition with one another, the interests of the organisation tend to take precedence over the interests of employees, and employees are subjected to a number of rules and policies enforced by supervisors. These conditions that are created by the organisation can be viewed as stimulating negative interpersonal relations between employees, whether this be relations between a supervisor who feels that he/she is appropriately enforcing disciplinary measures, or a co-worker who feels that aggressiveness is the appropriate response to competitive pressures within the organisation. Moreover, organisations that operate in a manner in which rules and policies must be followed by all employees may influence employees to feel comfortable holding others to similarly strict standards. The roots of these practices instituted by the organisation may be viewed as stemming from capitalist forces that influence organisations to view employees as a means or tool for generating profits.

Focusing at the organisational-level, Salin (2003) suggests that organisational culture can be intentionally developed in a way that institutionalises wide power imbalances. In other words, workplace bullying may indirectly be encouraged by those with authority through wider power imbalances. Furthermore, Neuman and Baron (1998) assert that some organisations may desire a certain level of 'toughness' in their employees. A number of other researchers have also suggested that workplace bullying may be presumed desirable and an important aspect of organisational culture (e.g. Bulutlar and Unler Oz 2009; Harvey *et al.* 2009). Moreover, these perspectives share some consistency with critical perspectives in organisational studies. For instance, Delbridge and Ezzamel (2005, p. 606) assert that senior management may engage in "managing culture in order to control employees through the influence of their values and beliefs."

Functionalist approaches to research inherently position the causes of workplace bullying to emanate from: 1) characteristics rooted at the individual-level (e.g. personality traits, demographic factors); 2) factors at the group-level (e.g., team dynamics, group norms); and/or 3) factors at the organisational-level (e.g. organisational leadership, culture) (Samnani and Singh 2012). A more critical perspective would suggest that, "Subordination is not related to personality clashes between individuals but a more Taylorist approach based on impersonal laws applied to supervisors and subordinates" (Liefooghe and Davey 2001, p. 387). Hence, the former perspectives neglect the possibility that the root of workplace bullying may be stemming from, and be a by-product of, broader forces of the capitalist system.

As compared with functionalist approaches to workplace bullying, few researchers have examined workplace bullying using a critical lens. Of the few researchers that do use a critical approach, Liefooghe and Davey (2001) assert that organisations facilitate the interpersonal processes of workplace bullying. Moreover, they position the organisation as the bully. Without providing a definition of workplace bullying, Liefooghe and Davey (2001) found that participants often indicated practices such as withdrawing opportunities for working overtime, using quantitative measures for evaluation and performance management, and sick leave policies as examples of bullying. Moreover, participants also recognised that managers themselves were also subjected to these same practices, which helped transfer the blame away from any specific manager and onto the organisation.

While similar qualitative research approaches as those discussed for interpretivism can be adopted when working within a critical management theory paradigm, an analytic technique called discourse analysis is possible. For example, within this paradigm, management is seen to employ a number of tactics in order to enforce excessive workloads and monitor employees' tasks with little resistance and retaliation, or even detection. Moreover, Lutgen-Sandvik *et al.* (2007) found that only one-third of the employees who had been subjected to bullying acts, as defined by the researchers, had self-identified as targets. In other words, two-thirds of the targeted employees did not indicate being bullied despite experiencing behaviours that these researchers had classified as bullying. This suggests that a considerable percentage of 'targets' may not be recognising bullying when they are subjected to it. One of the ways in which management can engage in workplace bullying without detection is through the use of discursive practices (see Delbridge and Ezzamel 2005). To illustrate, management may stress fierce competition to employees and emphasise the need to be competitive, cost effective, and productive (Thompson and Smith 2001). This represents a way in which employees can be induced into accepting various forms of managerial control, and workplace bullying as legitimate. Moreover, capitalist forces help organisations justify such practices to employees.

This notion of the use of discursive practices also appears in the employee commitment literature. There had been a shift in the management literature in the 1980s from using the term 'control' to more recently referring to an employee's compliance to these practices as 'commitment' (Thompson and Harley 2007). This shift reflects a way in which forms of control can be subtly exercised through the use of discourse that positively portrays employees' acceptance of control. Critical perspectives suggest that employees are often conditioned in a way that makes them want to be, and feel the need to be, controlled (O'Doherty and Willmott 2001; King and Learmonth 2014). Furthermore, employee conditioning is apparent in the workforce. For example, employees who comply with management authority are referred to as loyal and committed, while employees who undertake additional workloads are described as demonstrating organisational citizenship behaviours (Carpenter *et al.* 2014).

Several forms of workplace bullying that have been identified in the literature may not appear to be bullying to a more general audience; however, this is largely a result of the conditioning of individuals through discursive practices to become compliant with various control mechanisms in the workplace. Nevertheless, Liefooghe and Davey (2001, p. 385) found that some employees associated workplace bullying with the word "discipline". Furthermore, managers in their sample would often threaten to 'discipline' employees if they did not meet certain standards that they were being evaluated against (Liefooghe and Davey 2001). The word 'discipline' is typically used by management as a more politically correct version of the word 'punishment'. Thus, this example represents one such discursive practice managers use that enables them to discreetly engage in workplace bullying.

The definition of workplace bullying has remained considerably broad and encompasses a number of different forms (Samnani and Singh 2012). For instance, threats have typically been reported as a form of workplace bullying (Fox and Stallworth 2005). While threats are often perceived in the form of physical violence or harassment, Liefooghe and Davey (2001) argue that the constant awareness that one can be terminated from his or her job constitutes a threat. Furthermore, in several organisations the potential for employees to be replaced by machines or by other individuals represents a persistent threat.

In addition, the use of 'discipline' for actions or performance that does not meet management's standards also represents a constant threat to employees.

A recent study explored the ways in which bullying complaints were handled by human resource departments (Harrington *et al.* 2013). Harrington *et al.* (2013) found that human resources practitioners tended to attribute managerial bullying behaviours to legitimate practices related to managing employee performance. In this study, therefore, managerialist and capitalist discourses were used to protect the interests of the organisation over the interests of the targeted employee (Harrington *et al.* 2013). Overall, the use of discursive practices enables management to legitimate threats to employees often in the name of being competitive and profitable, factors that capitalism motivates. The capitalist system, which focuses on increasing capital, facilitates management practices whereby profitability and competition are emphasised at the expense of employees. Hence, if one shifts the focus of workplace bullying away from interpersonal issues and towards broader systemic forces, the system of capitalism can be perceived as the actual bully.

Postmodernism and workplace victimisation

The postmodernist paradigm suggests that there is no single 'truth'; rather, that there are multiple truths (Cooper and Burrell 1988). This approach, similar to the interpretivist and critical management theory paradigms, draws upon a subjective approach to understanding and examining phenomena (Samnani 2013). This section will focus on Foucauldian concepts of control and power.

Hutchinson *et al.* (2006) examine the phenomenon of workplace bullying, particularly in the nursing profession, by applying Foucauldian analysis and suggesting that workplace bullying is a form of power exercised by management over employees. Furthermore, they argue that senior management implements practices such as performance evaluation, training, and quality management to enforce disciplinary power and maintain their domination over employees through the use of, what comes to be known as, "legitimate" practices. Hutchinson *et al.* (2006) take a similar stance to Liefooghe and Davey (2001) on workplace bullying in asserting that:

> Organisations and management structures have been able to remain immune from any further consideration as to their role in perpetuating bullying . . . by depicting it as something different and less significant than it really is, and by generating the belief that bullying is solely a nurse-to-nurse phenomenon and a form of interpersonal conflict.
>
> (Hutchinson *et al.* 2006, p. 120)

The following continues to use a Foucauldian perspective to discuss concepts of control and surveillance, but also draws again on discursive practices since these can also, similar to the critical management theory perspective, be useful tools for understanding within the postmodernist paradigm. Researchers have asserted that the traditional Taylorist management practices have been modified to integrate softer and indirect forms of control (Thompson and Smith 2009). For instance, the excessive monitoring of an employee's work, an act considered to be workplace bullying (Bulutlar and Unler Oz 2009), does not necessarily need to take the form of a supervisor physically observing the work of an employee. Examples of modified forms of control and monitoring include the use of company-employed 'shoppers' in the retail industry and electronic monitoring preventing employee deviance from heavily scripted interactions in the call centre industry (Smith and Thompson 1998). These forms of control and surveillance of employees' work represent ways in which management continues its close monitoring of employees, but through different surveillance practices that are more concealed and subtle. Moreover, these forms of monitoring and control typically become accepted by employees as legitimate despite serving the same function as a manager watching over an employee's shoulder (Hutchinson *et al.* 2006). Finally, because employees are conditioned to perceive these practices as legitimate, they would not normally refer to these practices as bullying, monitoring, or as a form of control.

Klein (1991) argues that many work systems such as Just-In-Time (JIT), Total Quality Management (TQM), and other continuous improvement systems often lead to work intensification for employees. Moreover, work systems often incorporate mechanisms of peer- and self-monitoring as an additional form of control (Smith and Thompson 1998). In other words, control and monitoring take on forms that accomplish the same original goal, while significantly increasing the workloads of employees. Furthermore, as Hutchinson *et al.* (2006, p. 121) assert, "Techniques such as quality management, output measurement, performance management, industry benchmarking, case management, procedure manuals, and proscribed payment systems can be seen as forms of disciplinary technique, reinforcing power within organisations." What is more, Smith and Thompson (1998) argue that work systems such as TQM involve an even greater degree of monitoring and control of both employees and work teams than the more traditional work systems. While these systems have been found to result in increased firm performance (e.g. Appelbaum *et al.* 2000), they are typically accompanied with negative impacts on employees in the form of increased workloads and stress (Thompson and Harley 2007; King and Learmonth 2014).

As discussed earlier, the terminology used for these work systems often carry positive connotations but tend to be used in order to condition employees into accepting and even desiring these types of work. The types of terminology often associated with such work include high involvement work practices, high performance work systems, challenging multi-skilled work, and high trust environments (Smith and Thompson 1998; Boxall and Macky 2014). However, Burke and Cooper (2008) contend that work systems such as those of high involvement work practices often result in work intensification. Furthermore, as mentioned earlier, excessive workloads represent a form of bullying in the workplace. Therefore, since work intensification has been identified as a form of control (Smith and Thompson 1998), and high involvement work systems and other such work practices result in work intensification and modified forms of surveillance (Delbridge 2000; Thompson and Harley 2007; Boxall and Macky 2014), these work systems can, in turn, be viewed as a form of workplace bullying that the system imposes on employees through the application of modified traditional Tayloristic methods (Harrington *et al.* 2013).

Conclusion

This chapter highlighted methodological and paradigmatic approaches that can be taken to enrich our understanding of workplace victimisation. In sum, using an interpretivist paradigm can help researchers understand the meanings that employees attach to their experiences of workplace victimisation. Furthermore, using a critical lens provides an alternative way of understanding workplace bullying, and in particular, how and why it occurs. Rather than focusing on interpersonal issues or organisational culture as the cause of workplace bullying, the focus shifts to the broader system and its role in stimulating bullying situations in organisations. To neglect how economic, social, and institutional forces influence employees into engaging in workplace bullying limits our understanding of its broader roots. Furthermore, identifying workplace bullying as a mechanism of control through the postmodernist paradigm enriches the understanding of the rationale behind the actions of perpetrators.

In order to thoroughly understand important concepts such as symbols, power, and/or control in workplace bullying, qualitative research appears to be appropriate as a research design for non-functionalist approaches. Researchers can use methods such as narratives, interviews, focus groups, and/or ethnography from perpetrators and/or targeted employees, to better understand the phenomenon. Using a critical framework, for example, would help pinpoint broader notions of control and power relations and how these are intertwined with workplace bullying. Furthermore, researchers can also investigate ethnic and gender relations in organisations, which may tend to reflect the patriarchal systems in broader society. While the importance of also identifying the individual- and organisational-level issues involved in victimisation is not denied, a critical perspective enables further understanding of the stimulants of workplace bullying by analysing the role of societal-level factors. Therefore, researchers should investigate workplace victimisation from within a variety of paradigms in order to help develop a more balanced, well-rounded body of scholarship.

References

Agervold, M. and Mikkelsen, E. G., 2004. Relationships between bullying, psycho-social work environment and individual stress reactions. *Work and Stress*, 18(4), 336–51.

Appelbaum, E., Bailey, T., Berg, P. and Kalleberg, A. L., 2000. *Manufacturing advantage: Why high performance work systems pay off*. Ithaca, NY: Cornell University Press.

Aquino, K. and Thau, S., 2009. Workplace victimization: Aggression from the target's perspective. *Annual Review of Psychology*, 60(1), 717–41.

Boxall, P. and Macky, K., 2014. High involvement work processes, work intensification and employee well-being. *Work, Employment and Society*, 28(6), 963–84.

Brand, V., 2009. Empirical business ethics research and paradigm analysis. *Journal of Business Ethics*, 86(4), 429–49.

Bulutlar, F. and Unler Oz, E., 2009. The effects of ethical climates on bullying behaviour in the workplace. *Journal of Business Ethics*, 86(3), 273–95.

Burke, R. J. and Cooper, C. L., 2008. *The long work hours culture: Causes, consequences and choices*. Bingley: Emerald Group Publishing.

Burrell, G. and Morgan, G., 1979. *Sociological paradigms and organisational analysis*. London: Heinemen Education Books, Ltd.

Carpenter, N. C., Berry, C. M. and Houston, L., 2014. A meta-analytic comparison of self-reported and other-reported organizational citizenship behavior. *Journal of Organizational Behavior*, 35(4), 547–74.

Cooper, R. and Burrell, G., 1988. Modernism, postmodernism and organizational analysis: An introduction. *Organization Studies*, 9(1), 91–112.

Creswell, J. W., 2013. *Research design: Qualitative, quantitative, and mixed methods approaches*. Thousand Oaks, CA: Sage.

Delbridge, R., 2000. *Life on the line in contemporary manufacturing*. Oxford: Oxford University Press.

Delbridge, R. and Ezzamel, M., 2005. The strength of difference: Contemporary conceptions of Control. *Organization*, 12(5), 603–18.

Escartin, J., Rodríguez-Carballeira, A., Zapf, D., Porrúa, C. and Martín-Peña, J., 2009. Perceived severity of various bullying behaviors at work and the relevance of exposure to bullying. *Work and Stress*, 23(3), 191–205.

Foucault, M., 1977. *Discipline and punish: The birth of the prison*. Harmondsworth: Penguin.

Fox, S. and Stallworth, L. E., 2005. Racial/ethnic bullying: Exploring links between bullying and racism in the US workplace. *Journal of Vocational Behavior*, 66(3), 438–56.

Gill, M. J., 2014. The possibilities of phenomenology for organizational research. *Organizational Research Methods*, 17(2), 118–37.

Harrington, S., Warren, S. and Rayner, C., 2013. Human resource management practitioners' responses to workplace bullying: Cycles of symbolic violence. *Organization*, DOI: 10.1177/1350508413516175, pp. 1–22.

Harvey, M., Treadway, D., Heames, J. T. and Duke, A., 2009. Bullying in the 21st century global organization: An ethical perspective. *Journal of Business Ethics*, 85(1), 27–40.

Hershcovis, S. M., 2011. "Incivility, social undermining, bullying . . . oh my!": A call to reconcile constructs within workplace aggression research. *Journal of Organizational Behavior*, 32(3), 499–519.

Hutchinson, M., Vickers, M., Jackson, D. and Wilkes, L., 2006. Workplace bullying in nursing: Towards a more critical organizational perspective. *Nursing Inquiry*, 13(2), 118–26.

Jones, A. and Woolley, J., 2014. The email-diary: A promising research tool for the 21st century. *Qualitative Research*, DOI: 10.1177/1468794114561347, 1–17.

King, D. and Learmonth, M., 2014. Can critical management studies ever be "practical"? A case study in engaged scholarship. *Human Relations*, DOI: 10.1177/0018726714528254, 1–23.

Klein, J., 1991. The human cost of manufacturing reform. *Harvard Business Review*, March- April, 62–6.

Liefooghe, A.P.D. and Davey, K.M., 2001. Accounts of workplace bullying: The role of the organization. *European Journal of Work and Organizational Psychology*, 10(4), 375–92.

Lutgen-Sandvik, P., Tracy, S.J. and Alberts, J.K., 2007. Burned by bullying in the American workplace: Prevalence, perception, degree, and impact. *Journal of Management Studies*, 44(6), 837–62.

Mavin, S., Grandy, G. and Williams, J., 2014. Experiences of women elite leaders doing gender: Intra-gender micro-violence between women. *British Journal of Management*, 25(3), 439–55.

Neuman, J.H. and Baron, R.A., 1998. Workplace violence and workplace aggression: Evidence concerning specific forms, potential causes, and preferred targets. *Journal of Management*, 24(3), 391–419.

O'Doherty, D. and Willmott, H., 2001. The question of subjectivity and the labor process. *International Studies of Management and Organization*, 30(4), 112–32.

Omari, M., 2007. *Towards dignity and respect: An exploration of the nature, causes and consequences of workplace bullying*. Saarbrücken: VDM Verlag Dr. Müller.

Persson, R., Hogh, A., Hansen, Å.M., Nordander, C., Ohlsson, K., Balogh, I., Österberg, K. and Ørbæk, P., 2009. Prsonality trait scores among occupationally active bullied persons and witnesses to bullying. *Motivation and Emotion*, 33(4), 387–99.

Robinson, S.L., Wang, W. and Kiewitz, C., 2014. Coworkers behaving badly: The impact of co-worker deviant behavior upon individual employees. *Annual Review of Organizational Psychology and Organizational Behavior*, 1(1), 123–43.

Salin, D., 2003. Ways of explaining workplace bullying: A review of enabling, motivating and precipitating structures and processes in the work environment. *Human Relations*, 56(10), 1213–32.

Samnani, A.-K., 2013. Embracing new directions in workplace bullying research: A paradigmatic approach. *Journal of Management Inquiry*, 22(1), 26–36.

Samnani, A.-K. and Singh, P., 2012. 20 years of workplace bullying research: A review of the antecedents and consequences of bullying in the workplace. *Aggression and Violent Behavior*, 17(6), 581–9.

Schat, A.C.H., Frone, M.R. and Kelloway, E.K., 2006. Prevalence of workplace aggression in the U.S. workforce: Findings from a national study. *In:* E.K. Kelloway, J. Barling and J. Hurrell, eds., Handbook of workplace violence. Thousand Oaks, CA: Sage.

Schilpzand, P., de Pater, I.E. and Erez, A., 2014. Workplace incivility: A review of the literature and agenda for future research. *Journal of Organizational Behavior*, DOI: 10.1002/job.1976, 1–32.

Skogstad, A., Einarsen, S., Torsheim, T., Aasland, M.S. and Hetland, H., 2007. The destructiveness of laissez-faire leadership behavior. *Journal of Occupational Health Psychology*, 8(1), 110–22.

Smith, C. and Thompson, P., 1998. Re-evaluating the labour process debate. *Economic and Industrial Democracy*, 19(4), 551–77.

Thompson, P. and Harley, B., 2007. HRM and the worker: Labor process theory. *In:* P. Boxall, J. Purcell and P. Wright, eds., *The Oxford handbook of human resource management*. Oxford: Oxford University Press.

Thompson, P. and Smith, C., 2001. Follow the redbrick road: Reflections on pathways in and out of the labor process debate. *International Studies of Management and Organization,* 30(4), 40–67.

Thompson, P. and Smith, C., 2009. Waving, not drowning: Explaining and exploring the resilience of labor process theory. *Employee Responsibilities and Rights Journal,* 21(3), 253–62.

Tracy, S. J., Lutgen-Sandvik, P. and Alberts, J. K., 2006. Nightmares, demons, and slaves: Exploring the painful metaphors of workplace bullying. *Management Communication Quarterly,* 20(2), 148–85.

Vannini, P. and Franzese, A., 2008. The authenticity of self: Conceptualization, personal experience, and practice. *Sociology Compass,* 2(5), 1621–37.

Vickers, M. H., 2014.Workplace bullying as workplace corruption: A higher education, creative nonfiction case study. *Administration and Society,* 46(8), 960–85.

Yamada, D. C., 2004. Crafting a legislative response to workplace bullying. *Employee Rights and Employment Policy Journal,* 8(2), 476–521.

Zábrodská, K., Ellwood, C., Zaeemdar, S. and Mudrak, J., 2014. Workplace bullying as sensemaking: An analysis of target and actor perspectives on initial hostile interactions. *Culture and Organization,* DOI: 10.1080/14759551.2014.894514, 1–22.

3 Floorcraft

Researching subjective phenomena

Megan Paull and Antonia Girardi

Introduction

In the critically acclaimed movie *Dancing in Jaffa,* four-time world ballroom dancing champion Pierre Dulaine showcases how dance can transcend geographical and cultural boundaries and be a positive force for real change (see Dancing in Jaffa 2015). Dulaine explores the stories of three children who are forced to 'dance with the enemy' and in so doing raises awareness of the challenges involved in dealing with sensitive topics such as personal identity, segregation and racial prejudice. In the workplace, interpersonal relations can be just as challenging and workplace conflict has many manifestations.

Workplace abuse, incivility and bullying (WAIB) are sensitive topics which can be considered to be part of the dark side of organisational research (Linstead *et al.* 2014). In this chapter WAIB refers to a sub-set of those behaviours that harm others, including verbal and psychological abuse (Linstead *et al.* 2014). The evidence from the literature is that the manifestation of abuse, incivility and bullying can be found in workplaces the world over. It is only by tackling research into sensitive, often denied and certainly taboo subjects, that these can be considered and ameliorated. Research into sensitive topics, however, can be complex and difficult, and requires that researchers exercise caution (Liamputtong 2007), much like the floorcraft required of ballroom dancers.[1]

Interactions in the workplace might be compared to the interactions on a dance floor, with the workplace culture being likened to the tone and style of the ballroom, and the interactions between the workers to those between the dancers, based on the music being played, and the preference of the dancers. Whether the music indicates a waltz, a tango, a salsa or a barn dance, there is a cultural dimension which can be seen in the movement of the individuals, and their interpretation of the music. It is these nuances which can influence the interpretation of the acts of others, and which researchers may seek to explore in their investigations of WAIB.

Specifically, cross-cultural dimensions of human interactions are complex; undertaking cross-cultural research is "full of ethical and methodological challenges" (Liamputtong 2010, p. 18). The positioning of the researcher as a cross-cultural researcher, as a researcher of sensitive subjects, or both, has important implications. Jacobson *et al.* (2014) advise that it is essential for the researcher to be mindful of themselves and of the participants in their research, their cultural background, and the influence this may have, not only on the behaviour under investigation, but also on participant interaction with the researcher and gatekeepers; and on researcher interpretation of the data.

Quality research requires that the researcher takes care, not only of the paradigmatic considerations (Samnani 2013, and Samnani this volume), but also of the practicalities of undertaking the research in a way that will yield useful and informative outcomes. Such research comes from skilled researchers who have been mentored and trained, and have the agility and capability to adapt their research style to the requirements of the research and the researched. The researcher has a responsibility to take care of themselves, to not put themselves in the way of psychological or physical harm (Liamputtong 2007). Empathy with participants is likely to influence how data is obtained, but researchers must also protect themselves, participants and other stakeholders such as gatekeepers. In the design and execution of research, just as in the choreography and performance of dance, there is a responsibility to ensure that there is clear focus, that the researcher is agile, and that more difficult research is not attempted without practice and experience.

WAIB research has been undertaken in a wide range of industries (including health and education), and with myriad approaches. Quantitative approaches, including those which have employed the now widely translated Negative Acts Questionnaire (see Einarsen and Raknes 1997), have sought to establish what sorts of behaviours are present, and to gain indicative understanding of the prevalence of these (Balducci *et al.* 2012, Berry *et al.* 2012). Qualitative approaches have sought to gather the stories of those involved, to explore differing perspectives or to add depth to the perspectives provided by quantitative research (Dhar 2012, Turk *et al.* 2014). More recently there have been studies undertaken which seek the methodological gains of mixed methods, providing insights at a range of levels in the same study (McLaughlin *et al.* 2012, D'Cruz and Rayner 2013, Gilbert and Raffo 2013). What is apparent from the extant literature is that the interactions of workers naturally involve essential elements of the cultures of workplaces, and that it is not only workplace culture, but also ethnic culture which contributes to the expression of WAIB and related behaviours (Jacobson *et al.* 2014).

This chapter considers the practical aspects of researching the subjective phenomena of workplace abuse, incivility and bullying. Central to this is the capability and experience of the researcher, both with the phenomenon itself and with research. Different paradigm, researcher and gatekeeper goals influence the design of the research: access to sensitive data, how sensitive data is to be handled and translated across language and cultural divides, and how interpretation of static events can be meaningfully understood and disseminated to various audiences. Our perspective encourages the researcher to 'step off the dance floor and get on the balcony' to design (choreograph) and conduct (perform) quality research.

Designing research into workplace abuse, incivility and bullying

Research design is crucial to useful outcomes in research (Creswell 2013). The research process presents opportunities for researchers to make decisions in the definition and refinement of research objectives, the selection of a research approach, and conduct of the research, before disseminating outcomes to the intended audience(s). These decisions are not considered in isolation and require 'floorcraft' – skills needed to navigate an awareness of self, partners and others so as to adjust to the space available and militate against collisions and injury. Expert floorcraft is underpinned by mutual respect and trust for one another, and enables the different partnerships and participants to find a way to work together.

In designing research on sensitive topics, a number of key characteristics must be acknowledged and addressed. The first of these is the framing of the research question. While textbooks on research methods often posit the notion that the research question dictates the manner and method of research, it is more often the case that the approach is determined by a range of factors. It is thus important to see the research design as an iterative process requiring fine-tuning of each aspect, irrespective of paradigm.

For instance, in developing the research question it is important to frame the research appropriately, and in all paradigms this includes working out what definitions or approaches to terminology will be adopted. Decisions about definitions will influence not only the research question, but also the design of the research overall. There is still limited consensus on a definition of workplace bullying (Cowan 2012), despite there being efforts to achieve this, and there are similar differences about definitions of abuse, although incivility seems more settled (see Schilpzand *et al.* 2014). The literature points to three approaches in use for research into WAIB. The first is the adoption of an existing definition which has been operationalised or is in use in, for example, the law. A second approach is to use an *a priori* definition developed from the extant literature for the purposes of the particular research project (e.g. Lee *et al.* 2014). The third approach is not to offer a direct definition, but to draw on the participants' own understanding of the phenomenon. In qualitative research this can mean either offering a definition or terminology and seeking participant responses within that frame, seeking to develop a definition based on informant/participant feedback, or asking participants to offer their own definition or terminology.

Research questions and definitions devised by novice researchers, or newcomers to a particular topic area, can provide vital fresh insights into the phenomenon under investigation. It is, however, important that both beginner and experienced researchers focus on the selection of the appropriate question, and frame it in such a way that it takes into account the intended topic, the intended participants, the style and skill of the researcher(s), the time frame and resources available, and the likelihood of getting access to relevant stakeholders as participants.

Although the stage is often set by the research problem or question, which may have arisen because of a critical incident (Omari 2007), management dilemma (Shallcross *et al.* 2013) or theoretical question (Hutchinson *et al.* 2010), the interaction of the researcher and gatekeeper at the entry to the ballroom will necessarily inform the design of the research process. The researcher and the gatekeeper will need to take a balcony view to better consider the respective paradigms which inform their research approaches (see Samnani this volume), as well as their individual skills and experiences; all while considering the ethnic and organisational cultural contexts within which the research takes place.

The second characteristic to be considered in designing research on sensitive topics relates to selecting the research approach. Two fundamental decisions need to be made. The first in terms of methodology (quantitative, qualitative or mixed methods research); and the second in terms of the selection of the research method (including, for example, observation techniques, surveys, experiments, storytelling and lived experiences, ethnographic accounts, authoethnography, grounded theory and content analysis). The selection of methodology and method, whilst connected with the primary research objectives, needs to be flexible in order to take into account the interactions between the researcher, the gatekeepers and the potential research participants.

Given that WAIB research is a growing field, there are a range of existing studies on which researchers can draw in the design process. In quantitative, qualitative and mixed methods research it behoves researchers to consider the extant literature and historical data to ensure that, as the field grows, it is possible to compare and contrast new findings as well as to add to the body of knowledge. This can also help to refine the research objectives and thereby the selection of the research approach.

Quantitative researchers, usually operating in the positivist paradigm, seek to consider the hallmarks of measures of reliability and validity in the development of quality measurement instruments. There are some existing instruments in the WAIB field with which researchers should become familiar, even if only to critique them or develop alternatives. The most well-known in the WAIB field is the Negative Acts Questionnaire (NAQ) (Einarsen *et al.* 1994 cited in Bergen Bullying Research Group 2014), which has been revised (NAQ-R) (Hoel 1999 cited in Bergen Bullying Research Group 2014) and translated into several languages including Spanish (see Jiménez *et al.* 2007) and Japanese (see Tsuno *et al.* 2010).

While somewhat controversial, the questionnaire is now the basis of over 60 studies in 40 countries. A recent in-house review of the instrument has provided detailed information for those considering its use (Einarsen *et al.* 2009). Its owners, the Bergen Bullying Research Group, are well-known academics in the field of psychology researching workplace bullying (e.g. Einarsen and Nielsen 2015).

Quantitative instruments developed by other researchers have often included elements of the NAQ or NAQ-R in combination with other scales already in use. An example of this is the work of Balducci *et al.* (2012), whose recent work has explored the relationship between workaholism and aggression in the workplace. The NAQ-R was combined with the Dutch Workaholism Scale, and the Job-related Affective Well-being Scale (JAWS; Giorgi 2012) combined the NAQ-R with UNICLIMA, an instrument designed to measure organisational climate, as well as a health scale in order to examine the impact of workplace bullying on a group of employees and consider whether climate was an antecedent or consequence of the bullying. Key to the choices made by researchers in these studies is the selection of instruments which have already been validated.

Other recent work, including that of Abu Al Rub and Al-Asmar (2014), has drawn on an instrument developed by the World Health Organisation (WHO), International Council of Nurses (ICN), International Labour Organisation (ILO) and Public Services International (PSI) and published in 2003. This questionnaire is part of a world-wide joint effort to ameliorate conditions in healthcare and includes workplace bullying and harassment as forms of psychological violence but also physical violence (ILO *et al.* 2003).

Quantitative researchers have also used other approaches. Pilch and Turska (2015), for example, used the Unethical Behaviour Questionnaire (UBQ) which had been developed tens years earlier, while Beattie and Griffin (2014a, 2014b) employed diary surveys. New scales have been developed more recently, including the Hospital Aggressive Behaviour Scale – Coworkers and Superiors (HABS–CS) (Waschgler *et al.* 2013), designed to differentiate between sources of workplace bullying. It is important for researchers to consider the purpose of their work, and the nature of the existing instruments, before deciding to employ these or develop new scales.

Qualitative research in the WAIB field has been limited to date, and aside from the more usual reasons associated with getting qualitative research published (Wolcott 2009), it is also the case that qualitative research requires an increased level of trust between the researcher and the participants, as well as a level of skill from the researcher in dealing with an emotionally sensitive subject (Lofland *et al.* 2006, Liamputtong 2007). Qualitative researchers have myriad approaches which can be adopted in their exploration of WAIB. Storytelling seems to be a focus taking precedence over observation (see Jackson *et al.* 2011), with one researcher heeding the calls of Tracy *et al.* (2006) for more qualitative approaches and using creative writing as a tool to develop a semi-fictional case study (Vickers 2014). Recent work includes focus groups (Clendon and Walker 2012, Lee *et al.* 2012), interviews (D'Cruz and Noronha 2014, Doshy and Wang 2014), open-ended ongoing questionnaires (Willis 2012), surveys which collected stories (Guneri-Cangarli *et al.* 2013), and stories themselves (Omari 2007).

There is a small level of Mixed Methods Research (MMR) in the field. As MMR grows as a recognised approach to research (Tashakkori and Teddlie 2010, Creswell and Plano-Clark 2013), its value to WAIB research is becoming apparent. In the period since 2012, a limited number of studies have demonstrated the value of the breadth and depth offered by MMR (e.g. Alexander *et al.* 2012, Whitaker 2012). The employment of mixed methods offers the researcher the opportunity to draw on the quantitative work done to date in the field, and on the depth offered by qualitative methods. MMR, however, requires that researchers have skills across the multiple methods employed, is time consuming, and like all research projects, requires planning as to how the data will be collected and how it will be analysed, interpreted and integrated (Tashakkori and Teddlie 2010, Creswell and Plano-Clark 2013).

It is likely that for many researchers the selection of methodology and research process will be dependent on personal preferences including the research tradition(s) in which they are schooled and trained. The choice of approach is somewhat akin to the choice of dance style, in that such a choice posits research in the domain, leaving other choices up to the individual – such as partner, music and steps. The style and skill of the researcher(s) is an important consideration. 'What' and 'how' questions are then shaped on that basis. Similarly, gatekeeper negotiation may lead to consideration of the approach, with organisational culture and political considerations influencing how research is shaped. While it is agreed that the best research is designed with obtaining quality data as the primary consideration, the practicalities of obtaining data must dictate that researchers not ignore the others on the dance floor.

The design of the research will be improved if it takes into account the cultural context in which the research is being undertaken. This includes, but is not limited to, language and customs. Being aware of the language involved can include considering unintended consequences of translation from one language into another, for both the instruments of enquiry, and the stories and perspectives of the participants. For instruments this involves the standard practice of translation and back translation to ensure accuracy (e.g. Takaki *et al.* 2010). Techniques including parallel or double translation (see Douglas and Craig 2007) may offer additional benefits. Often as a precursor to undertaking research it is necessary to establish the meaning of key words and phrases, as discussed above (e.g. Lee *et al.* 2014). It can also be necessary to establish protocols for discussing difficult subjects in different cultures, often more difficult where the researchers are from another culture.

Increasingly, cross-cultural research is being undertaken to investigate WAIB, with recent work making comparisons across six continents (Power *et al.* 2013), between specific countries (Jacobson *et al.* 2014), or comparing one specific culture to the growing body of knowledge about WAIB (Turk *et al.* 2014). Cross-cultural studies which seek to compare findings require that language and research methods which have been refined to acknowledge differences remain consistent enough to allow for comparison. Researchers need to ensure that ethical considerations are met, practical challenges are anticipated and that the appropriate skills are employed. The role of the researcher as a cross-cultural researcher, a researcher of sensitive subjects, or both, must be acknowledged and understood.

Accessing sensitive data

In order to gather data for research into WAIB, researchers must first negotiate a pathway to those whose experience they need to understand. This means persuading gatekeepers and individuals to open up and share information about a subject that creates emotional responses which can range from denial and defensiveness to despair and depression. This might be in the form of an anonymous survey, online or at a distance, or by way of an interview or conversation at close quarters. Before researchers engage with those with firsthand experience, they must first negotiate access via a range of gatekeepers.

Gatekeepers are individuals at the 'gate' of organisations, personal assistants, boards and managers, as well as decision makers such as ethics committees or boards of review. They are important in the conduct of quality research, no matter the subject. Gatekeepers seek to protect and defend organisations and individuals by controlling access, for a range of reasons. Researchers need to respect their role and negotiate a pathway with them effectively. Such negotiations require preparation and planning and a considered view of the role played by the individuals who take this on (Lofland *et al.* 2006).

The process of gaining access is based on the development of trust. Trust is based on clear communication, good planning and the integrity of the behaviour of the researcher. Applying for and receiving ethics approval for intended research is a part of the development of trust. Ethics committees are the custodians of a level of quality and protection in research that balances the potential for harm with the need to know about the phenomenon under investigation. The researcher therefore should prepare well by planning and proposing research which will yield valuable insights and data, while offering the necessary protections to those who consent to participate. This means considering such things as the wording of questions, the response to distress, anger or despair, the avenues to support and the right of the individual to say no. The level of gatekeeping by ethics committees or their equivalents varies from country to country, and the different roles and rules in each location must also be a consideration for cross-cultural researchers (see NHMRC 2007/2014). Good planning and preparation can make the pathway through ethics approval less complex. Researchers have the opportunity to benefit from the feedback and support provided by committee members who will approach the process from a variety of perspectives.

Organisational gatekeepers can also make a great contribution to research by providing the researcher with early insights into the culture of organisations, and organisational processes. Gatekeeper negotiation requires a sensitive touch, like any new partnership, which respects the needs and rights of the gatekeeper as much as the importance of the research.

Handling sensitive data – do you speak my language?

The previous discussion has reinforced that researchers investigating WAIB have a responsibility to ensure that the data they seek access to balance the two priorities of advancing knowledge and protecting all those who choose to provide data. In gathering data the researcher needs to develop a relationship with the participants, not only the gatekeepers. Part of the development of the relationship is in gaining informed consent, and in developing a rapport based on trust in the research process. Gaining this trust, however, requires not only keeping the confidentiality of participants but by paying particular attention to not betraying the trust of other participants by passing on, confirming or hinting at confidential information from others in an identifiable way. Rapport building is a skill which requires different levels of aptitude depending on the nature of the data gathering process. In a survey or questionnaire-based data gathering exercise, part of the process is protected in the anonymity of the data provided by participants. In qualitative processes this may require skill in managing, for example, the interview or observation process. In a mixed methods approach researchers may require skills in both areas.

Data gathering on sensitive subjects is likely to include a requirement for the researcher to express empathy, to frame questions appropriately, and yet to not express any judgement or partiality to the participants. In WAIB research this includes working to make sure targets/victims feel heard and supported without adding to their distress, to encourage individuals against whom allegations of WAIB have been made to open up and talk without judgement, and to get good information from bystanders and witnesses, without adding to any emotional responses they may be having with respect to guilt or anger. It is also important, and likely to be a requirement under ethics approvals, to ensure participants are directed to adequate support, should they need it. Getting good data relies on skillful relationship-building both with gatekeepers and other partners including the researched.

Part of the skill in data gathering is cultural awareness (Jacobson *et al.* 2014). The language in use is an exercise of this awareness. In English there have been conventions associated with quantitative studies which have involved asking participants to identify 'negative acts' rather than directly asking about bullying (Balducci *et al.* 2012), but these have had to be carefully translated for use in other languages (Tsuno *et al.* 2010).

In other studies where stories have been collected by researchers it has been important to provide the opportunity for participants to tell their story in their own language, even when data has been collected by way of an English instrument (e.g. Guneri-Cangarli *et al.* 2013). Of the research which has focused on definitional issues, differences in cultural terms have been identified to be linguistically based and/or linked to actual cultural differences. For instance, Lee *et al.* (2012) specifically investigated the use of the slang term *wang-ta* as it relates to exclusion behaviours. The collectivistic nature of South Korean society is reflected in the behaviour, as well as understanding of, its meaning and impact.

Nuances associated with cultural norms may not emerge if the research approach to gathering data does not recognise the differences in language which may contribute to different understandings. Cultural norms may also influence the interpretation of data. Of the research which has reported on the frequency and/or occurrence of WAIB actions, sociocultural characteristics have been identified as contributing to the incidences. For instance, D'Cruz and Rayner (2013) report that superiors emerged as a predominant source of bullying, but that 'cross-level co-bullying', where a personal focus was emphasised, can be explained as reflecting the Indian ethos – a pluralistic society, hierarchically organised.

Analysis of the data, interpretation, theorising and the development of findings and recommendations requires that the researcher acknowledge their own position in the research (to be discussed later), but also that tools are selected which are appropriate to the study. In addition the purpose and design of the study should contemplate the method of analysis at the outset. Consideration must also be given to the process of secondary analysis of primary datasets and how this can be especially applied to exploring sensitive issues (see Long-Sutehall *et al.* 2011 re: qualitative data). This approach can provide the opportunity to revisit data and apply a new perspective or conceptual focus. Considerations, if this approach is undertaken, include the presumption of informed consent in secondary analysis. Long-Sutehall *et al.* (2011) suggest that if the aim of the secondary study meets the intentions of the primary research, then consent gained in the primary research may be sufficient to undertake the secondary analysis.

The fundamental position of the researcher and the paradigmatic lens with which the researcher views the research is a critical consideration in the development of the research design and access considerations.

Disclosure and dissemination

Reporting findings on WAIB has similar considerations to data collection. This includes being mindful of the participants in the research as well as of the audiences who will access the findings. Participants' trust in the research process is often based on the assurances of confidentiality. Gatekeeper approval is likely to be based on similar assurances. In addition, both gatekeepers and participants will potentially be affected by the results as they are reported, and as a consequence it is necessary to be mindful of the manner and style of reporting. These effects are likely to be magnified if research has been carried out in a small number of organisations, or with a small number of participants, and with qualitative rather than quantitative processes. In all types of data there is likely to be evidence which needs careful handling with respect to reporting. In contrast, taking too cautious an approach can lead to failure to tell the story in the data or to offer a true and correct record, which does the participants, and the wider community, a disservice.

Dissemination of findings is an important step in the research process (Cameron and Price 2009). Research which contributes to the body of scientific knowledge needs to be carefully reported, including a clear outline of the methodology and approach so that other researchers can evaluate the outcome, and replicate the approach. Careful selection of an appropriate outlet such as a peer reviewed journal, edited book or official research report will dictate the manner and style of reporting. In-house summaries and reports need to be just as carefully crafted. There is a responsibility associated with quality research to ensure that findings are communicated back to participants in a manner and form that is understandable and accessible while all of the considerations of confidentiality and anonymity are respected. Decision making when it comes to reporting is heavily influenced by the fundamental position of the researcher and the paradigmatic lens with which the researcher views the research. The researcher must listen carefully to the music and execute the dance with grace and style.

The researcher

Central to the study of phenomena as sensitive as WAIB is the researcher. Researcher values, attitudes, skills and experience influence the research and in turn are influenced by the research process as it unfolds. The position of the researcher relative to the researched and the context in which the research is being undertaken cannot be underestimated. Of particular importance when considering research in a cross-cultural context is the position of the researcher not only relative to the topic, in this case WAIB, but also relative to the cultural dimensions, both organisational and ethnic.

In terms of the cultural context in which the research is taking place, some published research is silent and does not specifically address the role of cultural or ethnic background as factors explaining work behaviours (for instance, see Priesemuth 2013, Klaussner 2014). In other conceptual models, the broader ethnic culture or society and organisational culture are considered important backdrops (see Branch *et al.* 2013). The synthesis of Samnani and Singh (2012) present national-level culture as an important factor influencing workplace bullying. In their conceptual model, national culture is subsumed under broad social factors which influence workplace bullying. These authors use the well-known dimensions of power distance, masculinity/femininity and individualism/collectivism (citing Hofstede 1980; see Omari and Sharma this volume) as a critical lens within which to view the influence culture may have on the perpetrator/target relationship, as well as organisational and group norm antecedents of bullying behaviours.

Seo *et al.* (2012) is an example of a specific study focusing on the cultural dimensions' influence on bullying in a single country. Power *et al.* (2013) observe that the confounding of cultural norms and understanding the differences in perceptions of bullying behaviours and incidence adds another layer of complexity in understanding sensitive subjects, when comparing cultural contexts. Understanding how national culture affects organisational policies and practices has been flagged by Jacobson *et al.* (2014) as important for future research.

The globalisation of the workforce increases the number and nature of cross-cultural relationships within the same organisation necessitating that the researcher be mindful of cultural factors at each stage of the research process. The active consideration of what has taken place during the research process can contribute to the sense-making of research into WAIB. A number of tools and techniques are available which afford the researcher opportunity to reflect on their experiences as an insider or outsider of the organisational and cultural contexts, but also of their relationship with the phenomenon under investigation.

As noted by Alvesson *et al.* (2008, p. 480), "reflective research has been attracting increasing attention in organization and management theory. . . ." Reflective practice and reflexivity in research are skills. Researchers first encounter the need for these when determining the positioning of their research both within a paradigm (see Samnani this volume) and the particular context. An example of this is the adoption of a research journal to document the reasons for key decisions (see Cameron and Price 2009). This journal can be utilised throughout the research process, and can present an opportunity for reflexivity much as a mirror would for a dancer to consider their form.

Easterby-Smith and Malina (1999) recommend mirroring and contrasting as two processes that can help researchers to gain insight into themselves and the research process. Increased self-awareness that arises from these practices will enhance the outcome of the research. Lofland *et al.* (2006, p. 3) refer to the privileged position of researcher as a "participant in and witness to" the lives of others. From a practical perspective, research teams which consist of researchers with outsider and insider experiences (Brannick and Coghlan 2007) can provide a way for researchers to have simultaneous insider experiences of multiple contexts and cultures; this is particularly beneficial in cross-cultural research (e.g. Omari *et al.* 2014).

During data analysis and interpretation the role of reflection takes on prominence when the researcher has personal experiences which could influence decision making and interpretation or sense-making (Sobre-Denton 2010). A conscious choice should be made about how to incorporate or set aside self-disclosure, for example, when the WAIB researcher has been the subject of accusations of bullying, or conversely been a target or bystander (Liamputtong 2007). Alvesson *et al.* (2008), for example, recommend being mindful of personal filters and using multi-voicing techniques by asking questions about the relationship between the researcher, gatekeepers and study participants. Options for reflective practice are not confined to the research team, and can include critical friends, reference groups and higher degree supervisory panels.

Writing up research offers an additional reflective opportunity, not only in the process of writing, but also in the peer review process offered by academic journals and edited publications. Irrespective of the choice of paradigm and associated conventions, the researcher by virtue of publishing undertakes an evaluative process. In the social sciences the absence of pure data means that all data is subject to interpretation. In this era of evidence based decision making it is important that quality research is not compromised by ill-attention to floorcraft, including the awareness of self which accompanies skilled research.

Concluding comments

The conduct of research into human behaviours is complex, and never more so than when the behaviour being investigated is one which is the subject of denials and taboos (Liamputtong 2007). This is no less so than for research into workplace abuse, incivility and bullying. This chapter has outlined key considerations in the investigation of these behaviours, and presented the role and positioning of the researcher as fundamental.

The determination of the size and scope of the research project is an underlying factor in its design. It is not only the research question, or the project brief, which will determine size. Research project management includes factors such as budget, time and access to other resources (Cameron and Price 2009).

The need for quality research into workplace abuse, incivility and bullying is still present, and in order to achieve quality outcomes there are three key elements which the researcher must bear in mind:

- The first is that it is important for the research to take many different forms so that the phenomenon of workplace abuse, incivility and bullying and its related issues are considered from many perspectives and in many different ways. This is not unlike the linkage of choreography to the music.
- The second is that it is important in WAIB research that there is room for the voices of all of the stakeholders to be given priority. Targets, bystanders, (alleged) perpetrators and others including boards, customers and the public, as well as those charged with prevention, management and follow up of incidents, all deserve to be heard in the search for answers. This is much like creating and utlising space in the ballroom.
- The third element is that the research which is undertaken needs to inform efforts to ameliorate workplace abuse, incivility and bullying. It needs to translate into the development of policies and approaches for the prevention, reduction, follow up and management of incidents. In this way organisations and workplaces will be able to work towards the creation of a culture of dignity and respect.

If these goals are part of the researcher's approach to workplace abuse, incivility and bullying, their efforts will serve to foster a stronger nexus between research and practice in tackling this complex subjective phenomenon. However the centrality of the researcher to the research is of paramount importance in attaining the goal of quality research into this sensitive area. This central role for the researcher is not confined to WAIB research, but in such research the need for the researcher to be both sensitive and reflexive requires careful consideration, skill and practice much like the floorcraft required of dancers in the ballroom.

Note

1 While the term 'floorcraft' was proposed by the second author due to her knowledge of ballroom dancing, we do acknowledge that others have previously referred to research using a dance analogy (e.g. Janesick 1994).

References

Abu Al Rub, R. F., and Al-Asmar, A. H., 2014. Psychological violence in the workplace among Jordanian hospital nurses. *Journal of Transcultural Nursing: Official Journal of the Transcultural Nursing Society, 25* (1), 6–14.

Alexander, M., MacLaren, A., O'Gorman, K., and Taheri, B., 2012. "He just didn't seem to understand the banter": Bullying or simply establishing social cohesion? *Tourism Management, 33* (5), 1245–55.

Alvesson, M., Hardy, C., and Harley, B., 2008. Reflecting on reflexivity: Reflexive textual practices in organization and management theory. *Journal of Management Studies, 45* (3), 480–501.

Balducci, C., Cecchin, M., Fraccaroli, F., and Schaufeli, W. B., 2012. Exploring the relationship between workaholism and workplace aggressive behaviour: The role of job-related emotion. *Personality and Individual Differences, 53* (5), 629–34.

Beattie, L., and Griffin, B., 2014a. Day-level fluctuations in stress and engagement in response to workplace incivility: A diary study. *Work & Stress, 28* (2), 124–42.

Beattie, L., and Griffin, B., 2014b. Accounting for within-person differences in how people respond to daily incivility at work. *Journal of Occupational and Organizational Psychology, 87* (3), 625–44.

Bergen Bullying Research Group, 2014. Negative Acts Questionnaire (NAQ). See www.uib.no/en/rg/bbrg/44045/naq.

Berry, P. A., Gillespie, G. L., Gates, D., and Schafer, J., 2012. Novice nurse productivity following workplace bullying. *Journal of Nursing Scholarship, 44* (1), 80–7.

Branch, S., Ramsay, S., and Barker, M., 2013. Workplace bullying, mobbing and general harassment: A review. *International Journal of Management Reviews, 15* (3), 280–99.

Brannick, T., and Coghlan, D., 2007. In defense of being "native": The case for insider academic research. *Organizational Research Methods, 10* (1), 59–74.

Cameron, S., and Price, D., 2009. *Business research methods: A practical approach.* London: CIPD.

Clendon, J., and Walker, L., 2012. "Being young": A qualitative study of younger nurses' experiences in the workplace. *International Nursing Review, 59* (4), 555–61.

Cowan, R. L., 2012. It's complicated: Defining workplace bullying from the human resource professional's perspective. *Management Communication Quarterly, 26* (3), 377–403.

Creswell, J. W., 2013. *Research design: Qualitative, quantitative, and mixed methods approaches.* London: Sage.

Creswell, J. W., and Plano Clark, V. L., 2013. *Desiging and conducting mixed methods research.* (2nd ed.). London: Sage.

Dancing in Jaffa, 2015. Available from www.dancinginjaffa.com.

D'Cruz, P., and Noronha, E., 2014. Workplace bullying in the context of organisational change: The significance of pluralism. *Industrial Relations Journal, 45* (1), 2–21.

D'Cruz, P., and Rayner, C., 2013. Bullying in the Indian workplace: A study of the ITES-BPO sector. *Economic and Industrial Democracy, 34* (4), 597–619.

Dhar, R. L., 2012. Why do they bully? Bullying behaviour and its implication on the bullied. *Journal of Workplace Behavioural Health, 27* (2), 79–99.

Doshy, P. V., and Wang, J., 2014. Workplace incivility: What do targets say about it? *American Journal of Management, 14* (1/2), 30–42.

Douglas, S. P., and Craig, C. S., 2007. Collaborative and iterative translation: An alternative approach to back translation. *Journal of International Marketing, 15* (1), 30–43.

Easterby-Smith, M., and Malina, D., 1999. Cross-cultural collaborative research: Toward reflexivity. *Academy of Management Journal, 42* (1), 76–86.

Einarsen, S., Hoel, H., and Notelaers, G. 2009. Measuring bullying and harassment at work: Validity, factor structure, and psychometric properties of the Negative Acts Questionnaire – Revised. Work & Stress, 23 (1), 24–44.

Einarsen, S. and Nielsen, M.B., 2015. Workplace bullying as an antecedent of mental health problems: A five-year prospective and representative study. International Archives of Occupational & Environmental Health, 88 (2) 131–42.

Einarsen, S., and Raknes, B.I. 1997. Harassment in the workplace and the victimization of men. *Violence and Victims, 12* (3), 247–63.

Gilbert, J.A., and Raffo, D.M., 2013. Gender, conflict, and workplace bullying: Is civility policy the silver bullet? *Journal of Managerial Issues, 25* (1), 79–98.

Giorgi, G., 2012. Workplace bullying in academia creates a negative work environment. An Italian study. *Employee Responsibilities and Rights Journal, 24* (4), 261–75.

Guneri-Cangarli, B., Paull, M., and Omari, M. 2013. Workplace bullying in Turkey and Australia: A preliminary comparative investigation. Paper presented at the *EURAM 2013 Democratising Management 13th Annual Conference of the European Academy of Management,* Istanbul, 26th to 29th June.

Hutchinson, M., Wilkes, L., Jackson, D., and Vickers, M.H., 2010. Integrating individual, work group and organizational factors: Testing a multidimensional model of bullying in the nursing workplace. *Journal of Nursing Management, 18* (2), 173–81.

ILO – see International Labour Office

International Labour Office (ILO), World Health Organisation (WHO), International Council of Nurses (ICN), and Public Services International (PSI), 2003. Joint programme on workplace violence in the health sector. Available at www.who.int/violence_injury_prevention/violence/interpersonal/en/WVquestionnaire.pdf.

Jackson, D., Hutchinson, M., Everett, B., Mannix, J., Peters, K., Weaver, R., and Salamonson, Y., 2011. Struggling for legitimacy: Nursing students' stories of organisational aggression, resilience and resistance. *Nursing Inquiry, 18* (2), 102–10.

Jacobson, K.J., Hood, J.N., and Van Buren, H.J., 2014. Workplace bullying across cultures: A research agenda. *International Journal of Cross Cultural Management, 14* (1), 47–65.

Janesick, V.J., 1994. The dance of qualitative research design: Metaphor, methodolatry, and meaning. In N.K. Denzin and Y.S. Lincoln (Eds.), *Handbook of qualitative research*. Thousand Oaks, CA: Sage, pp. 209–19.

Jiménez, B.M., Muñoz, A.R., Gamarra, M.M., and Herrer, M.G., 2007. Assessing workplace bullying: Spanish validation of a reduced version of the Negative Acts Questionnaire. *The Spanish Journal of Psychology, 10* (02), 449–57.

Klaussner, S., 2014. Engulfed in the abyss: The emergence of abusive supervision as an escalating process of supervisor-subordinate interaction. *Human Relations, 67* (3), 311–32.

Lee, H., Kim, H., and Park, J., 2014. Work-related risk factors for workplace violence among Korean employees. *Journal of Occupational Health, 56* (1), 12–20.

Lee, S., Smith, P.K., and Monks, C.P., 2012. Meaning and usage of a term for bullying-like phenomena in South Korea: A lifespan perspective. *Journal of Language and Social Psychology, 31* (3), 342–9.

Liamputtong, P., 2007. *Researching the vulnerable*. London: Sage.

Liamputtong, P., 2010. Cross-cultural research and qualitative inquiry. *Turkish Online Journal of Qualitative Inquiry, 1* (1), 16–29.

Linstead, S., Maréchal, G., and Griffin, R.W., 2014. Theorizing and researching the dark side of organization. *Organization Studies, 35* (2), 165–88.

Lofland, J., Snow, D., Anderson, L., and Lofland, L.H., 2006. *Analyzing social settings: A guide to qualitative observation and analysis.* (4th ed.). Belmont, CA: Wadsworth.

Long-Sutehall, T., Sque, M., and Addington-Hall, J., 2011. Secondary analysis of qualitative data: A valuable method for exploring sensitive issues with an elusive population? *Journal of Research in Nursing, 16* (4) 335–44.

McLaughlin, H., Uggen, C., and Blackstone, A., 2012. Sexual harassment, workplace authority, and the paradox of power. *American Sociological Review, 77* (4), 625–47.

National Health and Medical Research Council (NHMRC), Australian Research Council (ARC) and Australian Vice-Chancellors' Committee (AVCC), 2007/2014. *National statement on ethical conduct in human research 2007 (Updated March 2014).* Canberra: Commonwealth of Australia.

NHMRC – see National Health and Medical Research Council

Omari, M., 2007. *Towards dignity and respect: An exploration of the nature, causes and consequences of workplace bullying.* Saarbrücken: VDM Verlag Dr. Müller.

Omari, M., Paull, M., D'Cruz, P., and Guneri-Cangarli, B., 2014. Fair game: The influence of cultural norms in creating sanctioned targets in the workplace. Proceedings of the *9th International Conference on Workplace Bullying & Harassment,* Milan, Italy, 17th to 21st June.

Pilch, I., and Turska, E., 2015. Relationships between Machiavellianism, organizational culture, and workplace bullying: Emotional abuse from the target's and the perpetrator's perspective. *Journal of Business Ethics, 128* (1), 83–93.

Power, J.L., *et al.,* 2013. Acceptability of workplace bullying: A comparative study on six continents. *Journal of Business Research, 66* (3), 374–80.

Priesemuth, M., 2013. Stand up and speak up: Employees' prosocial reactions to observed abusive supervision. *Business & Society, 52* (4), 649–65.

Samnani, A.-K., 2013. Is this bullying?: Understanding target and witness reactions. *Journal of Managerial Psychology, 28* (3), 290–305.

Samnani, A.-K., and Singh, P., 2012. 20 years of workplace bullying research: A review of the antecedents and consequences of bullying in the workplace. *Aggression and Violent Behavior, 17* (6), 581–9.

Schilpzand, P., De Pater, I.E., and Erez, A., 2014. Workplace incivility: A review of the literature and agenda for future research. *Journal of Organizational Behavior,* DOI: 10.1002/job.1976.

Seo, Y.N., Leather, P., and Coyne, I., 2012. South Korean culture and history: The implications for workplace bullying. *Aggression and Violent Behaviour, 17* (5), 419–22.

Shallcross, L., Ramsay, S., and Barker, M., 2013. Severe workplace conflict: The experience of mobbing. *Negotiation and Conflict Management Research, 6* (3), 191–213.

Sobre-Denton, M.S., 2010. Stories from the cage: Autoethnographic sensemaking of workplace bullying, gender discrimination, and white privilege. *Journal of Contemporary Ethnography, 41*(2), 220–50.

Takaki, J., *et al.,* 2010. Assessment of workplace bullying and harassment: Reliability and validity of a Japanese version of the negative acts questionnaire. *Journal of Occupational Health, 52* (1), 74–81.

Tashakkori, A., and Teddlie, C., (Eds.), 2010. *Sage handbook of mixed methods in social and behavioral research.* (2nd ed.). Thousand Oaks, CA: Sage.

Tracy, S.J., Lutgen-Sandvik, P., and Alberts, J.K., 2006. Nightmares, demons, and slaves exploring the painful metaphors of workplace bullying. *Management Communication Quarterly, 20* (2), 148–85.

Tsuno, K., Kawakami, N., Inoue, A., and Abe, K., 2010. Measuring workplace bullying: Reliability and validity of the Japanese version of the negative acts questionnaire. *Journal of Occupational Health, 52* (4), 216–6.

Turk, M., Davas, A., Tanik, F.A., and Montgomery, A.J., 2014. Organizational stressors, work/family interface and the role of gender in the hospital: Experiences from Turkey. *British Journal of Health Psychology, 19* (2), 442–58.

Vickers, M.H., 2014. Telling tales to share multiple truths: Disability and workplace bullying – A semi-fiction case study. *Employee Responsibilities and Rights Journal, 27*(1), 27–45.

Waschgler, K., Ruiz-Hernández, J.A., Llor-Esteban, B., and Jiménez-Barbero, J.A., 2013. Vertical and lateral workplace bullying in nursing: Development of the hospital aggressive behaviour scale. *Journal of Interpersonal Violence, 28* (12), 2389–412.

Whitaker, T., 2012. Social workers and workplace bullying: Perceptions, responses and implications. *Work: A Journal of Prevention, Assessment and Rehabilitation, 42* (1), 115–23.

Willis, P., 2012. Witnesses on the periphery: Young lesbian, gay, bisexual and queer employees witnessing homophobic exchanges in Australian workplaces. *Human Relations, 65* (12), 1589–610.

Wolcott, H.F., 2009. *Writing up qualitative research.* (3rd ed.). Thousand Oaks, CA: Sage.

4 In the eye of the beholder

Ethnic culture as a lens

Maryam Omari and Manish Sharma

Introduction

It is said that 'diversity is the spice of life'; that is, differences add interest and 'flavour', but what if the spice is unpalatable, unfamiliar, hard to reconcile/digest, or just too exotic? Will it still add 'flavour' or will it cause discomfort or frustration? Human nature is such that people are comfortable with notions that are known to them; this provides certainty and stability. Differences can often cause unpredictability, and may require some degree of flexibility in being able to see multiple potential perspectives; tolerance, understanding, and eventually acceptance come from the ability to appreciate and reconcile differences.

Ethnic culture (hereafter referred to as culture) is multi-dimensional and provides a lens through which behaviours are perceived and interpreted. There are many famous and well-used cultural frameworks which compartmentalise value systems, attitudes, and resultant standards of behaviour. Often, stereotypes are used for ease of explanation and categorisation; however, caution must be exercised as diversity can be seen even within a seemingly homogenous group (Steers *et al.* 2013). The same behaviour may also be interpreted and construed differently by diverse groups if the points of reference, core values, and attitudes are not the same: resulting in an 'eye of the beholder'[1] perspective.

Culture has received limited attention in the workplace bullying literature (Samnani 2013). This chapter will commence by discussing culture and the notions of diversity and ethnocentrism. It will then briefly discuss various well-known, and some lesser known, frameworks for classifying culture. The chapter will form a frame of reference for ensuing country and culture specific chapters on workplace abuse, incivility, and bullying.

Culture

The word 'culture' has been derived from Latin and relates to "cult or worship" (Warner and Joynt 2011, p. 3). Culture can be described as a lens through which different behaviours are observed, interpreted, and experienced. Behaviour may not have the same meaning in different (cultural) settings; hence, the 'eye of the beholder' title for this chapter. Different interpretations of the same act or behaviour may cause confusion among those experiencing them who are not members of the relevant community. Outsiders with little or no understanding of differences can easily violate accepted norms in the community, resulting in offence, conflict, or inappropriate behaviours (an aspect that will be returned to later in this chapter).

The study of culture, and differences and similarities between various groups or communities, has long been of interest to people from all walks of life. Trailblazers in the field, such as Ruth Benedict (1887–1948) and Margaret Mead (1901–1978) often sparked controversy through their findings and methods, one of which was immersion in the cultures being studied. This lived experience was thought to provide valuable insights into a culture as it allowed a window into deep-seated value systems which influence attitudes and therefore behaviours (Steers *et al.* 2013). As this book has a focus on workplace abuse, incivility, and bullying from different cultural and methodological perspectives, author self-reports will provide unique insights into the interpretation of behaviours in different cultural contexts.

There are many definitions of culture. Fundamentally, most incorporate the notions of shared and learned values resulting in unique languages, symbols, and rules governing human interactions. Cameron and Quinn (2011, p. 19) contend that "people are unaware of their culture until it is challenged, until they experience a new culture, or until it is made overt and explicit". Beamer and Varner (2001, p. 3) describe culture as a "property of a community of people". This, a simple and elegant description, will be adopted as the frame of reference in this chapter.

Diversity

Social and group identification (Tajfel 1982; Tolman 1943 cited in Ashford and Mael 1989) and the Attraction-Selection-Assimilation thesis (Baron and Byrne 2004) purport that people more readily relate to, like, and are at ease with those who are similar to them (Standen *et al.* 2014). Omari *et al.* (2014) found that cultural norms are responsible for setting diversity tolerance thresholds. This in turn places value, be it high or low, on those who are seen as the 'same' or 'different' to the dominant group. There is much evidence suggesting that humans are comfortable and at ease with similar others.

It is well documented, especially in the change management literature, that differences, and therefore unknowns, can result in sceptical outlooks, lack of trust, and at the extreme, fear (e.g., Cummings and Worley 2008). In a cultural context, those who are different and do not 'fit in' are not considered worthy of 'membership' of the main group, and may come to be accepted as "fair game" or "sanctioned targets" and subjected to abuse and negative behaviours (Omari *et al.* 2014, p. 167). De Janasz *et al.* (2007) contend that a lack of diversity tolerance is a key influencing factor in negative behaviours, with stereotypes, prejudice, ethnocentrism, discrimination, and harassment all playing their part.

McPhail *et al.* (2015, p. 170) provide a composite model of diversity based on earlier work by Gardenswartz and Rowe (2003) and Loden and Rosener (1991). Of specific interest here are the internal and external dimensions of diversity, at the heart of which is personality. The internal dimensions include: ethnicity, race, age, gender, sexual orientation, and physical ability; and the external factors are: geographic location, income, personal habits, recreational habits, religion, educational background, work experience, appearance, personal status, and marital status. It is easy to see how the elements of the internal and external dimensions of the model are highly interrelated: geographic location, religion, personal appearance, ethnicity, and race. The model confirms assertions made that cultures are homogenous but allow for individuality; therefore cultures can explain but *not* predict behaviour (Steers *et al.* 2013). The Mcphail *et al.* (2015) model represents this individuality by placing personality at the heart of diversity.

Gannon and Pillai (2013) contend that fluency in a language does not necessarily result in understanding. This can be readily seen in countries such as Australia, the US, the UK, Canada, New Zealand, Singapore, and India, which all have English as an official language but which have different local cultures. As an example, the beach culture of Australia understands 'thongs' as being casual footwear (referred to as 'flip-flops' in the US). In the US, however, a 'thong' is understood to be a revealing form of underwear (referred to as a 'G-string' in Australia). Misunderstandings can be further amplified for non-native speakers, where often the spoken word is translated literally, such as this sign from a Japanese hotel: "You are invited to take advantage of our chambermaid" (McFarlin and Sweeney 2013, p. 92).

Jokes, sarcasm, light hearted banter, and the use of humour may be perceived in a negative light by non-native speakers of a language and may possibly be construed as outright insults. For example, in the casual Australian culture friends often address each other using derogatory terms or even swear words. This is seen as a sign of affection, 'mateship', or both being members of the same community or in-group. Outsiders viewing such interactions with little understanding of the cultural context may become confused, translate the verbal communication literally, and be offended by the language used, or the interactions taking place.

Silence also has different meaning in different cultural contexts (Beamer and Varner 2001). The Confucian Asian cultures use silence as part of conversation, giving time for reflection and meaning; however, the present oriented western cultures are generally uncomfortable with silence, as it is ambiguous. It is easy to see how misunderstandings can arise in the workplace given different cultural perspectives. In multicultural societies such as Australia and the US, the migrant population learns to speak English, and this to some extent assists in understanding the country, its culture, and context. English is the global language of work; therefore there is less incentive for native English speakers to learn other languages. With this goes the inability to gain an appreciation and understanding of other cultures, and of the subtleties inherent in communication across different cultural contexts.

There are many examples of victimisation based on characteristics which make an individual different from others or the dominant group: racism, discrimination, prejudice, homophobia, sexism, and ageism. Salin and Hoel (2013) argue that bullying is a gendered phenomenon which affects exposure, interpretation, and the lived experience of the victim. Lim and Cortina (2005) found that incivility and sexual harassment against female employees were related constructs with gendered harassment bridging the two, and having implications for well-being. Hoel *et al.* (2014) report that lesbians, gays, and bisexuals are more than twice as likely to be bullied and discriminated against as heterosexuals.

A study of bullying in nursing in the UK found race, and the related notions of being different and having less power, to be influencing factors in inappropriate workplace interactions (Allan *et al.* 2009). In the US, white employees were found to be more reactive to incivility than the racial minorities in the country (Kern and Grandey 2009) with similar causal factors being at play.

Diversity as a result of physical or mental disability has also been identified as a trigger for negative behaviours. Richards (2012) found that inclusion was an issue for adults with Asperger's Syndrome, and that this in turn affected their employment experiences in a negative manner. Fevre *et al.* (2013) identified that different types of disability were associated with different types of ill-treatment, and that employees with long-term illnesses and disabilities were more likely to be targets of a broader range of negative behaviours at work.

It is easy to see how diversity and diversity intolerance, both overt and covert, can result in workplace problems. Issues and confusion in perception, understanding, communication, and interactions can happen due to differences, including those of a cultural nature. This can have significant implications for employees, organisations, and beyond (Omari 2007). The breakdown in understanding can result in conflict (individual and organisational) and lead to negative workplace behaviours such as abuse, incivility, and bullying.

Ethnocentrism

Beamer and Varner (2001, p. 16) contend that most people see their own culture as natural and right, and assess other cultures by how closely they resemble their own. Triandis (1990) described this comparison to 'our' standards as ethnocentrism, and saw it as the basis for the creation of 'us' and 'them', resulting in in-group out-group behaviour. Here, those who are considered to belong to 'us' are seen as normal, are favoured in comparison to others, and granted concessions and benefits; whereas those who are considered 'them' may be seen as different or foreign, and are hard to reconcile in terms of behaviour or standing.

Acceptable standards of behaviour and conduct are generally rule-bound, and based on fundamental notions of right and wrong (Cameron and Quinn 2011). Within a culture, members of the community have a shared understanding of these expectations and demonstrate this through compliance with unwritten rules. Individuals either 'fit', and are therefore considered insiders by demonstrating appropriate behaviours, or they do not. In multicultural settings conflict can easily arise as a result of different frames of reference and norms of behaviour.

It is worth recounting a story to further reinforce this. An acquaintance of Chinese descent recently had a baby. A visitor of Middle Eastern descent took the time to see the mother and baby at the hospital and presented them with a gift. The new mother politely accepted the gift and set it on a side table unopened. After some time, and polite conversation, the Middle Eastern visitor left extremely offended by the behaviour of the new mother. When asked why, the visitor indicated that it was extremely rude of the new mother not to open the present in her presence and say how much she loved or needed it, this being customary in her own culture. The new mother, however, was completely oblivious to the offence she had caused, as in her Chinese culture it would have been very rude to open the present in front of the person giving it, as it may have resulted in the 'loss of face', an extremely important concept in Asian cultures. This is not a workplace example; however, it strives to make the point that if such (at face value) benign behaviours can readily cause offence, and possibly conflict in social settings, then the implications of these misunderstandings in the workplace may be more serious and pronounced.

The frameworks

The notion of culture itself is diverse both in nature and interpretation, leading to different dimensions and understandings. Members of communities tend to conduct themselves in accordance with given norms and within the cultural settings of those communities. This may lead to individuals behaving in different ways in the same situations, or people interpreting the same behaviour in different ways. Various cultural frameworks have been developed to assist in the understanding of the relevant dimensions and elements of culture; a few chosen ones will be described below.

Hofstede

With over 180 studies published in over 40 business and psychology journals, the Hofstede framework is not the oldest, but arguably one of the most frequently cited, and also at times, controversial (Kirkman *et al.* 2006). The framework is based on work conducted by Geert Hofstede between 1967–1973 at IBM in over 70 countries. Hofstede (1980) defined culture as the collective programming of the mind which distinguishes the members of one human group from another. The framework was established with four dimensions: power distance; individualism vs collectivism; masculinity vs femininity; and uncertainty avoidance. A fifth dimension, long-term orientation, was added in 1991 based on the work of Bond to incorporate the Confucian perspective and Asian cultures. More recently, in 2010, another dimension has been added based on the work of Minkov: indulgence vs restraint orientation (Hofstede Centre 2015). The six dimensions currently comprising the Hofstede framework are:

- Power distance – Ranked high or low, power distance is the extent to which individuals believe that power in establishments is distributed unequally. It also relates to the way in which society handles inequalities amongst people and groups. In high power distance societies everyone has their 'place' which determines their standing or status in society.
- Individualism vs collectivism – Individualism is referred to as a preference for a loosely knit social framework, wherein individuals are expected to look after themselves and their immediate families. Collectivism, at the other end of the continuum, is defined as a tightly held social framework, wherein individuals expect relatives, clan, or other members of the in-group to look after them in exchange for loyalty.
- Masculinity vs femininity – In masculine cultures, there is a marked preference for achievement, heroism, and assertiveness as well as material success. In feminine cultures, there is a preference for relationships, modesty, caring for the weak, and quality of life.
- Uncertainty avoidance – Also ranked high or low, uncertainty avoidance is the level to which individuals feel uncomfortable with uncertainty and ambiguity. The main aspect of this dimension relates to whether society wishes to control the future or let it happen. Countries with high uncertainty avoidance follow rigid codes of beliefs and behaviour.
- Long-term orientation – Also known as Confucian dynamism, long-term orientation refers to long-term vs short-term orientation. Long-term orientation refers to future oriented values such as persistence and thrift, whereas short-term orientation refers to past and present oriented values such as respect for tradition and fulfilling social obligations.
- Indulgence vs restraint – Indulgent communities strive for the enjoyment of life and having fun, whereas restraint based cultures adhere to strict social norms and 'hold back'.

Trompenaars and Hampden-Turner

Trompenaars in association with Hampden-Turner offer an alternative framework based on work that commenced in 1985 and continues to the present day (Trompenaars Hampden-Turner Culture for Business 2015). The distinctiveness of their perspective lies in the framework not being wholly engaged in investigating country based stereotypes, but emphasising the need to understand individuals with reference to their respective cultural setting, and while "doing business and managing" (p. 1). Trompenaars and Hampden-Turner (2012) devised three main dimensions: relationships with people, attitude to time, and relationship with the environment, with the first dimension comprising five elements.

- Relationships with people
    - Universalism vs particularism – Universalism relates to establishing broad general rules, that is, the same rules applying to all regardless. Particularist societies on the other hand deal with exceptions. This means, one rule for one group, and another for other groups, in effect resulting in what may be seen as differential and preferential treatment of people depending on who they are, and what relationships exist between the parties.
    - Individualism vs collectivism – Individualism focuses on the rights of the individuals and the belief that a person should be allowed to grow as well as fail on their own. In collectivism, the group, clan, and family are of paramount importance and come before an individual's interests.
    - Specific vs diffuse – In the specific orientated cultures, relationships between individuals are well defined, and work-life issues segregated; that is, there is a public sphere and a private one. For those with diffuse orientation, work-life issues are intermingled, cross over, and overlap, resulting in blurred lines of distinction.
    - Neutral vs affective – Those with a neutral orientation seldom display emotions publicly; here, controlled feelings form the hallmark of behaviour. Those with an affective stance are, however, open with their inner feelings and emotions, and visible signs such gesturing, smiling, and body language are used to convey messages.
    - Achievement vs ascription – In achievement based settings, status is achieved through performance. For ascription based orientations, status is gained through other means, such as personal and family connections, standing in the community, and seniority.
- Attitude towards time – Different cultures ascribe different meanings to the past, present, and future. In past oriented cultures, people tend to show respect for ancestors, as well as older people, and generally take things in a traditional and historic context. In present oriented cultures, people enjoy the present day activities and relationships. In future oriented cultures, people derive satisfaction from discussing future potentials, prospects, and opportunities for achievement.
- Relationship with the environment – This dimension deals with how individuals relate to their natural environment. People from internal oriented cultures have a more dominant attitude, a rigid focus on their own functions, and are not very comfortable with change. People from external oriented cultures are generally more flexible and willing to compromise, as there is a high level of emphasis on harmony, and a level of acceptance towards change.

Globe

The 'Global Leadership and Organizational Behavior Effectiveness' (GLOBE) project led by House commenced in 1991. An all-inclusive work from this study was published in 2004 based on results from around 17,300 middle managers from 951 organisations in the food processing, financial services, and telecommunications services industries. This project identified a number of cultural dimensions (House et al. 2004; Steers *et al.* 2013), some of which use similar terminology and overlap with earlier discussed frameworks.

- Power distance – Described as the level to which individuals in a culture expect power to be distributed equally. Similar to Hofstede's framework, in high power distance settings, societies are divided, and powerbases are stable with limited, if any, movement between groups.
- Uncertainty avoidance – Defined as the extent to which a collective entity may rely on social norms, rules, and procedures to eliminate the level of unpredictability of future events. High uncertainty avoidance cultures are marked by formalised social interactions, and reliance of laws and rules.
- Humane orientation – Relates to the level to which a collective would encourage as well as reward individuals for being fair, generous, caring, and kind to others. Cultures high on human orientation value altruism, the interests of others, belonging, and affiliation.
- Institutional collectivism – The level to which organisational practices encourage as well as reward collective distribution of resources and collective action. Strong, cohesive groups and the importance of the greater good are representative of high institutional collectivism.
- In-group collectivism – The degree to which individuals express pride, loyalty, and cohesiveness in their organisations or families. Individual contribution to the group is a hallmark of high in-group collectivism, as is organisations taking on a paternalist approach to the management of their staff.
- Assertiveness – The extent to which individuals are assertive, confrontational, and aggressive in their relationships with others. In high assertiveness cultures, communication is unambiguous, hard work is valued, and tough behaviour revered.
- Gender egalitarianism – The level to which the collective minimises the inequality of genders. Women participate strongly, and are awarded equal status in high gender egalitarianism cultures.
- Future orientation – Individual indulgence in future oriented behaviours, such as delaying gratification, planning, or investing in the future, are the focus of this dimension. Organisations strive towards economic success, are adaptive, and display flexible practices in high future orientated settings.
- Performance orientation – Referred to as the level to which a collective encourages and rewards group members for certain types of performance improvement and excellence. High performance orientated cultures value assertiveness, competition, and materialism.

Kluckhohn and Strodtbeck

The foundations for the Value Orientation Method (VOM) were laid in the 1940s and 1950s by anthropologists with the Harvard Values Project. This project established that people across cultures could respond to problems in at least three possible orientations at the two ends of the continuum and the midpoint across six dimensions (Kluckhohn and Strodtbeck 1961).

- Relationship with nature – This value refers to beliefs about the relationship between an individual and nature. People can be subordinate to nature, where they believe that life is largely determined by external forces, such as fate and destiny. There could also be harmonious coexistence, or the belief that people can master, conquer, and control nature.
- Relationship with people – This orientation is concerned with forms of social organisation. The hierarchical or lineal viewpoint is concerned with the natural order of relations, where some people are born to lead, whereas others are followers. In group orientated cultures, people have equal status and everyone shares in the decision making process. The individualistic perspective sees social structure being based on individuals with people having complete control over their own destiny.
- Human activities – This orientation focuses on the mode of activity. One mode is the alternative of 'being', where it is enough to live in the moment and just 'be'. Here it is not necessary to accomplish great things in life to feel life has been worthwhile. Alternatively, the focus can be on 'becoming' with an emphasis on inner development and growth. There is also the 'doing' orientation with an emphasis on goals and accomplishments where if people work hard, their efforts will be rewarded.
- Relationship with time – Here, people may relate to the past, where they learn from history, and strive to continue past traditions, or they may relate to the present, where they enjoy the 'here and now' without much concern for the past or future. The third perspective is future focused, wherein planning and goal setting are important in order to grow and change.
- Human nature – This dimension focuses on the basic nature of people. People can be evil, in that most cannot be trusted, are bad, and need to be controlled; mixed or neutral, both good and evil people coexist in the world; and good, most people are born good and are pure at heart.

Hall's framework

Hall (1966), an anthropologist and cross-cultural researcher, offered yet another cultural framework based on three main indicators: context, space, and time.

- Context – Here, two main elements were identified: high and low. In a high context culture, there are numerous hidden contextual elements that are the key to understanding rules, including non-verbal communication and gestures; this can be a daunting task for a person from outside the culture. In a low context environment, very little is taken for granted, and the spoken word is what counts in communication. This at times may result in lengthy explanations as everything is quite descriptively explicit; there may be less chance of misunderstanding, especially for outsiders.

- Space – The high territoriality perspective indicates that some people, as well as nations, are more territorial than others, and have a greater concern for securing their space. The low territoriality perspective is prevalent where some people ascribe little value to material ownership of space, and are comfortable in sharing territory and ownership.
- Time – People who are monochronic in terms of their orientation to time tend to do one thing at a time; this usually involves a high level of planning and scheduling. Whereas people who are polychronic value human interaction over time and material things, they often get things done, but without the limitation of any particular time frame.

Core cultural dimensions

Steers *et al.* (2013) acknowledge that each of these existing cultural frameworks make important contributions to the field. They offer a composite five-factor model referring to Core Cultural Dimensions and drawing on key aspects of earlier frameworks.

- Power distribution – This dimension covers equality and privilege and the way power is distributed in society, whether egalitarian or in a hierarchical manner.
- Social organisation – Where distinction is made between value being placed primarily on the individual or the group.
- Environmental relationships – Society's relationship with the environment is about control or harmony.
- Time/work patterns – The distinction made here is whether people tackle work in a linear and sequential, or non-linear and more complex polychronic, manner.
- Uncertainty and social control – The primary concern of this dimension is the value placed on rule-based or relationship-based perspectives.

Gannon and Pillai

Based on work which commenced in 1988 by Gannon, Gannon and Pillai's (2013) unique work on cultural metaphors focuses on a wide range of issues including: religion, public behaviour, lifestyle, space, greeting behaviour, group behaviour, political structure, food and eating behaviour, and class. Their work was initially criticised for portraying stereotypes, but these classifications are useful as they unearth deep cultural values, and therefore the shaping of attitudes and behaviours. Gannon and Pillai's (2013) book clusters countries into groups of nations based on similar characteristics and orientations. The main classifications are discussed below.

- Authority ranking cultures – These cultures have a high degree of collectivism, accompanied by a high degree of power distance. Here, both superiors and subordinates have obligations towards one another which transcend their job descriptions. Countries belonging to this group include: Turkey, Poland, Thailand, Japan, Saudi Arabia, Vietnam, and Korea.
- Scandinavian and other egalitarian cultures: Sweden, Finland, and Denmark fall within the Scandinavian egalitarian grouping. These and other egalitarian societies (e.g., Germany, Ireland, Canada, and France) are 'equality matching' cultures, with a low degree of power distance, and a high degree of individualism. This unique perspective leads to a cultural setting wherein individuals are highly valued and are largely autonomous at the same time, resulting from a low level of power distance.
- Market pricing cultures – These cultures are based on the paradigm that it is possible to compare individuals through a common unit of measurement, along with a true zero point. The zero point referred to is zero money, meaning everything is evaluated and judged by this one criterion. Britain and the US are prominent examples of such cultures.
- Cleft national cultures – The countries in this cluster are distinctive and diverse including: Israel, Malaysia, Nigeria, Italy (with a distinction between the north and south), and Belgium. Here national identity is difficult to form as the ethnic groups are so distinct in terms of values, and groups are generally separated from each other as they do not share the same religions or cultural values.
- Base cultures and diffusion – During the past century, migration of people across national borders has increased exponentially. When people move across countries, their deep-seated beliefs, norms, and values follow. The Chinese in Singapore and British settlers in Australia, the US, and Canada are good examples. The national cultures of the settled nations bear a significant affinity to their main migrant cohorts.

As can be seen, the frameworks above have some differences, yet many common dimensions and elements in classifying and categorising norms, values, beliefs, and behaviours. Given factors such as the globalised workplace, the advent and growth of multinational corporations, and popular media, some convergence of values and therefore standards of behaviour in certain cultures and countries are evident over time. Any one framework may not be able to comprehensively cover all idiosyncrasies across all cultural settings; however, each provide valuable contributions in their own right, and assist in a deeper appreciation and understanding of the complex notion that is known as culture. A better understanding of cultural contexts will be extremely valuable in the study of workplace abuse, incivility, and bullying in modern diverse workplaces around the world.

What little is known

It is well documented that bullying is a subjective phenomenon (e.g., Omari 2007). Power *et al.* (2013) found that there are different experiences of workplace bullying in different cultural contexts. This contention is an emerging theme in a number of recent studies. Escartín *et al.* (2011) found similarities in the conceptualisation of workplace bullying between Central America and Southern Europe. Despite common languages, results showed that employees from the former emphasised the physical and overt, while the psychological and more covert aspect of workplace bullying was emphasised in the latter. Subtle differences in perception arise from these perspectives.

In a study of employees in Russia and New Zealand it was found that cultural differences and considerations such as value placed on in-groups affected ethical decision making processes (Kuntz *et al.* 2013) and therefore resultant behaviours. Zábrodská *et al.* (2014) contend that sensemaking (through a cultural veil) can magnify the power disparity between different parties in workplace bullying scenarios. There is also some evidence that self-reports of workplace bullying in Greece (a hierarchical society) are different to the northern European/ Scandinavian (egalitarian) countries (Galanaki and Papalexandris 2013). Similarly, in a comparative study (of the US and Japan) researchers found that culture moderated cyberbullying incidents with the rates being higher in the American versus Japanese cohorts (Barlett *et al.* 2014).

Differences between experiences of, and attitudes towards, workplace bullying in high power distance and egalitarian cultures have also been documented. A study in China found that "employees with low power distance react more negatively to abusive supervisors than do those with high power distance" (Wang *et al.* 2012, p. 56). Loh *et al.* (2010) also reported that in different cultural contexts, egalitarian countries with low power distance respond to bullying more negatively than hierarchical ones with higher power distance. Power *et al.* (2013) found that in Asia, where cultural norms dictate that people submit to the interests of the group and there is a strong acceptance of authority, workplace bullying is more tolerated. This may point to inappropriate behaviors and bullying being expected in work settings by those lower in the hierarchy.

In India (D'Cruz and Rayner 2012) and Turkey (Guneri-Cangarli *et al.* 2013), both hierarchical societies, superiors have been identified as the main source of bullying; however, in Australia, a more egalitarian society, peers were found to be 30 per cent of the perpetrator group (Omari 2007). Power *et al.* (2013) report that in more equality based cultures (such as Australia), targets suffer more when subjected to negative behaviors due to the expectation of fairness and equality. In a similar vein, bystanders observing workplace bullying in Australia felt more powerful and were reported to take more direct action against the behaviour than in Turkey (Guneri-Cangarli *et al.* 2013).

Power *et al.* (2013) also found that humane orientation was negatively correlated with acceptability of bullying, with employees in Confucian Asia considering bullying to be more acceptable than employees in Latin America (where personal connections are highly valued) and sub-Saharan Africa (which has a higher humane orientation), with Anglo country clusters showing lower acceptability of bullying. Hodgins (2014) contends that mistreatment is complex and more commonly identified in stronger, more egalitarian, and more equitable economies. This may not necessarily be attributed to the relative prevalence, severity, or the nature of negative behaviours, but the cultural lens through which the 'beholder' perceives that which unfolds.

Concluding comments

Outsiders in any setting may have difficulty accurately perceiving, understanding, and responding to behaviours emanating from deep-seated values. This can lead to misunderstanding, confusion, feeling threatened, and possibly conflict, in turn increasing the potential for negative and inappropriate behaviours. The aim of this chapter was to provide background information on different cultural frameworks for the ensuing country specific chapters.

Cultural convergence, especially in the younger population, has already taken root as a result of globalisation, technological advances, and the blurring of the boundaries between space and time (Guneri-Cangarli *et al.* 2013). Culture is, however, deep rooted and stable by nature (Schein 1992); regardless of the degree of convergence, diverse values, attitudes, and behaviours will continue to exist in different contexts. Cross-cultural competence is a key attribute required not only of expatriate employees, but increasingly of all members of modern societies, especially for those in multicultural workplaces. The potential for synergies, creative problem solving, innovation, and advancements may not be realised in a globalised world if different individuals and groups do not develop an appreciation, better and deeper understanding, and an acceptance of different ways.

Note

1 The expression 'beauty is in the eye of the beholder' refers to an understanding that different people interpret things in different ways.

References

Allan, H.T., Cowie, H. and Smith, P., 2009. Overseas nurses' experiences of discrimination: A case of racist bullying. *Journal of Nursing Management*, 17, 898–906.

Ashford, B.E. and Mael, F., 1989. Social identity theory and the organization. *The Academy of Management Review*, 14(9), 20–39.

Barlett, C.P., Gentile, D.A., Anderson, C.A., Suzuki, K., Sakamoto, A., Yamaoka, A. and Katsura, R., 2014. Cross-cultural differences in cyberbullying behaviour: A short-term longitudinal study. *Journal of Cross-Cultural Psychology*, 45(2), 300–13.

Baron, R.A. and Byrne, D., 2004. *Social psychology*. New Delhi: Pearson.

Beamer, L. and Warner, I., 2001. *Intercultural communication in the global workplace*. Boston: McGraw-Hill Irwin.

Cameron, K.S. and Quinn, R.E., 2011. *Diagnosing and changing organizational culture: Based on the competing values framework*. 3rd ed. San Francisco: Jossey-Bass.

Cummings, T.G. and Worley, C.G., 2008. *Organization change and development*. New Delhi: Cengage.

D'Cruz, P. and Rayner, C., 2012. Bullying in the Indian workplace: A study of the ITES-BPO sector. *Economic and Industrial Democracy*, 34(4), 597–619.

de Janasz, S., Wood, G., Gottschalk, L., Dowd, K.I. and Schneider, B., 2007. *Interpersonal skills in organisations*. Boston: McGraw-Hill Irwin.

Escartín, J., Zaph, D., Arrieta, C. and Rodriguez-Carballeira, A., 2011. Workers' perception of workplace bullying: A cross-cultural study. *European Journal of Work and Organizational Psychology*, 20(2), 178–205.

Fevre, R., Robinson, A., Lewis, D. and Jones, T., 2013. The ill-treatment of employees with disabilities in British workplaces. *Work, Employment and Society*, 27(2), 288–307.

Galanaki, E. and Papalexandris, N., 2013. Measuring workplace bullying in organisations. *The International Journal of Human Resource Management*, 24(11), 2107–30.

Gannon, M.J. and Pillai, R., 2013. *Understanding global cultures: Metaphorical journeys through 31 nationals, clusters of nations, continents, and diversity*. 5th ed. Thousand Oaks: Sage.

Gardenswartz, L. and Rowe, A., 2003. *Diverse teams at work: Capitalizing on the power of diversity*. 2nd ed. Available from: www.gardenswartzrowe.com/about. html#div [accessed 25 November 2014].

Guneri-Cangarli, B., Paull, M. and Omari, M., 2013. Workplace bullying in Turkey and Australia: A preliminary comparative investigation. In *Proceedings of the European Academy of Management Conference (EURAM)*, Istanbul, Turkey.

Hall, E.T., 1966. *The hidden dimension*. New York: Double Day Anchor Books.

Hodgins, M., 2014. Workplace mistreatment: Health, working environment and social and economic factors. *Health*, 6, 392–403.

Hoel, H., Lewis, D. and Einarsottir, A., 2014. *The ups and downs of LGBs' workplace experiences: Discrimination, bullying and harassment of lesbian, gay and bisexual employees in Britain*. Manchester: Manchester Business School.

Hofstede, G.H., 1980. *Culture's consequences: International differences in work-related values*. Newbury Park: Sage.

Hofstede Center, 2015. *National cultural dimensions* [online]. Available from: http://geert-hofstede.com/national-culture.html [accessed 7 January 2015].

House, R.J., Hanges, P.J., Javidan, M., Dorfman, P.W. and Gupta, V., 2004. *Culture, leadership and organisations: The GLOBE study of 62 societies*. Thousand Oaks: Sage.

Kern, J.H. and Grandey, A.A., 2009. Customer incivility as a social stressor: The role of race and racial identify for service employees. *Journal of Occupational Health Psychology*, 14(1), 46–57.

Kirkman, B.L., Lowe, K.B. and Gibson, B., 2006. A quarter century of Culture's Consequences: A review of the empirical research incorporating Hofstede's cultural values framework. *Journal of International Business Studies*, 37, 285–320.

Kluckhohn, F.R. and Strodtbeck, F.L., 1961. *Variations in value orientations.* Evanston: Row, Peterson.

Kuntz, J.R.C., Kuntz, J.R., Elenkov, D. and Nabirukhina, A., 2013. Characterizing ethical cases: A cross-cultural investigation of individual differences, organizational climate, and leadership on ethical decision-making. *Journal of Business Ethics,* 113, 317–31.

Lim, S. and Cortina, L.M., 2005. Interpersonal mistreatment in the workplace: The interface and impact of general incivility and sexual harassment. *Journal of Applied Psychology,* 90(3), 483–96.

McFarlin, D. and Sweeney, P., 2013. *International organizational behaviour: Transcending borders and cultures.* New York: Routledge.

McPhail, R., Jerrard, M. and Southcombe, A., 2015. *Employment relations: An integrated approach.* South Melbourne: Cengage.

Loden, M. and Rosener, J.B., 1991. *Workforce America! Managing employees as a vital resource.* Burr Ridge: Business One Irwin.

Loh, J., Restubog, S.L.D. and Zagenczyk, T.J., 2010. Consequences of workplace bullying on employee identification and satisfaction among Australians and Singaporeans. *Journal of Cross Cultural Psychology,* 41(2), 236–52.

Omari, M., 2007. *Towards dignity and respect: An exploration of the nature, causes and consequences of workplace bullying.* Saarbrücken: VDM Verlag Dr. Müller.

Omari, M., Paull, M., D'Cruz, P. and Guneri-Cangarli, B., 2014. Fair game: The influence of cultural norms in creating sanctioned targets in the workplace. In *Proceedings of the 9th International Conference on Workplace Bullying & Harassment,* Milan, Italy, 167–76.

Power, J.L. *et al.,* 2013. Acceptability of workplace bullying: A comparative study on six continents. *Journal of Business Research,* 66(3), 374–80.

Richards, J., 2012. Examining the exclusion of employees with Asperger Syndrome from the workplace. *Personnel Review,* 41(5), 630–46.

Salin, D. and Hoel, H., 2013. Workplace bullying as a gendered phenomenon. *Journal of Managerial Psychology,* 28(3), 235–51.

Samnani, A., 2013. The early stages of workplace bullying and how it becomes prolonged: The role of culture in predicting target responses. *Journal of Business Ethics,* 113, 119–32.

Schein, E., 1992. *Organizational culture and leadership: A dynamic view.* San Francisco: Jossey-Bass.

Standen, P., Paull, M. and Omari, M., 2014. Managing workplace bullying: Propositions from Heider's Balance theory. *Journal of Management and Organization,* 20(6), 733–48.

Steers, R.M., Nardon, L. and Sanchez-Runde, C.J., 2013. *Management across cultures: Developing global competencies.* 2nd ed. Cambridge: Cambridge University Press.

Tajfel, H., 1982. Introduction. In H. Tajfel, ed., *Social identity and intergroup relations.* European Studies in Social Psychology. Cambridge: Cambridge University Press.

Triandis, H.C., 1990. Theoretical concepts that are applicable to the analysis of ethnocentrism. In R.W. Brislin, ed., *Applied cross-cultural psychology.* Chicago: Sage, 34–55.

Trompenaars Hampden-Turner Culture for Business, 2015. *About* [online]. Available from: www2.thtconsulting.com/about/ [accessed 7 January 2015].

Trompenaars, F. and Hampden-Turner, C., 2012. *Riding the waves of culture: Understanding diversity in global business.* 3rd ed. London: Nicholas Brealey Publishing.

Wang, W., Mao, J., Wu, W. and Liu, J., 2012. Abusive supervision and workplace deviance: The mediating role of interactional justice and the moderating role of power distance. *Asia Pacific Journal of Human Resources,* 50, 43–60.

Warner, M. and Joynt, P., 2011. Introduction: Cross-cultural perspectives. In M. Warner and P. Joynt, eds., *Managing across cultures: Issues and perspectives.* 2nd ed. Hampshire: Cengage, 3–7.

Zábrodská, K., Ellwood, C., Zaeemdar, S. and Mudrak, J., 2014. Workplace bullying as sensemaking: An analysis of target and actor perspectives on initial hostile interactions. *Culture and Organization,* DOI: 10.1080/14759551.2014.894514. Available from: www.tandfonline.com/doi/abs/10.1080/14759551.2014.8945 14#.VLdXjYszC-I [accessed 7 January 2015].

5 India

A paradoxical context for workplace bullying

Premilla D'Cruz

Introduction

Across the globe and in the last 20 years, workplace bullying has been established as an extreme social stressor. Yet emergent research findings emphasise the relevance of national factors as influences on various facets of the phenomenon. Acknowledging the coexistence of universal characteristics and cultural specificities has triggered scholarly interest in country-linked studies of the problem. Contributing to the ongoing agenda through a focus on India, the present chapter highlights how this nation's paradoxical social context simultaneously recognises and denies, nurtures and quells, as well as addresses and overlooks the issue. Following a description of the country's dialectical backdrop, the chapter synthesises several Indian empirical inquiries chronicling the incidence of workplace bullying, target and bystander experiences, organisational responses, legal provisions and collectivisation options to highlight how sociocultural dynamics colour a worldwide entity, giving rise to nuances and subtleties that cannot be side-stepped in the quest for interventions.

This chapter covers Indian workplaces in the formal sector. This includes: both old economy and new economy, public and private (domestic, Indian MNC [multinational corporation] and foreign MNC) organisations. Employment patterns in these contexts now go beyond the conventional standard full-time permanent contracts to encompass various non-standard part-time temporary forms. The primary data in the Indian empirical studies cited in this chapter were gathered in English from white-collar employees, supervisors, managers and professionals whose educational qualifications ranged from high school diplomas to doctoral degrees, with the majority being either graduates or post-graduates.

The Indian context

Located in South Asia and identified as a subcontinent, India is the second largest country in the world by population, having 1.1 billion residents, and the seventh largest country by area, being one-third the size of the United States of America (USA). It is the world's biggest democracy since acquiring independence in 1947 after the British ceded control (Gannon and Pillai 2013), and 72 per cent of the population are of Indo-Aryan heritage, 80.5 per cent identify as Hindus and 41 per cent have Hindi as their first language (Central Intelligence Agency 2013), alongside a variety of social categories stemming from religious, caste, regional, gender and class bases.

India represents a paradox socially and economically (Gannon and Pillai 2013). Socially, notwithstanding the stereotype that Indian culture is collectivistic, humanistic and spiritual, the coexistence of individualism, personalised and identity-based interactions, and materialism brings in complexity. In spite of their other-oriented and other-worldly stance, Indians pursue individual interests, favour hierarchical and in-group relationships linked to social categories, and value power, status, success and security. Religious beliefs (promoting a fatalistic outlook), social contagion, and a resource-poor environment account for this contradictory context (Beteille 2006, Kakar and Kakar 2007, Sinha 2008). According to Beteille (2006), it is important to recognise that Indian society is pluralist but not liberal, with pluralism being hierarchically, not democratically, organised. Diversity is enacted within this framework.

Economically, India has achieved substantial success on many measures but remains a poor country. Since 2003, it has been identified as a member of the BRIC (Brazil, Russia, India and China) group, a cluster of nations expected to become wealthier by 2050 than most of the leading economic powers of today. Although India's gross national product per person has increased in recent years, it is still only US$ (United States dollar) 1,020, compared to US$46,350 in the United States and US$3,270 in China. Despite having the largest number of college-educated scientists and computer specialists in the world, and a middle class that is estimated at over 250 million people, 41.6 per cent of the population lives on less than US$1.25 per day (Wright and Gupta in Gannon and Pillai 2013).

Whereas dimensional cross-cultural models describe India as collectivistic, relationship-based, hierarchical, mastery-oriented and polychronic (Steers *et al.* 2013), Indian reality accords with Gannon and Pillai's (2013) metaphorical approach, which underscores the contradictions inherent in the country. Highlighting India's predominantly Hindu traditions through the dance of Shiva and contemporary diversity via a kaleidoscope, Gannon and Pillai (2013) emphasise that inequality, prejudice, patriarchy, deprivation and corruption coexist with familism, spiritualism, tolerance, materialism and modernity in a state of dynamic evolution.

Indian workplaces reflect this paradox. Despite the influences of Western industrialism initiated during British rule and continuing under globalisation (Sinha 1990, Noronha 2005, D'Cruz and Noronha 2012a), universalism, professionalism, rationality, functional specificity and contractual relations, privileging merit, competence, rules and interest-based/class-based associations (Slotkin 1960, Moore 1966, Smelser 1966) have not succeeded in replacing traditional sociocultural patterns. Thus, while Indian workplaces, of all the country's subcultures, are exposed to Western influences and therefore to assimilation, transformation, reassertion and recreation (Kakar *et al.* 2002), Indian organisations do not function as their counterparts do in the West (Sinha 1997). Instead, they reflect a confluence between Indian culture and Western industrialism (Sinha 1982, 1990, 1994, 1997, Kakar *et al.* 2002, Kakar and Kakar 2007), illustrating Ralston *et al.*'s (1993) concept of crossvergence (Budhwar 2009, D'Cruz and Noronha 2012a).

Resembling feudalistic set-ups (Budhwar 2000) driven by paternalistic leadership where authority outweighs benevolence, and sycophancy and ingratiation become fairly routine, workplaces in the subcontinent generally privilege the informal organisation (Kakar *et al.* 2002), allowing power distance, favouritism, discrimination, manipulative behaviours and corruption to persist (Sinha 1982, 1990, 1994, Noronha 2005, Kakar and Kakar 2007).

The incidence of workplace bullying in India

Sinha's (1990) position that Indian workplaces provide grounds for abuse is reinforced by empirical evidence gained through quantitative surveys (D'Cruz 2013, D'Cruz and Rayner 2013) and qualitative inquiries (D'Cruz 2012a, D'Cruz *et al.* 2014), evidencing the presence of workplace bullying across various industrial sectors including IT (information technology), ITES-BPO (information technology enabled services-business process outsourcing), defence/government administration/civil services, financial services, manufacturing, engineering, retail, travel and hospitality and communication.

Definitions of workplace bullying in the Indian context are distinguished from those found in the literature in three ways. First, bullying is considered to be mainly top-down, reflecting the power distance that characterises Indian society and workplaces despite contrary claims about growing equality contemporaneously (Sinha 1994, Aycan *et al.* 1999, Verma 2004, Kakar and Kakar 2007, Budhwar 2009). Second, taking personal credit for success and blaming others for failure indicates a common national attributional tendency towards the 'self-serving bias' (Verma 2004, Sinha 2008). Third, including category-based harassment in the rubric of workplace bullying emphasises the entrenchment of various social identities linked to religion, caste, region, gender and class in the Indian psyche (Xaxa 2001, Agnes 2002, Sundaram and Tendulkar 2003, Fernandes 2004, Hutnik 2004, Robinson 2004, Sridharan 2004, Beteille 2006, Kakar and Kakar 2007).

Beyond these three differences, definitions of workplace bullying in India remain consistent with universal conceptualisations alluded to around the world (see, for example, Tracy *et al.* 2006, Omari 2007, Einarsen *et al.* 2011). That is, as in Europe, North America and Australia, Indians also see bullying as unwanted negative abusive, intimidating and aggressive behaviours, involving the misuse of power, displayed directly and/or indirectly, by an individual and/or a group, to another individual and/or a group, publicly and/or privately, over a period of time. Person-related bullying comprises personal comments, jeering, teasing and spreading rumours, while task-related bullying comprises unmanageable workloads and deadlines, extending work hours, withholding leave and micromanagement. Workplace bullying is perceived as unfair and impinges on targets' rights, resulting in physical and emotional distress and adversely affecting job performance.

Establishing prevalence in India, D'Cruz and Rayner (2013), in a multi-city study using the Work Harassment Scale (Bjorkvist and Osterman 1992), found that 44.3 per cent of their sample had been subjected to bullying behaviours ranging from mild to very severe, and that 42.3 per cent of their respondents reported at least one negative act as being experienced often or very often. While the most frequent source of bullying behaviour was superiors (73.1 per cent), followed by peers (37.3 per cent) and subordinates (21.8 per cent), it was rare for peers and subordinates to bully on their own, pointing to the existence of cross-level co-bullying. Factor analysis of the bullied sample indicated that task-related bullying predominated in instances of downwards bullying whereas person-related bullying was associated with 'diffused' bullying comprising horizontal, upwards and cross-level co-bullying. The relevance of hierarchy and position as well as relationships, alignments and exchanges, integral to the Indian context, was reinforced. Obviously, sociocultural dynamics have a bearing on who bullies and why and how they bully.

Available data highlight that among the range of etiological factors, apart from power and authority referred to earlier, relational orientation, regional identity and perceived career threats are culture-specific triggers (D'Cruz 2012a, D'Cruz and Noronha 2013). Whereas the first aspect sets the stage for bullying because knowing about and discussing people on a personal level opens up the possibility of misbehaviour (D'Cruz 2012a), the second attests to the role of affiliation-linked social networks in Indian society whereby category-based harassment and workplace bullying are conflated (D'Cruz and Noronha 2013), and the third points to the scarcity of opportunities in the country which results in a high degree of competitiveness (Misra and Tripathi 2004). Other studies also speak of sexual harassment (Punwani 1997, Tejani 2004), caste discrimination (Jodhka and Newman 2007, Madheswaran and Attewell 2007) and religious intolerance (Noronha 2005, Thorat and Attewell 2007) at work, reinforcing the notion that bullying often confounds with category-based abuse in the Indian context due to the primacy of social identities here. Thus, notwithstanding the collectivistic, relational, humanistic and spiritual leanings of Indian society, workplace bullying is present, fuelled by individualism, hierarchical, personalised and identity-based exchanges and materialism.

Protagonists' experiences

As with the international literature on workplace bullying (Bloch 2012, Jenkins *et al.* 2012), empirical research in India has focused on targets and bystanders rather than on (alleged) perpetrators. Target outcomes reflect known trends, underscoring that, universally, bullying is an extreme social stressor at work (Zapf *et al.* 1996) which unleashes severe harm (Lutgen-Sandvik 2005).

Consistent with their counterparts across the globe (Hogh *et al.* 2011, Nielsen and Einarsen 2012, Samnani and Singh 2012), Indian targets report low self-esteem, poor self-confidence, sleep problems, anxiety, anger, depression, nervousness, insecurity, suspicion, bitterness, concentration difficulties, chronic fatigue and various somatic problems as psychological, behavioural and physiological effects (D'Cruz 2012a, D'Cruz and Noronha 2013). The adverse impact spills over onto work roles such that job-related morale, motivation, satisfaction, attendance, commitment, performance and productivity are hampered (D'Cruz 2012a).

That Indian targets rely more on emotion-focused coping strategies rather than problem-focused coping strategies, striving for well-being as well as preferring to quit and seek fresh employment in the long run (D'Cruz 2012a), concords with findings across the globe (Lutgen-Sandvik 2008, Hogh *et al.* 2011). Yet, with regard to emotion-focused coping strategies, while Indian targets engaged cognitive restructuring, affective blunting, compartmentalisation and social support, spiritualism stood out as another preferred option.

Spiritualism, which subsumed religious leanings and fatalism, facilitated coping in constructive ways so that targets could work through and 'be on top of' the problem, providing not only explanations underlying the experience, but also mechanisms for tackling the situation. Considering their predicament as *karma* through which they atoned for their past sins on the path to *moksha,* or as part of a bigger plan whose goal was unclear, Indian targets displayed preoccupation with the larger meaning of life, grappling with numerous existential questions such as the purpose of humankind, the reason for suffering, matters of goodness, propriety and fairness and so on. Reflection, meditation and prayer promoted a sense of comfort and balance, allowing positive energy to prevail. Accordingly, seeing their circumstances as a test of faith, a means of developing an orientation of detachment, which included a lack of expectations, self-reliance and fortitude, and a lesson in forgiveness, were key to targets maintaining their equilibrium (D'Cruz and Noronha 2010, 2012b). It is also possible that targets feel helpless as they confront powerful bullies, and spiritual leanings help them cope effectively with their vulnerability and inadequacy. That is, the hierarchical nature of Indian society where power distance predominates across a variety of social categories allows for an attitude of tolerance towards bullying such that targets 'bear with' the situation, since they are socialised not to question or differ with 'established' norms and practices. Not surprisingly, retaliation was not referred to here unlike allusions to counter-aggression in the literature elsewhere (Lee and Brotheridge 2006, Hauge *et al.* 2009, Jenkins *et al.* 2012).

Among the less preferred problem-focused coping strategies, which also include direct confrontation with the bully and informally referring the matter to a superior (D'Cruz 2012a; D'Cruz and Noronha 2013), filing formal complaints appeared more challenging for targets in India than in the West, due to the lack of intra-organisational redressal alternatives in some instances. What accounts for this lacuna, particularly as Indian firms adopt global managerial practices and espouse international calls for employee rights, remains to be ascertained. Yet where redressal facilities were available, as evidenced elsewhere, uncertainty about outcomes marked Indian targets' decision-making about options. Perceptions of personal circumstances vis-à-vis bully influence and organisational position linked to power distance and social networks affected their choices. Feeling unsure of receiving justice in such a situation, targets opined that a formal complaint would render them more vulnerable, impeding their survival in the organisation and their employability outside.

Seeking formal psychosocial interventions such as counselling and psychiatric services, common in the West, is not resorted to by Indian targets. Apart from the availability of such services within and outside workplaces being a relevant factor (Wang *et al.* 2007), the stigma invariably associated with the need for professional assistance (Patel and Thara 2003) operates as an important deterrent in the subcontinent. Reliance on social support thus necessarily implies informal sources such as family, friends and similar significant others.

Bystanders in the Indian context display heterogeneity varying from apathy to agency, and can be broadly classified into actively colluding with the bully, taking no stand and supporting the target (D'Cruz and Noronha 2011), mirroring study findings from other countries (van Heugten 2011, Paull *et al.* 2012, Mulder *et al.* 2013). While bystanders parallel targets in terms of adverse personal and work-related outcomes and engagement with emotion-focused coping strategies (D'Cruz and Noronha 2011), as also found universally (Rayner 1999, Hoel *et al.* 2011), the presence of spiritualism and its associated religious and fatalistic links in bystander accounts brings in the culture-specific nuances earlier referred to in the case of targets.

Sociocultural dynamics with regard to the experiences of Indian bystanders are apparent in the interplay between relational orientation and personal interest, which simultaneously bring to the fore the complexities of individualism and collectivism. Bystanders who supported targets behaved as such because of friendship, but later withheld overt assistance as self-protection prevailed when the former were subjected to negative vibes from the bully and/or other influential people in the organisation. Guilt and remorse stemming from compromises on humanistic values and interpersonal connections jostled with relief linked to safeguarding one's own position and materialistic pursuits. Bystanders who aligned with their bullying team leaders, while not themselves engaging in any misbehaviour towards the target, adopted a stance of allegiance to their superiors premised on the understanding that loyalty would accrue to individual gain (D'Cruz and Noronha 2011).

Organisational measures to address workplace bullying

Illustrating world-wide trends (Ferris 2009, Vartia and Leka 2011, Harrington *et al.* 2012), not only do organisation-based workplace bullying interventions in India encompass primary, secondary and tertiary levels (D'Cruz 2012a), but their effectiveness depends on the commitment of top management and human resources (HR) towards addressing the problem (D'Cruz and Noronha 2010, 2011).

In terms of primary prevention, anti-bullying policies or codes of conduct are most common, with awareness and training about appropriate behaviour, social sensitivity and interpersonal skills held during induction and/or later at periodic intervals, and sometimes considered to double up as bystander sensitisation, being also reported (D'Cruz 2012a). That misbehaviour takes place in spite of these measures raises questions about the efficacy of primary interventions as well as necessitates secondary and tertiary interventions. The effectiveness of prevention mechanisms is compromised not just by organisational commitment to their implementation (D'Cruz 2012a), but also by individual predispositions and interpersonal differences, as well as societal-specific factors such as competition over scarce resources (Misra and Tripathi 2004) and deep-seated cultural patterns about power, position, identity and relationships (Beteille 2006, Kakar and Kakar 2007, Sinha 2008).

The presence of abuse calls for redressal measures and psychosocial assistance. Redressal, generally claimed to be widely publicised across the organisation, could move from informal to formal processes, including complaints procedures, and could operate through direct meetings as well as helplines, dropboxes and emails which often allow anonymity to be maintained. A range of organisational actions such as counselling, mediation, transfers, warnings, suspension and dismissal can be resorted to (D'Cruz 2012a). As observed in other countries, Indian targets do not pursue formal avenues especially to the extent of filing complaints. They may take the matter up to a certain point and then decide to live with the problem or quit in favour of fresh employment if it is not solved, but refrain from seeking further resolution due to anticipation of greater victimisation, loss of reputation and career regression.

Reluctance could arise from the joint interplay of individual inhibitions, organisational factors and sociocultural issues. Acknowledging that one is a target could imply recognising personal inadequacy and asking for help could indicate weakness and helplessness, apart from rendering oneself open to being held responsible for the situation – and together these could reinforce existing stereotypes about particular social identities. Emphasising a stand of inferiority could take away from the quest for individualism and the assertion of status. Highlighting such problems in the workplace could amount to finding fault with the organisation, which could invite hostile reactions linked to power distance (challenging authority) and identification variance (being different). Those who persist maintain their desire for justice notwithstanding the concomitant challenges personally, socially and professionally.

As targets and bystanders look for redressal and lodge complaints, their reports on the effectiveness of such mechanisms vary, with escalation of conflict, exacerbation of harassment and experiences of unfairness and injustice predominating the discourse, and satisfactory resolution emerging only in a few instances (D'Cruz and Noronha 2010, 2011). Though this is also reported internationally, being attributed primarily to issues of power and politics at work (Niedl 1996, Zapf and Gross 2001, Lutgen-Sandvik 2005), India-specific factors cannot be overlooked. The dynamics that colour Indian humanistic tendencies, namely, personalised and identity-based exchanges privileging hierarchy and in-group relationships (Beteille 2006, Kakar and Kakar 2007, Sinha 2008), as well as the complexities that characterise Indian workplaces, namely, power distance, sycophancy, informalisation, favouritism and manipulation, are relevant (Pandey 1981, Sinha, 1982, 1990, 1994, Noronha 2005, Kakar and Kakar 2007). Thus, along with the espousal of Western industrialism, particularly in this contemporary age of globalisation where organisations seek to promote 'progressive' images at par with international standards, the Indian ethos continues to prevail, evidencing crossvergence (Kakar *et al.* 2002, Sinha 2008, Budhwar 2009, D'Cruz and Noronha, 2012a).

In keeping with attitudes towards psychosocial services common to Indian society, in-house support facilities are mainly informal, with external referrals to care professionals (such as doctors and psychologists who may either be organisation-affiliated or whose services are paid for by the organisation) being suggested and/or provided by some organisations but not always availed of by protagonists.

The Indian legislative framework

Though India has no law against workplace bullying so far, legislations against sexual, gender, caste, religious, disability and chronic stigmatising illness-related discrimination at work, as well as legislations guaranteeing employee rights, are in place (D'Cruz 2012a). Protection against workplace bullying comes from all these provisions with various relevant laws, particularly labour legislations, being drawn upon as required to support targets.

Lawyers and legal activists interviewed by D'Cruz and Rayner (2013) stated that while bullying occurs at the workplace across industrial sectors and organisational hierarchy, their familiarity with victimisation at work was in relation to sexual, caste, religious, disability and chronic stigmatising illness-related harassment, all of which often resulted in the transfer, suspension and/or termination of targets who then sought legal recourse. Lawyers and legal activists observed that targets of the aforementioned types of misbehaviour turn to litigation as a means of redressal only after certain thresholds have been crossed. That is, whereas below particular levels of violations, targets either seek fresh employment, live with the problem and/or seek out informal or formal intra-organisational solutions, following their transfer, suspension and/or termination, targets pursue legal recourse. Targets' former responses arise due to their spiritual leanings and/or their insight into the difficulties associated with problem resolution. Their latter responses are triggered by knowing that their rights have been wrongfully violated and they have a sound legal case.

Moreover, instances seeking legal redressal generally come from blue-collar workers rather than from white-collar employees and supervisory and managerial levels. While blue-collar workers acknowledge and seek the benefit of being covered by labour laws, white-collar employees hold that they are out of the purview of such provisions, though this is not true. Issues pertaining to social status, integral to the Indian sociocultural fabric, are responsible for the latter stand. Accordingly, white-collar employees, supervisors and managers usually do not seek legal action in relation to victimisation since they do not wish to adversely affect their reputation and hamper their opportunities in the job market. Hence, when they face discrimination, they just move to new jobs, sometimes without engaging intra-organisational informal or formal alternatives to resolve the matter (D'Cruz and Rayner 2013). The challenges linked to India's judicial system, namely dragging cases over time and operating in a partisan manner with shades of corruption and politicisation, as well as the exorbitant costs associated with litigation, operate as deterrents across the country's workforce (D'Cruz and Rayner 2013) and cannot be overlooked. At the same time, misuse of legislation, as has been seen in a few instances of sexual harassment and caste discrimination, must also be acknowledged.

On the one hand, rhetoric, ineffectiveness and gaps often mark organisational interventions, owing, to an extent, to sociocultural factors outlined earlier. On the other hand, legal requirements such as those linked to sexual harassment, caste discrimination, religious tolerance, or employee rights, mandate the institution and implementation of particular workplace measures entailing compulsory protection. Shortcomings, sometimes of a sociocultural nature as previously alluded to, creep in here too.

The collectivisation option

Despite association being a fundamental right under the Indian constitution, collectivisation is linked with old economy firms such as manufacturing, rather than new economy firms such as IT and ITES-BPO, and with blue-collar workers rather than white-collar employees. Indeed, the disdain for unionism displayed by emergent industries and contemporary employees not only resonates with Indians' status-conscious mentality, but also coheres with government and employer wishes for a conducive industrial relations climate for business to 'flourish'. This is to the extent that the former remains apathetic when the latter promotes the stance that labour laws and collectivisation are not applicable to certain industrial sectors and workforce categories (Noronha and D'Cruz 2009a). Further, though union membership shows an increase (Noronha and Beale 2012), union influence has weakened considerably (Noronha 2003), necessitating engagement with revitalisation strategies (Frege and Kelly 2003) to regain and maintain efficacy.

Nonetheless, as is true in other parts of the world (Ironside and Seifert 2003, Hoel and Beale 2006, Beale and Hoel 2011), collectivisation in India provides an avenue to tackle workplace bullying. Working on the issue directly with governments, policy makers, employer associations, trade bodies and organisations, and indirectly as protagonists' representatives, union initiatives speak to primary, secondary and tertiary prevention. Legislation, policies, directives and agreements at the national and/or regional level, as well as anti-bullying policies, codes of conduct, awareness and training, redressal mechanisms, psychosocial assistance and adherence to mandatory requirements at the organisational level, represent the outcomes of direct efforts. As employee representatives, unions not only educate their members on misbehaviour and its management, but also support targets informally and formally within and outside the workplace with advice, advocacy and legal assistance. Where bullies are members of unions, support against victimisation, advice and assistance for behaviour amendment, as well as help regarding appeals, may be provided on informal and/or formal bases. Bystanders as members of unions also stand to gain from the foregoing measures. It may be noted that where the complainant is in the wrong, unions can play a role in pointing this out to him/her, and assist in overcoming personal short-comings and sorting out situational complications informally or formally. Overall, similar to their counterparts abroad, unions in India aim towards zero-tolerance of misbehaviour at work.

That the absence of collectivisation exacerbates the risks associated with workplace bullying, leaving protagonists vulnerable (Ironside and Seifert 2003, Lewis and Rayner 2003), is true of India too, as D'Cruz and Noronha's (2010, 2011 and 2014) studies in the IT and ITES-BPO sectors where unions are not present demonstrates. Indeed, the universal espousal of unitarist HR manage-ment by modern workplaces, which leads employees to disregard collectivisation (Lewis and Rayner 2003, Noronha and D'Cruz 2009a, Beale and Hoel 2011), facilitated further in the Indian context by status-conscious considerations (Noronha and D'Cruz 2009b), leaves targets and bystanders to cope single-handedly with their difficult predicament when rhetoric in organisational ideology emerges. Moreover, the relationship between crossvergence and rhetoric cannot be ignored (D'Cruz and Noronha 2012a).

Yet, while pluralism serves as a counterpoint to managerialism (Ironside and Seifert 2003, Beale and Hoel 2011, D'Cruz 2014, D'Cruz and Noronha 2014), it is not without complications. Unions, despite their best endeavours, could fail in their attempts to resolve workplace bullying due to linkages between the bully and the employer, the bully's ability to beat the system, or the employer's indifference to the issue. Union influence could negatively impact the course of a bullying situation in terms of both the trajectory of the misbehaviour and the outcomes of intervention. Conflicts within a union or between two unions can arise if the target and the bully belong to the same or different set-ups. Not only can unions resort to various forms of misbehaviour, including physical violence and emotional abuse to push their agenda, but also their links with employers, industry groups and political parties could bring in complications for targets, bullies, bystanders, organisations and others involved, as has been observed in India. Further, unions are not untouched by sociocultural factors. Thus, while pursuing the laudable goal of employee rights, power struggles associated with hierarchy and category-based differences stemming from numer-ous social identities, both entrenched in the Indian ethos, colour union func-tioning. Position, relationships, alignments and exchanges play a role such that Indian unions reflect the dynamics of Indian society and workplaces, with adverse implications for their effectiveness (D'Cruz 2012b, Noronha and D'Cruz 2013).

The road ahead

The complexities of the Indian sociocultural landscape present a variety of context-specific challenges to researchers of workplace bullying. Whereas an adult literacy rate of 62.8 per cent (Wright and Gupta in Gannon and Pillai 2013) necessitates reliance on interviews and observations rather than questionnaires as methods of data collection, the myriad languages spoken in India (Gannon and Pillai 2013) have fallouts for matters of parity and consistency in understanding, communication and interpretation. Methodological issues emerge because not only is the use of behavioural measures constrained, but also the need for accurate and interchangeable translations is complicated.

That category-based harassment arising from social identities is conflated with workplace bullying in India has already been evidenced. Yet what cannot be ignored is the link between physical violence and emotional abuse at work. The concomitance of bodily harm and psychological aggression, often in conjunction with identity-related misbehaviour, reported by various blue-collar workers in the informal sector (Harriss-White and Gooptu 2001), warrants investigation and calls for revisiting the hallmarks of workplace bullying. Forces of power and corruption associated with hierarchy and materialism, reinforced by network-based alignments and exchanges, underlie these circumstances.

While it is intriguing to note the persistence of harassment in Indian workplaces despite anti-discrimination and anti-abuse legislations and numerous labour laws, the chances of such instances abating in the near future seem remote. The heightened individualistic and materialistic orientation of Generation Y (Lukose 2009), and the increasing competitiveness across the subcontinent due to the growing inequity unleashed by globalisation (Jayasuriya 2005), appear poised to reinforce misbehaviour in general. This is particularly relevant to workplaces, as these are seen as pathways to progress, and people spend a large part of their lives at work.

Strongly activated and resolutely maintained organisational cultures, spurred by virtuous leadership (Havard 2007) drawing on India's stereotyped benevolent paternalism (Kakar *et al.* 2002) and steeped in ethical climates (Simha and Cullen 2012), rooted in the spiritualism widely perceived as synonymous with the country, seem to be the best way forward. In actioning these alternatives, robust evidence of their efficacy and suitable modification of their application, based on ongoing systematic empirical inquiries, are recommended.

References

Agnes, F., 2002. Transgressing boundaries of gender and identity. *Economic and Political Weekly*, 37 (36), 3695–8.

Aycan, Z., Kanungo, R. N. and Sinha, J.B.P., 1999. Organisational culture and human resource management: the model of culture fit. *Journal of Cross-Cultural Psychology*, 30 (4), 501–26.

Beale, D. and Hoel, H., 2011. Workplace bullying and the employment relationship: exploring questions of prevention, control and context. *Work, Employment and Society*, 25 (1), 5–18.

Beteille, A., 2006. *Ideology and social science*. New Delhi: Penguin.
Bjorkqvist, K. and Osterman, K., 1992. *The work harassment scale*. Vasa: Abo Akademi University. Available from: www.vasa.abo.fi/svf/up/Scales/WHS-English. pdf [Accessed 20 November 2014].
Bloch, C., 2012. How do perpetrators experience bullying at the workplace? *International Journal of Work Organisation and Emotion*, 5 (2), 159–77.
Budhwar, P.S., 2000. Indian and British personnel specialists – understanding of the dynamics of their function: an empirical study. *International Business Review*, 9 (6), 727–53.
Budhwar, P.S., 2009. Introduction: human resource management in the Indian context. *In:* P.S. Budhwar and J. Bhatnagar, eds., *The changing face of people management in India*. London: Routledge, 3–19.
Central Intelligence Agency/CIA, 2013. *The world factbook*. Available from: www.cia. gov/library/publications/the—-world—-factbook/ [Accessed 20 November 2014].
D'Cruz, P., 2012a. *Workplace bullying in India*. New Delhi: Routledge.
D'Cruz, P., 2012b. The global re-organising of work and its implications for collective voice: insights from India's ITES-BPO sector. *Keynote address to the 26th AIRAANZ conference*, 9 February 2012, Gold Coast, Australia.
D'Cruz, P., 2013. *Workplace bullying in the Indian IT sector*. Unpublished report. IIM Ahmedabad, India.
D'Cruz, P., 2014. *Depersonalised bullying at work: from evidence to conceptualisation*. New Delhi: Springer.
D'Cruz, P. and Noronha, E., 2010. The exit coping response to workplace bullying: the contribution of inclusivist and exclusivist HRM strategies. *Employee Relations*, 32 (2), 102–20.
D'Cruz, P. and Noronha, E., 2011. The limits to workplace friendship: managerialist HRM and bystander behaviour in the context of workplace bullying. *Employee Relations*, 33 (3), 269–88.
D'Cruz, P. and Noronha, E., 2012a. High commitment management practices re-examined: the case of Indian call centres. *Economic and Industrial Democracy*, 33 (2), 185–205.
D'Cruz, P. and Noronha, E., 2012b. Clarifying my world: identity work in the context of workplace bullying. *The Qualitative Report*, 17 (6), 1–29.
D'Cruz, P. and Noronha, E., 2013. Navigating the extended reach: target experiences of cyberbullying at work. *Information and Organisation*, 23 (4), 324–43.
D'Cruz, P. and Noronha, E., 2014. Workplace bullying in the context of organisational change: the significance of pluralism. *Industrial Relations Journal*, 45 (1), 2–21.
D'Cruz, P., Noronha, E. and Beale, D., 2014. The workplace bullying-organisational change interface: emerging challenges for human resource management. *International Journal of Human Resource Management*, 25 (10), 1434–59.
D'Cruz, P. and Rayner, C., 2013. Bullying in the Indian workplace: a study of the ITES-BPO sector. *Economic and Industrial Democracy*, 34 (4), 597–619.
Einarsen, S., Hoel, H., Zapf, D. and Cooper, C.L., 2011. The concept of bullying at work: the European tradition. *In:* S. Einarsen, H. Hoel, D. Zapf and C.L. Cooper, eds., Bullying and harassment in the workplace. London: Taylor & Francis, 3–40.
Fernandes, L., 2004. The politics of forgetting: class politics, state power and the restructuring of urban space in India. *Urban Studies*, 41 (12), 2415–30.

Ferris, P.A., 2009. The role of the consulting psychologist in the prevention, detection, and correction of bullying and mobbing in the workplace. *Consulting Psychology Journal: Practice and Research*, 61 (3), 169–89.

Frege, C.M. and Kelly, J., 2003. Union revitalisation strategies in comparative perspective. *European Journal of Industrial Relations*, 9 (1), 7–24.

Gannon, M.J. and Pillai, R., 2013. *Understanding global cultures: metaphorical journeys through 31 nations, clusters of nations, continents and diversity*. Thousand Oaks, CA: Sage.

Harriss-White, B. and Gooptu, N., 2001. Mapping India's world of unorganised labour. *Socialist Register*, 37, 89–118.

Harrington, S., Rayner, C. and Warren, S., 2012. Too hot to handle? Trust and human resource practitioners' implementation of anti-bullying policy. *Human Resource Management Journal*, 22 (4), 392–408.

Havard, R., 2007. *Virtuous leadership*. New York, NY: Scepter.

Hauge, L.J., Skogstad, A. and Einarsen, S., 2009. Individual and situational predictors of workplace bullying: why do perpetrators engage in the bullying of others? *Work and Stress*, 23 (4), 349–58.

Hoel, H. and Beale, D., 2006. Workplace bullying, psychological perspectives and industrial relations: towards a contextualised and interdisciplinary approach. *British Journal of Industrial Relations*, 44 (2), 239–62.

Hoel, H., Sheehan, M.J., Cooper, C.L. and Einarsen, S., 2011. Organisational effects of workplace bullying. *In:* S. Einarsen, H. Hoel, D. Zapf and C.L. Cooper, eds., *Bullying and harassment in the workplace*. London: Taylor & Francis, 129–48.

Hogh, A., Mikkelsen, E.G. and Hansen, A.M., 2011. Individual consequences of workplace bullying/mobbing. *In:* S. Einarsen, H. Hoel, D. Zapf and C.L. Cooper, eds., *Bullying and harassment in the workplace*. London: Taylor & Francis, 107–28.

Hutnik, N., 2004. An intergroup perspective on ethnic minority identity. *In:* J. Pandey, ed., *Psychology in India revisited*. New Delhi: Sage, 216–60.

Ironside, M. and Seifert, R., 2003. Tackling bullying in the workplace: the collective dimension. *In:* S. Einarsen, H. Hoel, D. Zapf and C.L. Cooper, eds., *Bullying and emotional abuse in the workplace*. London: Taylor & Francis, 382–98.

Jayasuriya, S., 2005. Globalisation, equity and poverty: the South Asian experience. *In:* N.E. Dinello and L. Squire, eds., *Globalisation and equity: perspective from the developing world*. Cheltenham: Edward Elgar, 137–62.

Jenkins, M.F., Zapf, D., Winefield, H. and Sarris, A., 2012. Bullying allegations from the accused bully's perspective. *British Journal of Management*, 23 (4), 489–501.

Jodhka, S.S. and Newman, K., 2007. In the name of globalisation: meritocracy, productivity and the hidden language of caste. *Economic and Political Weekly*, 42 (41), 4125–32.

Kakar, S. and Kakar, K., 2007. *The Indians*. New Delhi: Penguin.

Kakar, S., Kakar, S., Kets de Vries, M.F.R. and Vrignaud, P., 2002. Leadership in Indian organisations from a comparative perspective. *International Journal of Cross-Cultural Management*, 2 (2), 239–50.

Lee, R.T. and Brotheridge, C.M., 2006. When prey turns predatory: workplace bullying as a predictor of counter aggression/bullying, coping and well-being. *European Journal of Work and Organisational Psychology*, 15 (3), 352–77.

Lewis, D. and Rayner, C., 2003. Bullying and human resource management: a wolf in sheep's clothing? *In:* S. Einarsen, H. Hoel, D. Zapf and C. L. Cooper, eds., *Bullying and emotional abuse in the workplace.* London: Taylor & Francis, 370–82.

Lukose, R. A., 2009. *Liberalisation's children: gender, youth, and consumer citizenship in globalising India.* Durham, NC: Duke University Press.

Lutgen-Sandvik, P., 2005. *Water smoothing stones: subordinate resistance to workplace bullying.* Unpublished Ph.D. thesis, University of Arizona, Tempe, USA.

Lutgen-Sandvik, P., 2008. Intensive remedial identity work: responses to workplace bullying trauma and stigmatisation. *Organisation,* 15 (1), 97–119.

Madheswaran, S. and Attewell, P., 2007. Caste discrimination in the Indian urban labour market: evidence from the National Sample Survey. *Economic and Political Weekly,* 42 (41), 4146–53.

Misra, G. and Tripathi, K. N., 2004. Psychological dimensions of poverty and deprivation. *In:* J. Pandey, ed., *Applied social and organisational psychology.* New Delhi: Sage, 118–215.

Moore, W. E., 1966. Industrialisation and social change. *In:* B. F. Hoselitz and W. E. Moore, eds., *Industrialisation and society.* Paris: UNESCO-Mouton, 299–370.

Mulder, R., Pouwelse, M., Lodewijkx, H. and Bolman, C., 2013. Workplace mobbing and bystanders' helping behaviour towards victims: the role of gender, perceived responsibility and anticipated stigma by association. *International Journal of Psychology* [online]. Available from: DOI: 10.1002/ijop.12018 [Accessed 21 September 2014].

Niedl, K., 1996. Mobbing and well-being: economic and personnel development implications. *European Journal of Work and Organisational Psychology,* 5 (2), 239–49.

Nielsen, M. B. and Einarsen, S., 2012. Outcomes of exposure to workplace bullying: a meta-analytic review. *Work and Stress,* 26 (4), 309–32.

Noronha, E., 2003. Indian trade unions: today and beyond tomorrow. *Indian Journal of Industrial Relations,* 39 (1), 95–107.

Noronha, E., 2005. *Ethnicity in industrial organisations.* New Delhi: Rawat.

Noronha, E. and Beale, D., 2012. India, neo-liberalism and union responses: unfinished business and protracted struggles. *In:* G. Gall, ed., *The international handbook of labour unions.* Cheltenham: Edward Elgar, 167–86.

Noronha, E. and D'Cruz, P., 2009a. *Employee identity in Indian call centres: the notion of professionalism.* New Delhi: Sage.

Noronha, E. and D'Cruz, P., 2009b. Organising call centre agents in India. *Industrial Relations Journal,* 40 (3), 215–34.

Noronha, E. and D'Cruz, P., 2013. Hope to despair: the experience of organising Indian call centre employees. *Indian Journal of Industrial Relations,* 48 (3), 471–86.

Omari, M., 2007. *Towards dignity and respect: an exploration of the nature, causes and consequences of workplace bullying.* Saarbrücken: VDM Verlag Dr. Müller.

Pandey, J., 1981. A note about social power through ingratiation among workers. *Journal of Occupational Psychology,* 54 (1), 65–7.

Patel, V. and Thara, R., 2003. The role of NGOs in mental health care. *In:* V. Patel and R. Thara, eds., *Meeting the mental health needs of developing countries: NGO innovations in India.* New Delhi: Sage, 1–20.

Paull, M., Omari, M. and Standen, P., 2012. When is a bystander not a bystander? A typology of the roles of bystanders in workplace bullying. *Asia Pacific Journal of Human Resources*, 50 (3), 351–66.

Punwani, J., 1997. Sexual harassment: is it enough to set guidelines? *Economic and Political Weekly*, 32 (42), 2645–6.

Ralston, D.A., Gustafson, D.J., Cheung, F.M. and Terpstra, R.H., 1993. Differences in managerial values: a study of US, Hong Kong and PRC managers. *Journal of International Business Studies*, 24 (2), 249–75.

Rayner, C., 1999. From research to implementation: finding leverage for prevention. *International Journal of Manpower*, 20 (1/2), 28–38.

Robinson, R., 2004. *Sociology of religion in India*. New Delhi: Sage.

Samnani, A.-K. and Singh, P., 2012. 20 years of workplace bullying research: a review of the antecedents and consequences of bullying in the workplace. *Aggression and Violent Behaviour*, 17 (6), 581–9.

Simha, A. and Cullen, J.B., 2012. Ethical climates and their effects on organisational outcomes: implications from the past and prophecies for the future. *Academy of Management Perspectives*, 26 (4), 20–34.

Sinha, J.B.P., 1982. *The nurturant task leader*. New Delhi: Concept.

Sinha, J.B.P., 1990. *Work culture in the Indian context*. New Delhi: Sage.

Sinha, J.B.P., 1994. Power dynamics in Indian organisations. *In:* R.N. Kanungo and M. Mendonca, eds., *Work motivation*. New Delhi: Sage, 213–29.

Sinha, J.B.P., 1997. A cultural perspective on organisational behaviour in India. *In:* C.P. Earley and M. Erez, eds., *New perspectives on international industrial/organisational psychology*. San Francisco, CA: Lexington Press, 53–74.

Sinha, J.B.P., 2008. *Culture and organisational behavior*. New Delhi: Sage.

Slotkin, J.S., 1960. *From field to factory: new industrial employees*. Glencoe, IL: Free Press.

Smelser, N.J., 1966. Mechanism of change and adjustment to change. *In:* B.F. Hoselitz and W.E. Moore, eds., *Industrialisation and society*. Paris: UNESCO Mouton, 32–54.

Sridharan, E., 2004. The growth and sectoral composition of India's middle class: its impact on the politics of economic liberalisation. *India Review*, 3 (4), 405–28.

Steers, R.M., Nardon, L. and Sanchez-Runder, C.J., 2013. *Management across cultures: developing global competencies*. Cambridge: Cambridge University Press.

Sundaram, K. and Tendulkar, S.D., 2003. Poverty among social and economic groups in India in 1990s. *Economic and Political Weekly*, 38 (50), 5263–76.

Tejani, S., 2004. Sexual harassment at the workplace: emerging problems and debates. *Economic and Political Weekly*, 39 (41), 4491–4.

Thorat, S. and Attewell, P., 2007. The legacy of social exclusion: a correspondence study of job discrimination in India. *Economic and Political Weekly*, 42 (41), 4141–5.

Tracy, S.J., Lutgen-Sandvik, P. and Alberts, J.K., 2006. Nightmares, demons, and slaves: exploring the painful metaphors of workplace bullying. *Management Communication Quarterly*, 20 (2), 148–85.

van Heugten, K., 2011. Theorising active bystanders as change agents in workplace bullying of social workers. *Families in Society*, 92 (2), 219–24.

Vartia, M. and Leka, S., 2011. Interventions for the management of bullying at work. *In:* S. Einarsen, H. Hoel, D. Zapf and C.L. Cooper, eds., *Bullying and harassment in the workplace.* London: Taylor & Francis, 359–80.

Verma, J., 2004. Social values. *In:* J. Pandey, ed., *Psychology in India revisited.* New Delhi: Sage, 60–117.

Wang, P.S., *et al.,* 2007. Use of mental health services for anxiety, mood, and substance disorders in 17 countries in the WHO world mental health surveys. *Lancet,* 370 (9590), 841–50.

Xaxa, V., 2001. Protective discrimination: why scheduled tribes lag behind scheduled castes. *Economic and Political Weekly,* 36 (29), 2765–72.

Zapf, D. and Gross, C., 2001. Conflict escalation and coping with workplace bullying: a replication and extension. *European Journal of Work and Organisational Psychology,* 10 (4), 497–522.

Zapf, D., Knorz, C. and Kulla, M., 1996. On the relationship between mobbing factors, and job content, social work environment, and health outcomes. *European Journal of Work and Organisational Psychology,* 5 (2), 215–37.

6   Turkey

East of West, west of East

Burcu Guneri-Cangarli

Introduction

Workplace bullying in Turkey has attracted increasing attention since 2000. In their daily lives, Turks may complain that they are being bullied by their superiors or peers, mostly superiors, without fully considering the actual definition. Turkish people believe that workplace bullying is a common occurrence. Is this due to the behaviour being widespread? Or because people cannot distinguish conflict from bullying? Or is it because Turkey's cultural characteristics, as well as socio-economic environment, may be seen to create predatory environments? In order to seek the answers to these questions, this chapter will focus on workplace bullying studies conducted in Turkey. Findings will be interpreted in accordance with socio-economic dynamics as well as cultural characteristics of the country.

Turkey: an overview

History

The Turkish Republic was founded in 1923 by Mustafa Kemal Ataturk after the demise of the Ottoman Empire which existed for around 600 years spanning the Middle East, Eastern Europe, and North Africa. In the last decades of the Empire, many nations declared their independence; Turks, as the ruling class, were the last in establishing a new and independent state. The first years of the young republic required radical reforms addressing various economic, legal, and social issues. The Ottoman Empire's legal system mainly depended on Sharia Law, which applies Islamic rules to a range of areas including crime, politics, and economics, as well as personal matters such as sexual relationships, hygiene, diet, prayer, everyday etiquette, and fasting. The founders of the Republic intended to create not only a new state, but also a new nation that would be able to adapt to modernity. Therefore, Turkey was founded as a secular state whose legal system mainly depends on continental law. Other reforms addressed restructuring the education system, the role of women in social and political life, the multi-party system, and the industry and banking systems (Kabasakal and Bodur 2007).

Ethnic profile and languages spoken

It is always said that Turkey is a mosaic, reflecting the different nationalities which lived under the rule of the Ottoman Empire; however, the majority of the population (89 per cent) define themselves as Turks. The second largest ethnic group is the Kurds (8 per cent), with Arabs and Zazas representing 1 per cent of the population. Other minority groups, such as Armenians, Greeks, and Jews make up the balance (Onder 1998). The official language of the country is Turkish. It is spoken as a mother tongue by 82.5 per cent of the population; this is followed by Kurdish (14.4 per cent) (Koc 2007). The recent civil war in Syria has affected regional dynamics and the ethnic profile of Turkey. It is estimated that, since 2011, more than 800,000 Syrians have migrated to the country (Dincer *et al.* 2013). It is expected that some will stay in Turkey long-term. Therefore, the Turkish government has issued some regulations increasing the rights of Syrians, including access to health and education services, and entry to the labour market. The government's expenditure on Syrian refugees, their cultural differences, and language barriers has been of concern to Turkish citizens.

Religion

Islam is the religion of the vast majority (99 per cent) of the population. Islamic rituals such as believing in God's will in their daily behaviours are quite common among Turkish people. *Bismillahir-rahmanir-rahim,* which means "In the name of the God, the Merciful, the Compassionate", is frequently uttered by Turks when they begin tasks. Moreover, *mashallah,* which means "God protects you from harm", is said just after making compliments or hearing good news about someone. Interestingly, a deeper look at the rituals shows traces of Shamanism, which was the religion of the Turks' ancestors who migrated from Middle Asia in the 4th Century (Ocak 2009).

Population

Compared to many countries in Europe, Turkey has a large population: 74.93 million. Statistics show that this number continues to grow at a rate of 13.7 per cent per year (TUIK 2014a). The majority of the population (76.8 per cent) lives in cities and metropolitan areas. Although the population has begun to age in recent years, it is still young, with an average age of 30.4 (TUIK 2014a). Turkey's young population offers some advantages, such as a large number of working age citizens, while it also brings certain challenges, such as the quality and dispersion of education and a high unemployment rate.

Education

Primary education, which lasts eight years, has been mandatory since 1996. The adult literacy rate has therefore been constantly increasing, and reached 94.1 per cent in 2012 (www.unicef.org/infobycountry/Turkey_statistics.html).

Inequalities in terms of access to education between men and women, however, still exist. Among 15–24-year-olds, 79 per cent of people who are illiterate are women (Uysal Kolasin and Guner 2010). The primary education enrolment rate is 99.5 per cent for men and 98.3 per cent for women. The gap between enrolment rates widens at secondary school level: 81.4 per cent for men and 76.2 per cent for women (www.unicef.org/infobycountry/Turkey_statistics. html). Access to university education has been quite limited in Turkey. In the recent past when only state universities existed, only a small proportion of students who passed the central exam were granted entry; however, in the last two decades, the number of universities established by private foundations has dramatically increased; allowing access to many others.

Politics and economy

When first founded in 1923, the Republic's main economic activities depended on agriculture. At that time, its Gross Domestic Product (GDP) was $570 million USD, with $47.5 as the annual income per person (Egilmez 2014). Until the 1980s Turkey operated a closed economy in which the State was the main investor. After which it opened its economy to the world. Opening the doors of the economy brought an influx of foreign investors and strengthened the private sector; however, it also made the economy more fragile and subject to external dynamics and crises.

During the 1990s and 2000s the Turkish economy survived three major economic crises: in 1994, 1998, and 2001. The resulting hardship destroyed people's trust in political parties as many lost their jobs and savings. At that time, a newly established political party, "Justice and Development", appeared as a new hope. The Justice and Development Party came to power in 2002, and applied a new strategy to the Turkish economy. Although some argue that this new strategy makes the economy more fragile due to the huge account deficit, other economic indicators point to significant development. Since then the nation's GDP has been on the rise from $231 billion USD (in 2001) to $820.2 billion USD (in 2013) (Egilmez 2014, The World Bank 2014), while annual income per person reached $10,950 in 2013 (The World Bank 2014).

In line with global and technological developments, the relative importance of different sectors for GDP has changed. Early on, agriculture was the driving sector with a 43 per cent share; currently it generates only 9 per cent of the total, while manufacturing is responsible for 30 per cent, and services 61 per cent (Egilmez 2014).

Despite economic developments, unemployment is still a major problem due to the size and youthfulness of Turkey's population. Participation in the workforce is relatively low: 49.1 per cent, with a 10.2 per cent unemployment rate (TUIK 2014b). Youth unemployment rates are a more serious problem at 17 per cent. Also noteworthy is the difference between men and women's workforce participation rates: 70 per cent and 28.7 per cent, respectively.

The major critiques of the Justice and Development Party's actions are not related to the economy but to its performance on human development and democratic rights. For instance, in spite of its economic boost, Turkey still suffers significant income distribution inequalities. The Gini coefficient, which scores inequalities in income distribution where 0 is perfect equality and 100 perfect inequality, was calculated at 40.0 in 2011 (The World Bank 2014). Considering that the Organisation for Economic Co-operation and Development's (OECD) average was 32 in the same year, 40.0 represented high inequality. Moreover, Turkey has failed to improve its position in the Human Development Index (HDI) in line with its improvement of economic indicators. The value was 0.722 HDI in 2012, which is below the average of countries in Europe and Central Asia at 0.733 (UNDP 2013).

Business life

Small and medium sized enterprises (SMEs) are dominant in Turkey (at 98 per cent of businesses), providing 78 per cent of total employment. An Economic Survey of Turkey in 2014 prepared by the OECD underlines the importance of SMEs in Turkey, as well as their problems. Their main challenge relates to productivity. Labour productivity in SMEs constitutes less than 25 per cent of that of large companies. This is noteworthy as it demonstrates the largest gap of this kind among OECD countries (OECD 2014).

Of the companies in Turkey, 95 per cent are owned and managed by families. These businesses, which have relatively short life cycles (average of 24 years) due to lack of institutionalism and professionalism, create certain challenges in the Turkish labour market (ASO 2005). These SMEs and family businesses do not generally have effective and modern human resource management practices (Aycan 2001). Moreover, labour unions are weak and not widely dispersed, and membership is not encouraged by employers. Interestingly, employees also have low levels of trust in unions (Urhan 2005).

In line with the low effectiveness of labour unions and human resource management practices, the labour market suffers from job security and health and safety issues. These may lead to unfair workplace behaviours, sanctions, or work related accidents which may result in injury or even death. The Ministry of Labour and Social Security defends its position by pointing to the necessary regulations; however, ineffective control of employment practices is seen as a major problem (Aycan 2001).

Culture

Turkey has been described as the bridge between the East and West (Kabasakal and Bodur 2007), not necessarily belonging totally to either, but being an integral part of both. Turkish people have Eastern cultural values compared to the Europeans, but Western values compared to their Middle Eastern neighbours (Schwartz 2008); this brings a sense of belonging to both, though not fully to either. A frequently said proverb: "A Turk has no friend but only Turks in the world" reflects this predicament.

Gannon and Pillai (2013) describe Turkish culture by a "coffee house" metaphor. Turkish coffee houses are quite different to their counterparts in other countries. They provide a significant forum for communication and recreation, especially for men. In coffee houses, men, surrounded by friends and family members, feel integrated into the community. Relationships are very important in Turkey, and Gannon and Pillai (2013) portray Turkish people as "people who need people". In summary, just like the atmosphere in coffee houses, Turkish culture can be characterised by collectivism, male dominance, relationship, and family orientation.

Besides Gannon and Pillai (2013), Turkish culture is examined in the well-known cultural frameworks (e.g. Hofstede 1984, Trompenaars 1993, House *et al.* 2004, Schwartz 2008). There are similarities among the frameworks in terms of dimensions used to describe cultures, however, study-specific dimensions and findings exist, making separate references to each framework necessary in order to explain the complex dynamics of Turkish culture. For instance, the GLOBE researchers (House *et al.* 2004) put Turkey in the Middle East cluster, whereas Schwartz (2008) believes Turkey is one of eight societies that do not fit in the cultural characteristics of their regions.

High power distance/hierarchic society

According to both Hofstede (1984) and GLOBE (House *et al.* 2004), Turkey is a high power distance country where unequal distribution of power is accepted. Similarly, Schwartz (2008) classified Turkish culture as hierarchical, in which social power, authority, humility, and wealth are very important values. There are clear reflections of high power distance values in Turkish organisations and businesses. For instance, Turkish organisations are characterised by centralised hierarchical structures (Hofstede 1984). In a comparative study of 38 nations, Turkey was found to have the steepest hierarchy (Trompenaars and Hampden-Turner 1998). In line with hierarchical and centralised structures, business space and resources are generally allocated based on the person's "place" or standing in the organisational hierarchy rather than the necessities of work (Kabasakal and Bodur 2007). Regarding communication with superiors, Turkish employees are expected to show obedience (Fullagar *et al.* 2003); indirect and soft opposition is acceptable, however, direct opposition to superiors is not welcome (Kabasakal and Bodur 2007). In keeping with this, top-down, one-way performance evaluations in which only superiors assess the performance of subordinates are common in Turkish businesses (Aycan 2001).

Collectivist/embedded society

Like high power distance, collectivism is one of the cornerstones of Turkish culture. Turkey has been classified as: highly collectivist (Hofstede 1984,

Trompenaars 1993), an in-group collectivist (House *et al.* 2004), or embedded society (Schwartz 2008). It can be argued that the roots of collectivism stem from families with members of Turkish families strongly bonded to each other. There is a high level of trust, interdependency, and caring within the family (Kagitcibasi 1982). These characteristics extend to more distant relatives, and even people outside the family. Especially in large cities, *hemsherilik* (migrants sharing the same region of origin) may also attract help or cooperation (Kiray 1997). Therefore, it is very typical to ask even a total stranger "where are you from?" If the region is the same, it is interpreted as a sign that may mean the beginning of a close relationship. This is also an indicator of the notion of having things in common and "sameness" (see Omari and Sharma this volume).

Just like families, inside Turkish organisations signs of in-group collectivism are quite apparent. As previously mentioned, 95 per cent of businesses are family run (ASO 2005). It is always said that in business, trust among family members is stronger than members' trust in those outside the family. Therefore, top management is generally selected from family members because of their membership, rather than their competencies (Kabasakal and Bodur 2007). Even in businesses that are not family run, recruitment decisions are based on the suggestions of trusted people (Aycan 2001). In performance evaluations, individual performance is not as valued as group performance. Possibly for this reason, individual performance based reward systems generally do not work in the Turkish culture. For instance, each employee is selected as 'the employee of the month' on a rotational basis, rather than their outstanding performance (Gannon and Pillai 2013); this is believed to promote group harmony among workers.

In spite of its high score on in-group collectivism, Turkey scores low on institutional collectivism, which refers to the extent to which a society encourages and rewards collective work in institutional settings (House *et al.* 2004). In line with this finding, engagement in collective actions, such as membership of Non-Government Organisations (NGOs), is quite low. Turkish people are aware of the need to be more active in NGOs in order to protect their own rights, and improve the quality of life in the country (Kabasakal and Bodur 2007).

Affective/emotional society

Trompenaars (1993) classified Turkey as an affective society where emotions play an important role in interpersonal relationships. Similarly, Gannon and Pillai (2013) describe Turkish people as being rich in emotions. Accordingly, Turks tend to show their feelings plainly by laughing, smiling, scowling, and gesturing. Moreover, they expect other parties to reciprocate in terms of openly showing emotions. Those who use animated expressions during their speeches are considered good speakers (Trompenaars 1993).

As Turkish people strongly feel and live with their emotions, their reactions to positive or negative events may seem exaggerated to foreigners. In 2011, the

Dutch coach of the Turkish football team, Guus Hiddink, said that "In a country like Turkey things get very emotional" (www.mirror.co.uk/sport/football/news/ex-chelsea-manager-guus-hiddink-fears-3313457). This was in relation to the negative and heated reactions of Turkish fans just after their team lost. In turn, the Turkish media and football fans accused him of insensitivity.

The affective (Trompenaars 1993) nature of Turkish society is quite apparent in Turkish workplaces. As feelings quickly find their way into any discussion, task related conflicts may easily turn into interpersonal disputes. Similarly, giving negative feedback is very difficult, as people tend to take criticism personally; due to this many companies do not give performance feedback to employees (Aycan 2001).

Paternalist society

Paternalism, which is nurtured by high power distance, in-group collectivism, and affectivity, is a trademark of Turkish culture (Aycan 2006). As the leaders in Turkish organisations, paternalists play a parental role in their relationship with subordinates. Accordingly, they feel responsible for protecting the interests of and caring for their subordinates. In return, they expect unquestioning loyalty. Although this type of leadership is emotionally nurturing and satisfying for employees, it has a dark side; paternalism is associated with nepotism, and can have a harmful impact on perceptions of justice in organisations (Ertureten *et al.* 2013). Moreover, the expected unquestioning loyalty may seriously limit subordinates' freedom to act and speak.

Low future but faith oriented society

Turks are short-term oriented; for the long-term, they look to their faith. When referring to their future decisions and actions, they frequently say *kismet* or *inshallah,* which refers to the belief that their realisation depends on God's, rather than their own, will (Gannon and Pillai 2013). It can be said that this belief has both positive and negative sides. It has a positive side, because when bad and unavoidable events such as death or sickness of their beloved ones happen, Turks see the situation as the God's will. As a result, they more easily accept and adapt to such events, compared to Western societies. This orientation also has a negative side, since it decreases responsibility as a result of wrongdoing or inaction.

The practical results of short-term orientation in business life can be seen in any type of planning. Although the State Planning Organisation prepares five-year plans for government and state institutions, they are not generally applied (Kabasakal and Bodur 2007). Similarly, large organisations have planning departments and issue strategy documents, but long-term plans are filed away and forgotten. In SMEs, attitudes towards planning are even more pessimistic. Top managers believe that planning for the future is impossible due to economic volatilities (Aycan 2001). Similarly, employees believe that detailed career plans are not worth making because of the unstable external environment.

The first half of this chapter describes the main, but not necessarily all, cultural characteristics of Turkey. Other characteristics of Turkish culture not fully explored include: high assertiveness, low uncertainty avoidance, humane orientation, gender egalitarianism, and performance orientation (House *et al.* 2004). As the main focus of this chapter was to provide some context to workplace bullying incidents in Turkey in accordance with the country's business environment and culture, the decision was made to focus on the cultural characteristics which are most relevant to this negative behaviour.

Government preventative actions and legislation for workplace bullying in Turkey

In line with the increasing attention paid to workplace bullying in academia and the media, the Turkish government decided to engender effective intervention and prevention strategies. For this purpose, a public mandate entitled "Preventing Psychological Harassment at Work (Mobbing)" was issued in 2011 by the Prime Minister. According to the mandate, responsibility for prevention and intervention is given to employers along with support and control from the Ministry of Labour and Social Security. The Ministry has established a hotline, through which victims can get free support from experts (psychologists and lawyers) relating to ways to deal with workplace bullying. Statistics show that the hotline is well-used, with more than 11,000 calls since its establishment (Ministry of Labour and Social Security 2014). In addition, in 2012, the Ministry founded the "Council for the Prevention of Psychological Harassment at Work", with members from human rights institutions, the State Personnel Department, and the largest labour unions in Turkey. The Council, which assembles twice a year, actively works to increase public awareness of workplace bullying through seminars, training programs, and booklets.

In line with the increasing public awareness, there has been an increase in legal action against bullies and employer organisations. Courts refer to different yet similar definitions such as: "Mobbing includes any negative behaviour, violence, threat or humiliation which is applied systematically by peers or superiors" (Yargitay 2008, n.p.), or "Systematic hostile actions, hatred or emotional torture among employees or any of these negative actions can be exposed to employees by employers" (Cil 2011, pp. 477–8). Currently, court decisions refer to various provisions in labour law, obligations law, or civil law. This is due to a lack of provisions which specifically address workplace bullying (Limoncuoglu 2013). Therefore, courts usually base their decisions on whether the equality principle will be harmed, or on the principle of the protection of workers (Erdem and Parlak 2010). Decisions which favour the victims generally include payment for pecuniary and non-pecuniary damages; however, amounts paid for non-pecuniary damages are too low to discourage workplace bullying (Limoncuoglu 2013). Therefore, there is a need for provisions which specifically address workplace bullying in Turkey, with appropriate sanctions that can act as a deterrent.

Workplace bullying in Turkey

Definition

It is argued that workplace bullying is a serious, common and longstanding problem in Turkey, which began to receive attention in the 2000s. In the academic field, different terminology such as: workplace bullying (e.g. Asunakutlu and Safran 2006), psychological violence (e.g. Tutar 2004), deterrence (e.g. Bayrak Kok 2006), psychological workplace terror (e.g. Genc and Pamukoglu 2006), and mobbing (e.g. Halac and Bulut 2010) have been used. Popular media and consultancies prefer to use the term "mobbing", with roots back in the European literature (Leymann 1990). Since these terms have been used interchangeably in Turkish academic and employment settings, in this chapter the term "workplace bullying" will be used to refer to bullying and similar negative workplace behaviours.

Workplace bullying has been defined in Turkey as "any type of negative behaviour, humiliation, threat or violence which is shown by superiors or peers to an employee" (Tutar 2004, p. 11), or "targeting someone in the workplace through longstanding and repetitive negative behaviours" (Baykal 2005, p. 7); or "through creating systematic psychological pressure and unethical acts, decreasing targeted person(s)' performance and willingness to stay, thus leading to their voluntary dismissal" (Cobanoğlu 2005, pp. 21–2). These definitions have many commonalities with others developed and accepted in the international area. Turkish scholars generally prefer to use internationally accepted definitions (e.g. Einarsen *et al.* 2003, Leymann 1990); therefore, the impact of culture is not visible in the conceptualisation of terms in Turkey. As with their international counterparts, Turkish scholars use systematisation of the behaviour, perceived imbalance of power between the perpetrator and the victim, and the intention to harm to distinguish workplace bullying from conflict in Turkish academic settings (e.g. Ozturk 2011). Popular usage of the terms, however, indicates that people may label any negative act they experience as bullying, without thinking about the intention behind it, or its systematisation.

When the Turkish literature on workplace bullying is examined, it is clearly seen that the majority of research to date is quantitative, with very few qualitative studies available. This may be due to the quantitative research tradition in management studies in Turkey. Quantitative studies in the field focus on prevalence, scale development and adaptation, and antecedents and consequences of workplace bullying (e.g. Bayrak Kok 2006, Ozturk 2011, Soylu 2011, Palaz 2013), while the small number of qualitative studies have adopted a case study approach or made cross-cultural comparisons based on participant discourse (e.g. Guneri 2008, Guneri-Cangarli *et al.* 2013, Sahin 2013).

Prevalence rates

The reported rates of workplace bullying in Turkey are relatively high. For instance, a study conducted with 370 nursing students shows that 60 per cent were exposed to bullying during internships (Palaz 2013). In two separate studies sampling white-collar employees, 55 per cent (Bilgel *et al.* 2006) and 44.8 percent (Aytac *et al.* 2011) of participants reported that they were the victims of bullying. Similarly, Cemaloglu (2007) finds that 50 per cent of primary school teachers considered themselves victimised. One may argue that these extremely high prevalence rates are due to the measurement method, as utilising behavioural scales may result in inflated rates compared to the operationalisation of definitions (Salin 2001). However, in a study conducted with 288 public sector employees, operating with the definition method, Ozturk (2011) found a relatively high prevalence rate of 29 per cent. This suggests that workplace bullying is a serious and widespread problem in Turkey, regardless of the measurement and method.

Victims

Studies which focus on victims' personality traits and workplace bullying are quite rare in Turkey. There is an example of a study showing a positive relationship between neuroticism and psychoticism and being bullied (Deniz and Gulen-Ertosun 2010). As with research in the international sphere, Turks register their concern about these findings, as these personality characteristics may be developed as a direct result of being exposed to bullying. That is, there is a cause–effect conundrum; did the action or condition come first?

Also in line with international research, studies investigating the relationship between victims' demographics and being exposed to bullying in Turkey report conflicting findings. Some researchers report a positive relationship between age and being exposed to workplace bullying (e.g. Yilmaz *et al.* 2008), while others report a negative relationship (e.g. Koc and Urasoglu Bulut 2009), and yet others an insignificant relationship (e.g. Ozaralli and Torun 2007). Similar results are obtained for gender and marital status (Halac and Bulut 2010). Findings relating to demographics are not surprising considering the complex nature of bullying, and the difficulty of explaining such a complex phenomenon with demographics alone. Turkish researchers, however, have successfully shown relatively clear relationships between education, experience, and being exposed to bullying. Studies show that the likelihood of being victimised is higher for more educated but inexperienced people (e.g. Dogan Kilic 2009, Yilmaz *et al.* 2008). This can be explained by the hierarchical and collectivist structure of Turkish organisations, as such places can be difficult to navigate for new graduates. It may be that this cohort is insulted by their superiors for their inexperience, and in order for the superiors to boost their own egos. Moreover, as they are new comers, they are not yet seen as part of the in-group, therefore not getting the social support they need from their colleagues.

Perpetrators

There appears to be no study which collects data from alleged perpetrators in Turkey. From the victims' perspectives, perpetrators act with one of four main motives: (1) to convince targets to act in accordance with existing norms; (2) to eliminate or hold back high potential employees; (3) to overcome boredom; or (4) as a result of prejudicial attitudes towards victims' ethnicity, gender, or other characteristics (Yuceturk 2002). When motives are examined, reflections of Turkish cultural characteristics can be clearly seen. For instance, the first motive, to convince the victims to act in line with the existing norms, highlights collectivism, in which nonconformity to group norms deserves punishment. The second motive, to eliminate or hold back high potential employees, is frequently observed in Turkey, due to its assertive culture characterised by harsh competition. The final motive, prejudicial attitudes towards victims' ethnicity, gender, or other characteristics, may indicate in-group/out-group separation, which is frequently observed in collectivist cultures. Accordingly, a person may be bullied just because s/he is perceived as an out-group member.

The collectivist and relationship orientation of Turkey also shows itself in perpetrator tactics. As in these societies, relationships and others' opinions are quite important; perpetrators are aware that they can harm the victim through damaging relationships and reputation. Therefore, they first try to socially isolate the victim, and then harm their personal reputation (Halac and Bulut 2010). Other tactics, such as damaging work related outcomes or sabotage, often follow.

Observers

In Turkey, data on workplace bullying is generally collected from victims rather than other parties. No comprehensive study specifically explores observers' feelings and reactions towards bullying; only victims' reports have been identified. In case of supervisory bullying, victims generally report that "they [the observers] did nothing" or "they [the observers] were too afraid to intervene", or "they [the observers] try to support me behind the back of the perpetrator" (*sic*) (Guneri-Cangarli *et al.* 2013). Ozturk (2011) finds that observers are also negatively affected by workplace bullying, as they report lower levels of justice perception and organisational citizenship behaviours compared to non-observers. This leads to the question: why do observers do nothing or just show passive support although they are also negatively affected? Potentially, the answer lies in the cultural characteristics and socio-economics dynamics of Turkey. In high power distance societies, opposing superiors is difficult. Moreover, considering the volatile economic situation of the country and high unemployment rate, observers may be afraid of their employment security; therefore, support is passive or non-existent.

Management, leadership and organisational politics

Supervisors are the most reported group of perpetrators, followed by supervisor-peers and peers alone (e.g. Deniz *et al.* 2010). In line with this, Ozturk (2011) finds that among those bullied, 81.4 per cent are exposed to supervisory bullying. Moreover, in a qualitative study conducted with Turkish and Australian graduate students, when asked to reveal their most serious workplace bullying incidents, Turks report only supervisory incidents, while Australian counterparts mention supervisory and peer bullying (Guneri-Cangarli *et al.* 2013). Studies show that criticising management actions, or simply disagreeing with their opinions are among the common reasons for supervisory bullying in Turkey (e.g. Sahin 2013). This situation can be linked to power distance, as in high power distance societies' criticism from subordinates is unacceptable for those with power.

The relationship between leadership style and workplace bullying has also been investigated in Turkey. Turks perceive the authoritarian leadership style as positively related to supervisory bullying, while transactional and transformational leadership styles are negatively related (Ertureten *et al.* 2013). Results on the impact of paternalism, however, are conflicting. Ertureten *et al.* (2013) show that paternalist leadership negatively affects the risk of being exposed to supervisory bullying; conversely Soylu (2011) finds that it may be a contributing factor. This can be explained by the complex nature of paternalism. On the one hand, it is nurturing and protective, while on the other it requires unquestioning loyalty, which may create psychological pressure on subordinates, and limit their freedom (Ertureten *et al.* 2013).

The role of management in the prevention of workplace bullying is also frequently mentioned by victims. They believe that it is their managers' responsibility to stop or prevent bullying. Therefore, victims hold their managers responsible for their experiences, no matter who the bully is (Guneri-Cangarli 2009).

Apart from the mainstream research in the international arena, it is interesting to see that, in Turkey, workplace bullying has frequently been linked with organisational politics in which bullying behaviours are deliberately used to serve the interests of perpetrators (Samanci 2001, Guneri-Cangarli 2009). Accordingly, supervisors, and even peers, may perpetrate bullying in order to influence organisational decisions related to promotion, task assignments, dismissal, and performance management (Guneri-Cangarli 2009). Moreover, in a narrative study, Guneri (2008) found that perpetrators use bullying as a very effective political tactic which eventually causes the dismissal of the victim. Similarly, Samanci (2001) reported that workplace bullying is frequently used as a deliberate strategy by managers and owners, especially during periods of economic recession, causing the voluntary resignation of the victim, and avoiding severance payments. These findings point to the highly hierarchical and assertive nature of Turkish organisations where political behaviours are more common. Moreover, they are made possible by the weaknesses of the social security system, and the ineffectiveness of labour unions in Turkey.

Consequences

It can be argued that due to the collectivist and family oriented nature of Turkish society, victims are not as seriously affected as their counterparts in Western societies; that is, there may be some buffering due to social support from families and close friends (Baltas 2006). Empirical research provides evidence that victims of workplace bullying in Turkey often suffer from psychological problems such as loss of concentration, increased anger, and decreased motivation (Palaz 2013); Yildirim *et al.* (2007) found that 9 per cent of bullying victims seriously consider suicide.

The organisational consequences of workplace bullying in Turkey are similar to those found in other countries. Turkish researchers have detected productivity losses (Dikmetas *et al.* 2011); decreases in organisational commitment (e.g. Bulutlar and Unler Oz 2009) and job satisfaction (Ertureten *et al.* 2013); and perceptions of organisational injustice (Ozturk 2011). Other consequences include: increases in absenteeism (Asunakutlu and Safran 2006); turnover intentions (Ertureten *et al.* 2013); and burnout (Dikmetas *et al.* 2011). Findings highlight that workplace bullying is harmful not only for victims but also for organisations.

Coping behaviours

A common coping behaviour, unfortunately, is silence (Aytac *et al.* 2011). The main reasons for silence or taking no formal action are the lack of trust in existing regulations (Guneri-Cangarli *et al.* 2013), and the lack of organised social support for victims (e.g. Bilgel *et al.* 2006). Another frequently used coping strategy is to resign or propose a rotation (Ozaralli and Torun 2007). Alternatively, victims may try to be more effective and show higher performance levels in order to avoid being humiliated by managers (Yildirim *et al.* 2007). This may be interpreted as victims blaming themselves rather than their managers. This reaction is not surprising, considering the high power distance orientation of the society in which power holders are privileged. Victims rarely try to solve the issue by talking to the bully or reporting the situation to management. Thus, victims seem to need more social support and clearer regulations to actively cope with workplace bullying (Guneri-Cangarli *et al.* 2013).

Conclusion and future directions

This chapter examines the problem of workplace bullying in Turkey in accordance with its socio-economic dynamics and cultural characteristics. The prevalence of workplace bullying in Turkey, affecting around 40 per cent of employees, is high compared to many countries. The hierarchical, collectivist, assertive, and paternalist nature of Turkish society, combined with its volatile economy, may favour predatory environments. Decreasing the very high prevalence of bullying in workplaces will involve the cooperation of all parties; policy makers, labour unions, human resource managers, and academics, as well as employees themselves, including observers. For policy makers, effective regulation which specifically addresses workplace bullying, backed up with effective sanctions, would seem to be a logical first step. Moreover, it appears that the "Council for the

Prevention of Psychological Harassment at Work" has a larger role to play in improving public awareness. Labour unions should support the actions of the Council through training programs and providing advice, as well as psychological and legal support to victimised members. Similarly, human resource managers are responsible for awareness-raising and developing and using anti-bullying policies in organisations.

In view of Turkey's hierarchical, assertive, collectivist, and paternalist nature, awareness should be increased within companies of the type of behaviour, including leadership styles, that constitute bullying. Moreover, considering the fact that victims suffer more because of the lack of organised support, groups in companies can be established as preventative measures and to help, support, and buffer victims. In the academic field, more empirical research is needed to provide comprehensive data. Research, especially on perpetrators, observers, and cross-cultural comparisons, is needed to extend the knowledge base. Finally, observers should be aware that their silence indirectly supports bullying. Together with the above-mentioned preventative actions, activating observers may have a significant impact on decreasing the high prevalence of workplace bullying in collectivist Turkey.

References

ASO, 2005. *Aile şirketleri: Değişim ve süreklilik* (Family businesses: Change and sustainability). Ankara: Ankara Sanayi Odası Yayınları.

Asunakutlu, T., and Safran, B., 2006. Bullying (zorbalık) ve kontrol odagi (Bullying and locus of control). In Bingol, D. (ed.), *14th Ulusal Yonetim ve Organizasyon Kongresi Bildiri Kitapcigi,* 25–27 May, Erzurum: Ataturk University, 315–18.

Aycan, Z., 2001. Human resource management in Turkey: Current issues and future challenges. *International Journal of Manpower,* 22(3), 252–60.

Aycan, Z., 2006. Paternalism. In Kim, U., Yang, K.S., and Hwang, K.K. (eds.), *Indigenous and cultural psychology. Understanding people in context.* New York: Springer, 445–66.

Aytac, S., Bozkurt, V., Bayram, N., Yildiz, S., Aytac, M., Akinci, F.S., and Bilgel, N., 2011. Workplace violence: A study of Turkish workers. *International Journal of Occupational Safety and Ergonomics (JOSE),* 17(4), 385–402.

Baltas, A., 2006. *Adı yeni konmuş bir olgu: İşyerinde yıldırma* (Recently known phenomenon: Workplace bullying). Available from: www.baltasbaltas.com/web/makaleler/ck_3.htm (Accessed 26 Dec 2014).

Baykal, A.N., 2005. *Yutucu rekabet: Kanuni devrindeki mobbingden gunumuze* (Hard competition: Mobbing from Kanuni's time to today). Istanbul: Sistem.

Bayrak Kok, S., 2006. Is yasaminda psiko-siddet sarmali olarak yildirma (Bullying as a psycho-violence at work). In Bingol, D. (ed.), *14th Ulusal Yonetim ve Organizasyon Kongresi Bildiri Kitapcigi,* 25–27 May, Erzurum: Ataturk University, 161–70.

Bilgel, N., Aytac, S., and Bayram, N., 2006. Bullying in Turkish white-collar workers. *Occupational Medicine,* 56(4), 226–31.

Bulutlar, F., and Unler Oz, E., 2009. The effects of ethical climates on bullying behavior in the workplace. *Journal of Business Ethics*, 86, 273–95.

Cemaloglu, N., 2007. The exposure of primary school teachers to bullying: An analysis of various variables. *Social Behavior and Personality: An International Journal*, 35(6), 789–802.

Cil, S., 2011. *Is hukuku yargıtay ilke kararları* (Supreme Court appeals in labour law). Ankara: Turhan Kitabevi.

Cobanoglu, S., 2005. *Mobbing ve basa cikma yontemleri* (Mobbing and coping methods). Istanbul: Timas.

CSGB (Ministry of Labour and Social Security), 2014. *Is yerinde psikolojik taciz (mobbing): Bilgilendirme Rehberi* (Psychological harassment at work (mobbing): Introductory guide). Ankara: CSGB.

Deniz, N., and Guler Ertosun, O., 2010. The relationship between personality and being exposed to workplace bullying or mobbing. *Global Journal of Strategic Management*, 7, 129–42.

Dikmetas, E., Top, M., and Ergin, G., 2011. Asistan hekimlerin tükenmişlik ve mobbing düzeylerinin incelenmesi (Examining exposure to mobbing and burn-out syndrome on junior hospital doctors). *Türk Psikiyatri Dergisi*, 22(3), 137–49.

Dinçer, O.B., Federici, V., Ferris, E., Karaca, S., Kirisci, K., and Carmıklı, E.O., 2013. *Suriyeli Mülteciler ve Türkiye: Sonu Gelmeyen Misafirlik* (Syrian refugees and their endless stay). Ankara: International Strategic Research Organization (USAK).

Dogan Kilic, E., 2009. Psychological violence in learning organizations: A case study in Sanliurfa, Turkey. *Social Behavior and Personality*, 37(7), 869–80.

Egilmez, M., 2014. *Türkiye'de değişimin sosyo-ekonomik analizi* (Socio-economic analysis for change in Turkey). Available from: www.mahfiegilmez.com/2014/03/turkiyedeki-degisimin-sosyo-ekonomik.html (Accessed 9 Dec 2014).

Einarsen, S., Hoel, H., Zapf, D., and Cooper, C.L., 2003. The concept of bullying at work: The European tradition. In Einarsen, S., Hoel, H., Zapf, D., and Cooper, C.L. (eds.), *Bullying and emotional abuse in the workplace: International perspectives in research and practice*, London and New York: Taylor & Francis, 3–30.

Erdem, M.R., and Parlak, B. 2010. Turk ceza hukukunda mobbing (Mobbing in Turkish penal code). *TBB Dergisi*, 88, 271–86.

Ertureten, A., Cemalcilar, Z., and Aycan, Z., 2013. The relationship of downward mobbing with leadership style and organizational attitudes. *Journal of Business Ethics*, 116(1), 205–16.

Fullagar, C.J., Sumer, H.C., Sverke, M., and Slick, R., 2003. Managerial sex-role stereotyping: A cross cultural analysis. *International Journal of Cross Cultural Management*, 3(1), 93–107.

Gannon, M.J., and Pillai, R. 2013. *Understanding global cultures: Metaphorical journeys through 31 nations, continents, and diversity*. Thousand Oaks: Sage.

Genc, N., and Pamukoglu, E., 2006. Psikolojik isyeri teroru: Dr. Siyami Ersek Gogus ve Kalp Damar Cerrahisi Egitim ve Arastirma Hastanesi'nde bir uygulama (Psychological terror at work: A study in Dr. Siyami Ersek Hospital for Cardiovascular Diseases). In Bingol, D. (ed.), *14th Ulusal Yonetim ve Organizasyon Kongresi Bildiri Kitapcigi*, 25–27 May, Erzurum: Ataturk University, 319–29.

Guneri, B., 2008. The dark side of the relationships at work: The nature of bullying. In Katrinli, A. (ed.), *Real life stories of how people feel and behave in organizations.* Charleston: BookSurge Publishing, 167–91.

Guneri-Cangarli, B., 2009. Bullying behaviors as organizational political tactics. Unpublished PhD Thesis. Izmir University of Economics, Irzmir.

Guneri-Cangarli, B., Paull, M., and Omari, M., 2013. Workplace bullying in Turkey and Australia: A preliminary comparative investigation. Presentation in the *European Academy of Management Conference,* 26–29 June, Istanbul.

Halac, D.S., and Bulut, C., 2010. Mobbing: A review of Turkish literature. *Social Responsibility, Professional Ethics, and Management Proceedings of the 11th International Conference,* 24–27 November, Ankara.

Hofstede, G., 1984. *Culture's consequences: International differences in work-related values.* Thousand Oaks: Sage.

House, R.J., Hanges, P.J., Javidan, M., Dorfman, P.W., and Gupta, V., eds., 2004. *Culture, leadership, and organizations: The GLOBE study of 62 societies.* Thousand Oaks: Sage.

Kabasakal, H., and Bodur, M., 2007. Leadership and culture in Turkey: A multifaceted phenomenon. In Chhokar, J.S., Brodbeck, F.C., and House, R.J. (eds.), *Culture and leadership across the world: The GLOBE book of in-depth studies of 25 societies.* New York: Taylor & Francis, 835–74.

Kağitçibaşi, C., 1982. Sex Roles, Value of Children and Fertility, in C. Kağitçibaşi, C. and Sunar, D. (eds.) Sex Roles, Family and Community in Turkey, pp. 151–80. Bloomington, Indiana: Indiana University Turkish Studies Series 3.

Kiray, M., 1997. *Abandonment of the land and transformation to urban life. Human development report.* Ankara: United Nations Development Programme.

Koc, I., 2007. Turkiye'de Turkce ve Kurtce anadil nufuslarinin demografik farklilasma ve anadil duzeyleri (Demographic differentiation and mother tongue usage of Turkish and Kurdish groups in Turkey). *21. Yuzyil,* Jan-Feb-March, 179–86.

Koc, M., and Urasoglu Bulut, H. 2009. Ortaogretim ogretmenlerinde mobbing: Cinsiyet, yas ve lise turu degiskenleri acisindan incelenmesi (Mobbing among secondary school teachers: Examining the relationship with gender, age and school type). *International Online Journal of Educational Sciences,* 1(1), 64–80.

Leymann, H., 1990. Mobbing and psychological terror at workplaces. *Violence and Victims,* 5(2), 119–26.

Limoncuoglu, S.A., 2013. Is hukuku kapsaminda psikolojik tacizin değerlendirilmesi ve mağdurlarin kullanabilecekleri haklar (The analysis of psychological harassment within the scope of labour law and the rights of the victims). *TBB Dergisi,* 105, 51–88.

Ocak, A.Y. 2009. *Alevi ve Bektasi inanclarinin Islam oncesi temelleri* (Pre-Islam foundations of Alevi and Bektasi beliefs). Istanbul: Iletisim Yayinlari.

OECD, 2014. Economic survey of Turkey. Available from: www.oecd.org/turkey/economic-survey-turkey.htm (Accessed 17 Dec 2014).

Onder, A.T., 1998. *Türkiye'nin etnik yapısı* (Ethic structure of Turkey). Ankara: Bilim ve Sanat Dagitim.

Ozaralli, N., and Torun, A., 2007. Calisanlara uygulanan zorbaligin magdurlarin kisilik ozellikleri, negatif duygular ve isten ayrilma niyetleriyle iliskisi uzerine bir arastirma (A study on mobbing in relation with personality characteristics, negative feelings and intention to leave). In G. Yildiz (ed.), *15th Ulusal Yönetim ve Organizasyon Kongresi Bildiriler Kitabi*, 25–27 May, Sakarya University, Ankara, 938–47.

Ozturk, D. 2011. Workplace bullying: Its reflection upon organizational justice and organizational citizenship behavior perceptions among public sector employees. Unpublished Master's Thesis. Middle East Technical University, Ankara.

Palaz, S., 2013. Turkish nursing students' perceptions and experiences of bullying behavior in nursing education. *Journal of Nursing Education and Practice*, 3(1), 23–30.

Sahin, M., 2013. Mobbing olgusuna anatomik bir bakıs: Universite ozelinde vaka analizi (An anatomic view on mobbing: Case study in a university). *Akademik Bakıs Dergisi*, 38 (September-November), 1–20.

Salin, D., 2001. Prevalence and forms of bullying among business professionals: A comparison of two different strategies for measuring bullying. *European Journal of Work and Organizational Psychology*, 10(4), 425–41.

Samanci, A., 2001. Taciz, depresyon, istifa (Harassment, depression and resignation). Available from: www.radikal.com.tr/2001/01/22/yasam/01tac.shtml (Accessed 25 Dec 2014).

Schwartz, S.H., 2008. *Cultural value orientations: Nature and implications of national differences*. Available from: http://blogs.helsinki.fi/valuesandmorality/files/2009/09/Schwartz-Monograph-Cultural-Value-Orientations.pdf (Accessed 17 Dec 2014).

Soylu, S., 2011. Creating a family or loyalty-based framework: The effects of paternalistic leadership on workplace bullying. *Journal of Business Ethics*, 99(2), 217–31.

Trompenaars, F., 1993. *Riding the waves of culture: Understanding cultural diversity in business*. London: The Economist Books.

Trompenaars, F., and Hampden-Turner, C. 1998. *Riding the waves of culture: Understanding diversity in global business*. New York: McGraw-Hill.

TUIK, 2014a. *Adrese dayali nüfus kayit sistemi sonuclari, 2013* (Results of residency based population statistics, 2013). Available from: www.tuik.gov.tr/PreHaber Bultenleri.do?id=15974 (Accessed on 15 Dec 2014).

TUIK, 2014b. *Hanehalki isgucu istatistikleri, Subat 2014* (Household workforce statistics). Available from: www.tuik.gov.tr/PreHaberBultenleri.do?id=16007 (Accessed 10 Dec 2014).

Tutar, H., 2004. *Isyerlerinde Psikolojik Siddet* (Psychological violence at work). Ankara: Platin.

UNDP, 2013. *Human development report 2013: The rise of the south: Human progress in a diverse world*. Available from: www.tr.undp.org/content/dam/turkey/docs/Publications/hdr/Turkey.pdf (Accessed on 9 Dec 2014).

Urhan, B. 2005. Turkiye'de sendikal orgutlenmede yasanan guven ve dayanisma sorunlari (Trust and co-operation issues in labour unions in Turkey). *Calisma ve Toplum*, 1, 57–88.

Uysal-Kolasin, G., and Guner, D., 2010. *4 Millions 742 thousands women are illiterate*. Research Brief, Istanbul: BETAM.

World Bank Data. *Turkey*. Available from: http://data.worldbank.org/country/turkey (Accessed 9 Dec 2014).

Yargitay Kararları (Supreme Court of Appeals), 2008. Karar No. (Decision number): Y9HD 30.05.2008 E. 2007/9154 K. 2008/13307

Yildirim, D., Yildirim, A., and Timucin, A., 2007. Mobbing behaviors encountered by nurse teaching staff. *Nursing Ethics,* 14(4), 447–63.

Yilmaz, A., Ergun Ozler, D., and Mercan, N., 2008. Mobbing ve orgut iklimi iliskisine yonelik ampirik bir arastirma (An empirical research on mobbing and organizational climate relationship) *Elektronik Sosyal Bilimler Dergisi,* 7(26), 334–57.

Yuceturk, E.E., 2002. *Bilgi Caginda Orgutlerin Gorunmeyen Yuzu: Mobbing* (Hidden face of organizations in the information age: Mobbing). Available from: www.bilgiyonetimi.org/cm/pages/mkl_gos.php?nt=224 (Accessed 12 Dec 2014).

7 Greece

Incivility, bullying and forcing in the land of bullying gods and lesser mortals

Nikos Bozionelos

Introduction

This chapter aims to provide a comprehensive picture of workplace abuse in Greece. It will start in a somewhat unorthodox manner by introducing its methodology. Available research on abusive behaviour in the Greek work context, albeit useful, is very limited and, hence, insufficient to provide a complete picture. Accordingly, the author has resorted to additional resources. One such resource was his own native knowledge of Greek culture and experience of the Greek workplace. The author has work experience from quite disparate industries and occupations in the Greek context including the private sector (sales, marketing, telemarketing), the armed forces (where he served as both subordinate and line manager in the front line), and Greek academia, which is attached to the State. Despite its potential subjectivity, such knowledge and experience is a substantial descriptive and interpretative resource, partly because workplace abuse is a predominantly subjective experience that is largely shaped by actors' (targets' and perpetrators') cultural background, and the cultural context in which they find themselves. This was supplemented with material from interviews with three individuals who are involved in the human resource function of Greek firms. Interviews covered the theme of workplace abuse and attempted to extract a general picture, as well as to uncover nuances that are unique to the Greek environment. Though by no means exhaustive or flawless, the above methodology enabled the development of a broad picture of the situation with respect to workplace abuse in the Greek context.

Demographics and economy

Greece is geographically located in the south-east part of the European Continent, with a population of around 11 million (Greek Statistical Agency 2014). Politically Greece is a member of the European Union (it joined in 1981, much earlier than most current member states), and a member of most international diplomatic and humanitarian organisations including the United Nations (UN) and the Organisation for Economic Cooperation and Development (OECD) (European Union 2014). The official language, Modern Greek (a direct descendent of Ancient Greek, which has lent many terms to other modern languages), is the first language for the population, which is largely indigenous. Learning foreign languages is an integral part of the educational culture, and most Greeks are competent in at least one foreign language, that normally being English, followed by French.

Greece is at present hosting more than 2 million recent immigrants who live in the country along with the indigenous population (though official statistics present a lower number; Καθημερινή, 2013). The vast majority of these immigrants come from non-EU member states, and their status varies, from being illegal (meaning in many cases unrecorded and officially non-existent), to having a residence permit, and to a small few who have obtained Greek citizenship. Regardless of their status, these immigrants have had an impact on the economic and social (though not yet the political) life of the country. Very few immigrants, however, have made their way into mainstream Greek employment. The vast majority either work as 'free-lancers', mostly in manual or blue-collar jobs (e.g., agriculture, construction), or have started their own businesses that in many cases are part of the secondary economy and officially do not exist. Furthermore, it is very rare to find immigrants in white-collar positions in either the public or the private sector (Stratoudaki 2008, Papastergiou and Takou 2014). It is therefore the indigenous Greek population to whom reference is made in this chapter.

The economy of Greece is composed mostly of services, which represents in excess of 80 per cent of the Gross Domestic Product (GDP) and 70 per cent of employment (Enterprise Greece 2014), the disproportionately large public sector included. The vast majority of private sector firms (99.9 per cent) fall within the Small-Medium Enterprise (SME) category (i.e., they employ less than 250 employees) and account for more than 85 per cent of private sector employment (European Commission 2013). Firms with more than 250 employees are fewer than 500. Furthermore, only half a per cent (0.5 per cent) of SMEs employ more than 50 people, the rest being either micro-businesses (around 96 per cent) or smaller SMEs (around 3 per cent), employing less than 10 and 10–49 people, respectively (European Commission 2013). As can be inferred from their overwhelmingly micro- or small-SME character, the great majority of private sector firms are family owned (Vassiliadis and Vassiliadis 2014), which means that capital ownership and key positions are in the hands of individuals from a single family, or sometimes of a few friendly families.

History and culture

Greece has a very long history that extends back in excess of 9,000 years. The country has been exposed to a variety of influences which have shaped its modern culture. As a result, modern Greek culture is a complex amalgam of features, some of which appear contradictory yet co-exist (for example, strong power distance along with a detestation and distrust of authority; see Carl *et al.* 2004, Bozionelos and Kiamou 2008). The modern Greek State was founded in 1830.

Until that point, and for around 400 years, Greece was a semi-autonomous part of the Ottoman Empire. Prior to that, the region now known as Greece became part of the Roman Empire in 146 BC, and was part of the subsequent Byzantine Empire that emerged in the first centuries AD (History of the Greek Nation 2007). During its history, Greece has been exposed to the rationalism and intellectualism of ancient Greece and to the values of the Christian religion, but also to the influences of Islam (Mouzelis 2012). Modern Greek culture has elements of all these value systems. Furthermore, and especially after the Second World War, the political leadership of the country expended effort towards cultural mimicry of Western European countries (viewed as model states and worth imitation by most Greek governments). This has resulted in limited infusion of Western European cultural characteristics, though nowhere near what was hoped for. Therefore, the culture of modern Greece is still quite distanced from that of the core countries of the European Union.

Cultural profile

Most parsimonious models of national culture, including Hofstede's (1980) and the GLOBE project (House *et al.* 2004), contain Greece. These models place Greece within the Eastern European cultural cluster, along with countries such as Albania, Georgia, Hungary, Poland and Russia. Greece was not part of Trompenaars' (1993) study, which also has useful interpretive elements, but it is possible to extrapolate on Greece's relative position on the dimensions of that model by considering participant countries with presumably similar cultural characteristics to Greece (Bozionelos and Kiamou 2008). General models of culture, however, provide only a crude picture that does not normally allow fine-grained analysis and accurate interpretation of social, including workplace, behaviour. This necessitates parallel utilisation of country-specific cultural knowledge (Hofstede 1993, Bozionelos 2006). What is presented below, therefore, includes those cultural characteristics that appear most relevant to an understanding of workplace abuse in Greece. Some of these are found in generic models, while others are country-specific and necessitate hands-on knowledge of the local culture that can be acquired only by means of living and interacting within the Greek society for long periods.

Weak institutional vs. strong in-group collectivism, and the profound in-group–out-group polarisation

Greece finds itself in the last position on the GLOBE study's measure of Institutional Collectivism (Gelfand *et al.* 2004), which in essence indicates the extent to which people view their fate as interdependent with the fate of the collective (being the State, the community or the employer), and are willing to sacrifice personal convenience for its interests. This, in effect, means that Greeks consider their own fates as independent of that of the general collective/society, and they are therefore unwilling to abide by laws or even ethical guidelines if they do not see these as directly compatible with their own personal convenience or interests (also Voulgaris 2006). On the other hand, Greece scores moderately strongly on In-group Collectivism (Gelfand *et al.* 2004), which signifies whether members of a society identify themselves most closely with particular in-groups rather than the whole collective. Typical in-groups in the Greek society include the family (immediate and sometimes extended), networks of friendly families, and the political party to which one is sympathetic or affiliated (Bozionelos 2014).

Though present in every culture, the mentality of the in-group–out-group distinction is especially pronounced in Greek society (Triandis *et al.* 1968). Those who are viewed as in-group members (or 'our people' according to the Greek expression) are treated with warmth and are provided with strong support and favouritism by their fellow in-group members. Those who are viewed as belonging to the out-group are treated with suspicion and often with overt hostility (Triandis *et al.* 1968, Broome 1996). In everyday life Greeks automatically categorise others as members of their in-group or out-group, and adjust their behaviour accordingly. Neutrality is often interpreted as out-group sympathy and may have consequences that resemble overt out-group membership (Bozionelos 2014). As a result, being part of the 'right' in-group may have profound repercussions on many fronts, including how one is treated by peers and senior colleagues.

The profile of the country on the above three cultural features can explain the high levels of corruption (Greece occupies the top position amongst all 27 EU countries; Transparency International 2012) and of disrespect for the law in modern Greek society. An interesting demonstration of the latter is that Greece is the only country worldwide where there have been two antismoking laws but smoking continues uninterrupted in all public (including work) places. Disrespect for the law and regulations is also reflected in the wide discrepancy between official legislation, rules and procedures for workplace functioning (e.g., human resource systems, health and safety procedures) and what happens in reality (Bozionelos 2011). It is the norm, for example, that human resource systems (such as grievance procedures or performance appraisal) exist and function on paper, while in reality they are either mocked or are unpretentiously not effectuated. This means that even where systems that could work against workplace abuse are in place (e.g., grievance procedures, 360-degree feedback), the likelihood that these systems are utilised in any meaningful way is low.

The family as the prototypical in-group

The potent role of family as the prototypical in-group (many times followed by the political party one is sympathetic to or affiliated with) demands emphasis. The family is of paramount importance in Greek culture, and it is loyalty to the family and its perceived interests that largely guide social behaviour. This feature combined with the low Institutional Collectivism renders behaviours oriented towards the benefit of the family morally legitimate. Therefore, family-oriented behaviours are regularly performed, regardless of whether they (directly or collaterally) are to the detriment of outsiders or of the general collective. This occupies great importance within the context of workplace abuse, because the majority of firms in Greece are family owned. Family dominance and 'ownership' often also applies to individual agencies and departments of the public sector, and to political party leadership that many times extends to the government itself.

Low humane orientation

Greece occupies one of the very bottom positions in Humane Orientation (Kabasakal and Bodur 2004). This means low empathy and low concern or felt responsibility towards others and their well-being, as well as tendencies towards discrimination against disadvantaged groups. This cultural feature bears relevance to workplace abuse. It signifies that superiors, or those in power, have low concern for the feelings and well-being of their subordinates, or of those they perceive as less powerful. It also signifies that employees show low genuine interest for their colleagues, or are ill motivated to act (e.g., report the incident or intervene) if they witness workplace abuse. This is generally true with one exception: interest and concerns for others is higher if colleagues or subordinates are perceived to be members of their own in-group.

Low professionalism

Another cultural feature of Greece that is of importance within the context of workplace abuse is the generally low professionalism. Although there are certainly exceptions, Greeks generally perceive the roles imposed by their professions or occupations as secondary, and assign low importance to the appropriate and dutiful execution of tasks and activities contained within those roles. Low professionalism can, at least partly, be explained by the diffuse and affective nature of the Greek society, as extrapolated from Trompenaars' (1993) model. Being a Diffuse and Affective society means that people do not strongly distinguish personal from professional relationships, while overt displays of emotions are acceptable if not encouraged. This implies that Greeks allow personal preferences and dislikes to influence their behaviour and judgement in professional matters, while at the same time they lack the emotional management that professionalism often necessitates. Hence, for example, frustrations at a personal level with a colleague or a subordinate, or even a client, might be translated into abusive behaviour at a professional level and vice versa.

A trademark cultural characteristic of Greeks, *filotimo,* is in fact a reflection of the configuration of low professionalism and the strong obligation felt towards the in-group. *Filotimo* does not have a direct translation in the English language, but it is in essence in-role behaviour perceived, executed and understood as extra-role behaviour within the Greek context. Due to low professionalism it is common for job incumbents either to refuse to perform their tasks at all (especially in the public sector), or to perform these in a perfunctory way, unless performance of tasks is seen as an obligation towards their in-group. When that happens supervisors, colleagues or the public (in the case of the public sector) may try to evoke emotions of guilt and the feeling of being generous, kind and gentle at heart, in an effort to motivate them to do what they should do, or should have done, as part of their work roles. This is normally redundant in societies with strong professionalism (e.g., many Western European, North American, and some Far Eastern Societies).

Power distance and formality in superior–subordinate relationships

In line with the country's relative position on Power Distance (e.g., Hofstede 2001, Carl *et al.* 2004), there is generally substantial distance and strong formality in the relationship between superiors and subordinates in the Greek workplace (Bozionelos 2006). Most workplaces in Greece have power organisational cultures (Bourantas and Papadakis 1997, Bozionelos 2014; for the notion of power organisational culture, see Handy 1976). This means that in most workplaces, and especially in the private sector, the main motive is fear or at best extreme obligation. What, however, makes the situation more complicated are specific national cultural characteristics such as the in-group–out-group distinction, the importance of the family, and the key role of political ideology and political party affiliation. As a result, in many firms of the private sector, those who belong to the same family with those who are in key posts or are affiliated with them in some way, receive special treatment and enjoy protection, and hence are less likely to fall victim to abuse or be treated with incivility. This does not only hold for family-owned businesses, but also for subsidiaries of foreign multinationals, which are also often dominated by certain families. This also means that in the public sector people who share family ties or family friendship ties with those who are in key positions – and who normally have connections with popular political parties or the unions – also enjoy protection, making them less likely to be subjected to abuse.

Political ideology and political party affiliation

Finally, a cultural feature of consequence is the profound importance of political ideology and political party affiliation in Greek society; both of which have played a major role in social affairs throughout modern Greek history (see Bozionelos 2014). Political party affiliation is still the sole determinant of appointments, transfers and career progression in the overgrown (exactly because of that reason) public sector and sectors of similar nature (e.g., municipal government, part of academia); and sometimes also in the private sector. Political party affiliation is also directly linked with the protection an individual can expect from labour unions (whether as perpetrator or target of abuse) because unions in Greece are heavily politicised and typically controlled by particular political parties (e.g., Kouzis 2007, Tsakiris 2012).

The legislative framework for workplace abuse

There is no legal framework in Greece for any form of workplace abuse apart from sexual harassment. This means that it is at the discretion of individual employers whether to include abuse in their internal code of conduct, how to define it, and how or whether to establish policies and procedures to deal with it. The Greek labour law requires that every firm that employs more than 70 individuals compiles and ratifies a regulatory framework that sets rules on how the employer relates with employees, and how employees relate and interact with each other. This needs to be agreed upon and signed both by the firm and union representatives. There are a number of caveats on the implementation of this requirement: (1) many firms with more than 70 employees simply do not comply with the legislation. This is a consequence of the aforementioned cultural feature of low respect for law and regulations that is reinforced by the tolerance of state agencies and their agents; (2) the vast majority of firms in Greece do not meet the size requirement (70-plus employees); (3) even if a firm establishes a framework, the firm may choose not to explicitly include elements that touch upon abuse issues (given that there is no legal obligation), and much less set procedures about dealing with these; and (4) in the few cases of firms that have set regulatory frameworks that include abuse, taking action in case of abuse (which is very difficult to document in the first place) is very complicated, given that workplace abuse does not come under employment law, but under civil law instead. Hence, to effect disciplinary action the case has to go to a civil court, which is known, discouragingly, to take many years.

Some firms have their own internal codes of conduct, separate from any legislation and independent of the size of the firm. Again, however, many of these firms avoid explicit inclusion of topics of abuse in their code. In addition, it is very rare to have explicitly stated procedures to deal with abuse. Furthermore, given the discrepancy between formal systems and actual practice in the Greek environment, human resource systems that may reveal or document abuse, such as performance appraisal, often take place only nominally or remain 'on paper' only.

Workplace abuse

Being aware of the debate on the proliferation and usefulness of concepts that denote workplace abuse (e.g., Hershcovis 2011, Tepper and Henle 2011, Branch *et al.* 2013, Neall and Tuckey 2014), the choice has been to focus on incivility and bullying (with harassment and supervisory abuse seen as within bullying). In the present work, incivility is defined as uncivilised behaviour (such as threatening, swearing, shouting, being ironic or being rude and discourteous in general) towards another individual, or group of individuals, that is not necessarily repeated towards the same targets, or at least does not happen with consistency and frequency. Furthermore, perpetrators and targets of incivility might not interact regularly for work-related issues, and there is no conscious intention to harm the other individual. These features are in line with Anderson and Pearson's (1999) notion of incivility in the workplace. On the other hand, bullying refers to abusive behaviour directed towards a particular target that is consistent and sufficiently frequent (e.g., Einarsen *et al.* 2011). The distinction in terms of intention and frequency is important within the Greek context, and for that reason it was decided to treat those two constructs, incivility and bullying, separately. Subsequently, this chapter introduces the notion of 'forcing', a phenomenon highly prevalent in certain sectors within Greece, such as academia, which refers to explicitly obliging the target individual to perform tasks and activities that are contained in other individuals' (the perpetrators') work roles.

Incivility

Incivility in everyday life is strong in Greece and in most cases this extends to the workplace. The cultural profile of the country that includes low Institutional, and strong In-group Collectivism along with low Humane Orientation, may offer a partial explanation. Explanations that make use of country-specific characteristics may shed additional light on the reasons behind the phenomenon. Here, all accounts should be seen as complementary instead of mutually exclusive:

1. Politeness, which partly overlaps with civility, is often viewed within the Greek society as sign of hypocrisy. This has its roots in the high value the Greek society places (or used to place) on authenticity and forthrightness (Bozionelos and Kiamou 2008). In this sense, being polite to people one is not acquainted with or may not hold respect for is still seen by many Greeks as unauthentic or hypocritical behaviour. Hence, on many occasions people behave in an uncivilised manner to those they are not well acquainted with in order to be consistent with their self-image of forthrightness, but also display such an image to their social environment and especially to their in-group.
2. The strong in-group–out-group polarisation in the Greek culture that predisposes Greeks to automatically categorise others as either in-group or out-group members (Bozionelos 2014). Many people encountered in everyday work life are not sufficiently known; hence, they are likely to be automatically categorised as 'outsiders' (which is sometimes seen as tantamount to foes in the Greek culture). This imposes a requirement to treat them with indifference and/or incivility. Everyday Greek life is replete with cases where incumbent individuals (e.g., public or private sector employees) treat people from the public or unknown/little known colleagues from other departments with incivility, only to find out later (either by the other party him/herself or by third parties) that the target individual in fact belongs to their own in-group (this can be the same political party or union or a network of family friends). The typical reaction in such cases is not

embarrassment, but simply change in behaviour (to friendliness and obligingness) because treating out-group members with rudeness and/or unprofessionalism is culturally acceptable or even an imperative.

3. Incivility is often seen as the only way to achieve outcomes in civilian or professional life. As already seen, laws, legal regulations and formal procedures abound in Greece, but they are more often ignored than abided by, while professionalism is low. Therefore, in most cases it is fruitless for the affected individual to use the formal or legal route (e.g., launching a complaint or an appeal) to impose dutiful execution of tasks or to correct a wrongdoing. Hence, he or she may choose incivility, such as threatening or shouting at the wrongdoer or undutiful colleague or subordinate, as a means of exerting pressure towards proper execution of tasks. This is also a cultural feature in the sense that it is vicariously learnt through generations and viewed as a natural way of behaving for contesting one's rights or for achieving results.

4. Another reason – that may seem counter-intuitive at first – is the low level of serious violent behavior between individuals (this does not apply to groups) within the Greek culture. That is, under normal circumstances involving "average" individuals, it is rare for verbal confrontation to escalate into serious inter-personal violence. "Heated" conversations between Greeks normally stop at the verbal part and rarely extend into the physical part. Hence, incivility in Greece is unusual to escalate to intense physical violence with grave consequences – as it may in other societies, where it can lead to serious physical injury or death. This makes people less prone to take care of their cordiality towards fellow workers or citizens.

As an interesting illustration, the legislation for the public sector specifies that any issue or dispute within the sector, or between the sector and civilians, can only be resolved internally (i.e., via procedures and institutions within the public sector) and not through the civil judicial system. Public sector appointments and promotions are nearly exclusively decided by means of political party ties, while jobs are tenured. This means that however grave and obvious the wrongdoing or neglect, the person or persons responsible is unlikely to ever be held accountable, much less penalised. The wrongdoing itself is also unlikely to be redeemed through the formal route, and in the event that happens it will be after many years, even decades, through a system that is inherently slow and essentially designed to protect itself and its members. For that reason incivility (e.g., shouting with explicit language and threatening those who are seen as the wrongdoers) is often seen as the only way to correct a problem at an early stage or 'on the spot' in the public sector. This partly applies to the private sector too because, as seen, legislation is loose and internal regulations or codes are often non-existent or incomplete. In addition, the situation is greatly aggravated by the fact that many firms are small and family owned, which makes it very difficult for employees who do not belong or are not affiliated to the owning family to assert their rights via the formal or the legal route.

Bullying

The single empirical work available suggested a near 15 per cent prevalence of bullying in the Greek workplace (Galanaki and Papalexandris 2013). That rate was concluded with the use of the operational/behavioural criterion (Galanaki and Papalexandris 2013) that seems to be the least biased (e.g., Nielsen *et al.* 2010). This suggests a prevalence of workplace bullying at levels comparable to the Western European average, albeit higher than the 'model' Nordic countries (see Nielsen *et al.* 2009, Nielsen *et al.* 2010). Although that rate was characterised as "alarming" (Galanaki and Papalexandris 2013, p. 2126), there are reasons to believe that the actual prevalence is substantially higher:

1. The sample utilised to establish prevalence was composed of highly skilled individuals (mean years in education was nearly 16, meaning that the majority had completed tertiary education), in managerial positions (all of them had line management responsibilities), and were working mostly for large employers by Greek standards (well in excess of 1,000 employees) (see Galanaki and Papalexandris 2013). Considering that around 8 out of 10 Greeks in the private sector are simply subordinates in very small or small SMEs (European Commission 2013) that are either family owned or family dominated (see above), it is not unreasonable to assume that most Greeks find themselves in positions that are much more likely to invite, or at least not condemn, bullying behaviours. This is exacerbated by the fact that union presence, which may theoretically serve as a form of deterrence, is very weak in the private sector and virtually non-existent in small private firms in Greece (Kapsalis 2012).
2. Comparative research carried out at the same time suggests that acceptability of workplace bullying in Greek society is higher than in almost every other society in the world (Power *et al.* 2013).
3. The measurement of bullying largely relies on what is 'in the eye of the beholder': whether the self-report (i.e., where individuals decide themselves whether they have been victims of bullying), or the behavioural/operational criterion (where individuals simply report whether they have been subjected to certain behaviours and the verdict of whether bullying occurred is made with the use of a predefined operational criterion) is adopted (e.g., Nielsen *et al.* 2010). Considering the high acceptability of bullying in the Greek context, it is conceivable that many behaviours contained in bullying instruments are simply not noticed in Greece because they are viewed as 'normal' and 'expected'. The learning phenomenon of habituation (Thorpe 1963) refers to long-term exposure to an otherwise arresting stimulus, which eventually renders that stimulus unnoticeable because it is now part of the environment and is thus perceived as not needing immediate attention (Eisenstein *et al.* 2001). Therefore, individuals are likely to overlook behaviours or situations that occur around them with consistency and frequency, or of which they themselves are part (as victims or perpetrators or both), and to which they might otherwise have paid attention. Indeed, bullying

may be part of the culture of a workplace, which means that relevant behaviours comprise the norm (Robinson and O'Leary-Kelly 1998) and the natural way of doing things (Schein 2004).

Though this begs appropriate empirical demonstration, it is very likely, therefore, that the prevalence of bullying in the typical Greek workplace is substantially greater than what the sole available report indicates. The same is likely to hold for mobbing, which can be viewed as bullying exercised by a group of individuals towards the target (e.g., Leymann 1996, Tepper and Henle 2011). This is because of the profound role of the in-group–out-group distinction, with those who are not seen as belonging to the in-group being likely to be treated with hostility by in-group members. The low Humane Orientation must further contribute to the extensiveness and especially intensity and seriousness of mobbing in the Greek workplace.

It is interesting to note that the main reason behind bullying within the Greek work context is not to effect performance improvements, as it may be in some other cultures – for example, Confucian or Anglo-Saxon (see Power *et al.* 2013) – though performance correction may often be the pretence. Greece falls near the bottom among all ranked countries in most aspects of the cultural dimension of Performance Orientation (Javidan 2004), including whether leaders consider that striving for excellence in their own and in subordinates' performance can lead to desired outcomes (Javidan 2004). Hence, for example, the reasons for bullying on the part of the line manager must be tied to factors other than output concerns. The cultural configuration of the country that includes very low Humane Orientation, high subordinate–superior distance, weak Institutional and strong In-group Collectivism dictates that those in positions of power are culturally handed the right to behave as tyrants and potentially the expectation to do so (Bozionelos 2013). Tyranny, capriciousness and corruption on the part of the line manager and those in power are found in Greek folklore and in many modern jokes. The situation is aggravated by the widespread lack of merit-based ascendance to positions of power (in the public sector the sole criterion is political party affiliation and its attached connections, while in many parts of the private sector it is kinship or family friendship). This means that those in positions of power have not been subordinates in the real sense, so they have not had the opportunity to develop empathic views towards those with inferior position power.

Forcing

There is a practice in the Greek academic environment that certainly falls within workplace abuse, but it is sufficiently different from incivility and bullying to warrant separate treatment. It involves target individuals who are regularly forced to perform tasks and activities that are contained in the workloads of powerful others (see Bozionelos 2014). For this reason the term 'forcing' is coined. Target individuals receive no formal credit for this because the work is officially performed by the perpetrators and is recognised as an accomplishment of the perpetrators themselves. The only reward targets receive is being 'allowed' to exist within the system, sometimes with implied promises (and collateral threats), such as the renewal of their temporary contract, obtainment of a better contract or of a tenure-track job, or earning tenure or promotion. On the other hand, the implied negative consequence for non-compliance is 'removal' from the system or more serious abuse. This is an endemic phenomenon in Greek academia and involves targets such as doctoral students, teaching fellows in temporary contracts, untenured academic staff, and tenured staff who aspire to promotion (Bozionelos 2014).

The Greek academic system is rather unique because it is essentially controlled by a web of individuals who are linked with ties that are mostly family or political party related or both. These individuals form the in-group, who essentially control processes and outcomes that have to do with hiring, promotions and disciplinary action within the whole of academia (this situation is rooted in historical events and the cultural characteristics of the country, Bozionelos 2014, in press). Out-group members, or 'outsiders', are individuals without family or political connections with the 'in-group' or the popular political parties or the government. When outsiders try to enter academia – a highly prestigious occupation in Greece – obtain tenure or advance, they are forced to perform duties that are 'on paper' performed by members of the in-group. Such tasks and activities may include performing secretarial tasks, delivering teaching, marking and invigilating on behalf of in-group members and their affiliates, adding in-group members as co-authors in their papers, and preparing deliverables for in-group members' private businesses that are often run from within the higher education institution. Outsiders perform these tasks on behalf of those others over and above the tasks included in their own workloads. This is seen as 'natural', until or unless someone is exposed to a different system (e.g., Schein 2004).

Forcing is able to perpetuate itself because (1), as already seen, there is an absence of legal or even regulatory framework, but especially (2) because all key positions in the system, including the professoriates in virtually all higher education institutions in Greece, are controlled and occupied by the in-group. The members of that in-group have links (family, extended family or political ties) with the major political parties and the government, and often are in essence appointed by the government or the dominant political parties (Bozionelos 2014). In the hypothetical case that someone is 'foolish' enough to report an incident of forcing, the people to whom the report will be made, and who will deal with it, are the perpetrators or their accomplices.

In addition to 'forcing', incivility and bullying are also highly prevalent within the Greek academic environment, with bullying being normally directed from the in-group or those who aspire to join the in-group (thus they feel they have the necessary power and protection) towards outsiders (Bozionelos 2014). In fact, bullying and incivility may lay the foundations for forcing by means of inflicting fear and helplessness. Hence, apart from other typical forms of bullying, frequent acts include: public humiliation of outsiders (e.g., in the departmental assembly or in public spaces); in-private disgracing and degradation (i.e., the in-group member calling an outsider into the office to explain to the outsider his or her level of mediocrity, and that his or her fate depends on showing 'good character'); or especially designed 'rituals'. An interesting illustration is a particular university where affiliated staff – who have to apply anew for their job every year – are called to publicly apologise in front of the permanent in-group and their affiliates about any matter however trivial, such as failure to attend a meeting, lateness to return a report or having been late for a class. To make the apology, 'wrongdoers' are left to wait for many hours outside the amphi-theatre in which the hearing takes place, and the apology is typically followed by hostile questioning and degrading comments by the permanent staff.

Forcing also occurs in the lower ranks of the armed forces, and especially with conscripts, where the author has himself been a witness. Emotionally and physically weaker soldiers maybe forced by fellow soldiers to perform duties (e.g., cleaning, tidying, patrolling or guarding in difficult hours or locations) on behalf of others, and over and above their own duties. Forcing is different from hazing, initiation rituals in the armed forces (e.g., Ostvik and Rudmin 2001, Workplace Bullying Institute 2013): hazing is performed on a group basis (normally by the previous cohort to the cohort of newcomers), normally it is not directed towards duty-related activities, and it has finite duration; while forcing is performed on single individuals, is work/duty-oriented, and may continue for most or the full length of the target's service. Forcing is unusual in civilian environments but also in the officer ranks of the armed forces.

Apart from the Greek academic environment where the phenomenon is of substantial proportions, forcing apparently exists in limited degrees within small private Greek firms. As seen, these firms are typically family-owned, so family members and their affiliates have absolute control. Forcing may also sometimes be present in larger Greek firms dominated by a single or a small number of families who show strong favouritism to their own members and affiliates. Finally, forcing may also be observed within the Greek public sector, with targets being temporary employees. Temporary employees in the Greek public sector are hired on a rolling one-year basis (i.e., their contract is renewed every year without any provision for becoming permanent). These employees are often individuals with strong qualifications, but without the political party connections that are required for a permanent tenured public sector job. The official line is that they are hired to cover 'seasonal' or 'unforeseen' needs, but the actual reason is to undertake the work that is supposed to be carried out by the permanent staff who are grossly underperforming. It might be argued, however, that in no other work environment within Greece is forcing likely to be as widespread, intense and endemic as within Greek academia.

Summary and directions for future work

This chapter discussed workplace abuse within the Greek context, where a complex cultural configuration backed by a non-existent legislative framework apparently leads to a strong prevalence of both incivility and bullying in its various forms. In addition, the examples of Greek academia, primarily, and of the low ranks of the military, secondarily, illustrated the phenomenon of forcing, a distinct form of workplace abuse.

A potential avenue for future research is measuring bullying using reports from individuals who have been exposed to cultures with very different profiles. For example, individuals who have worked for many years in a Nordic culture (where there is sensitivity and substantive measures against it) and then move to an indigenous firm in Greece or another Eastern European country (where theoretically bullying is strong; Bozionelos 2013, Power *et al.* 2013), and vice versa. Such a study may provide the necessary cultural contrast to remove the effects of habituation in the detection and establishment of prevalence of workplace abuse, so more meaningful comparisons between cultures may be made. This line of work can also be of benefit in the area of international mobility of workers because it can inform multinational firms about what reactions they should expect from individuals who move between different cultures and workplaces, so they can develop analogous human resource systems (Baruch and Bozionelos 2010).

In addition, future studies may compare the strength of relationship between bullying and its negative outcomes, such as health-related problems and impoverished work attitudes for recipients (e.g., Samnani and Singh 2012) across cultures. Habituation and sensitisation, seen as the opposite of habituation (Eisenstein *et al.* 2001), may be at work along with cultural expectations. Hence, the strength of the relationship may not be proportional: for example, the effects of bullying in the Greek workplace may be of a smaller magnitude than in the Nordic workplace despite the fact that incivility and bullying are apparently much more prevalent and serious in the former, simply because of the effect of habituation and sensitisation. Recent empirical research lends some indirect support to this conjecture (Loh *et al.* 2010). This also invites the possibility of relationships that differ according to the level of analysis. In environments where bullying is relatively absent, the consequences of bullying acts on single individuals may be serious, while in environments with high prevalence of bullying the consequences for a single individual may be relatively minor due to their being inured to its effects. On the other hand, the pattern of effect at the group, unit and organisational level may be the reverse. In cultures with low prevalence of bullying within sensitised societies, a bullying incident may have serious consequences for a single or a few individuals, but the presence of an anti-bullying culture, along with relevant regulatory frameworks that are actually enforced, may contain its effects and seal the rest of the group. On the other hand, bullying acts may create ripple effects with serious repercussions for the group and the organisation (e.g., Heames and Harvey 2006) in cultures with strong acceptance of bullying that are embedded in environments without regulatory or legal frameworks.

This chapter made use of the author's personal experience and cultural knowledge from the perspective of an insider to develop an account for workplace abuse within the context of a particular country. Without invoking the author's personal experience, this chapter would not have been feasible. Such an approach directs us towards novel, and for some unconventional, methods for the study of workplace abuse, such as autoethnography (Ellis 2004). Here, the researcher's personal experience and cultural lens are valuable inputs and analytical tools, and offer insights that more mainstream methods, which assume detachment and objectivity, may not be able to do.

Finally, it is unlikely that Greece is the only country where forcing occurs. For instance, Greece shares many cultural characteristics with the other countries of the Eastern European cluster (Bakacsi *et al.* 2002), which renders these countries potential hosts of the forcing phenomenon. Beyond consequences that are parallel to those of incivility and bullying, forcing may have serious implications in other domains such as performance appraisal and individual accountability. Future work, therefore, may focus on its further substantiation as a phenomenon in various cultures and sectors, on the refinement of its definition, establishment as a construct, and on the development of instruments to further investigate it.

References

Anderson, M., and Pearson, C. M. (1999). Tit for tat? The spiraling effect of incivility in the workplace. *Academy of Management Review, 24,* 452–71.

Bakacsi, G., Sandor, T., Andras, K., and Viktor, I. (2002). Eastern European cluster: Tradition and transition. *Journal of World Business, 37,* 69–80.

Baruch, Y., and Bozionelos, N. (2010). Career issues. In S. Zedeck (Ed.), *APA handbook of industrial and organizational psychology, volume 2: Selecting & developing members of the organization* (pp. 67–113). Washington, DC: American Psychological Association.

Bourantas, D., and Papadakis, V. (1997). Greek management: Diagnosis and prognosis. *International Studies of Management and Organization, 26*(3), 13–32.

Bozionelos, N. (2006). Mentoring and expressive network resources: Their relationship with career success and emotional exhaustion among Hellenes employees involved in emotion work. *International Journal of Human Resource Management, 17,* 362–78.

Bozionelos, N. (2011). Performance appraisal in the Greek public sector: What happens on paper vs. what [does not] happen[s] in reality. In H. van Emmerik, N. Bozionelos, and H. Guenter (Chairs), *Ways of measuring and monitoring employees' performance and well-being in different cultures.* Symposium conducted at the International Conference of the Eastern Academy of Management, 26–30 June, Bangalore, India.

Bozionelos, N. (2013). Country cultures make their mark on workplace bullying. *International HR Adviser, 55,* 11–12.

Bozionelos, N. (2014). Career patterns in Greek academia: Social capital and intelligent careers, but for whom? *Career Development International, 19*(3), 264–94.

Bozionelos, N. (in press). Social capital and careers: Indisputable evidence and note for caution. In A. De Vos and B.I.J.M. Van der Heijden (Eds.), *Handbook of research on sustainable careers.* Northampton, MA: Edward Elgar Publishing.

Bozionelos, N., and Kiamou, K. (2008). Emotion work in the Hellenic frontline services environment: How it relates to emotional exhaustion and work attitudes. *International Journal of Human Resource Management, 19,* 1108–30.

Branch, S., Ramsay, S., and Barker, M. (2013). Workplace bullying, mobbing and general harassment: A review. *International Journal of Management Reviews, 15,* 280–99.

Broome, B. J. (1996). *Exploring the Greek mosaic: A guide to intercultural communication in Greece.* Yarmouth, ME: Intercultural Press.

Carl, D., Gupta, V., and Javidan, M. (2004). Power distance. In R. J. House, P. J. Hanges, M. Javidan, P. W. Dorfman, and V. Gupta (Eds.), *Culture, leadership, and organizations: The GLOBE study of 62 societies* (pp. 513–63). Thousand Oaks, CA: Sage.

Einarsen, S., Hoel, H., Zapf, D., and Cooper, C. L. (2011). The concept of bullying and harassment at work: The European tradition. In S. Einarsen (Ed.), *Bullying and harassment in the workplace: Developments in theory, research, and practice* (pp. 3–40). Boca Raton, FL: Taylor & Francis.

Eisenstein, E. M., Eisenstein, D., and Smith, J. C. (2001). The evolutionary significance of habituation and sensitization across phylogeny: A behavioral homeostasis model. *Integrative Physiological and Behavioral Science, 36,* 251–65.

Ellis, C. (2004). *The ethnographic I: A methodological novel about autoethnography.* Walnut Creek, CA: AltaMira Press.

Enterprise Greece (2014). Human capital [Ανθρώπινο Κεφάλαιο]. Retrieved from www.investingreece.gov.gr/default.asp?pid=19&la=2.

European Commission (2013). *2013 SBA fact sheet: Greece.* Brussels: European Commission.

European Union (2014). *Greece.* Retrieved from www.http://europa.eu.

Galaniaki, E., and Papalexandris, N. (2013). Measuring workplace bullying in organisations. *International Journal of Human Resource Management, 24,* 2107–30.

Gelfand, M. J., Bhawuk, D.P.S., Nishii, L. H., and Bechtold, D. J. (2004). Individualism and collectivism. In R. J. House, P. J. Hanges, M. Javidan, P. W. Dorfman, and V. Gupta (Eds.), *Culture, leadership, and organizations: The GLOBE study of 62 societies* (pp. 437–512). Thousand Oaks, CA: Sage.

Greek Statistical Agency [Ελληνική Στατιστική Αρχή] (2014). *Η Ελλάδα με αριθμούς, 2014* [Greece in numbers, 2014]. Πειραιάς, Ελλάδα: Ελληνική Στατιστική Αρχή.

Handy, C. B. (1976). *Understanding organizations.* Oxford: Oxford University Press.

Heames, J., and Harvey, M. (2006). Workplace bullying: A cross-level assessment. *Management Decision, 44,* 1214–30.

Hershcovis, M. S. (2011). 'Incivility, social undermining, bullying . . . oh my!': A call to reconcile constructs within workplace aggression research. *Journal of Organizational Behavior, 32,* 499–519.

History of the Greek Nation [Ιστορία του Ελληνικού Έθνους] (2007). Αθήνα: Εκδοτική Αθηνών.

Hofstede, G. (1993). Cultural constraints in management theories. *Academy of Management Executive, 7,* 81–94.

Hofstede, G. (1980). *Culture's consequences: International differences in work-related values.* Beverly Hills, CA: Sage.

Hofstede, G. (2001). *Culture's consequences: Comparing values, behaviors, institutions, and organizations across nations.* Thousand Oaks, CA: Sage.

House, R. J., Hanges, P. J., Javidan, M., Dorfman, P. W., and Gupta, V. (2004). *Culture, leadership, and organizations: The GLOBE Study of 62 Societies.* Thousand Oaks, CA: Sage.

Javidan, M. (2004). Performance orientation. In R. J. House, P. J. Hanges, M. Javidan, P. W. Dorfman, and V. Gupta (Eds.), *Culture, leadership, and organizations: The GLOBE study of 62 societies* (pp. 239–81). Thousand Oaks, CA: Sage.

Kabasakal, H., and Bodur, M. (2004). Humane orientation in societies, organizations and leader attributes. In R. J. House, P. J. Hanges, M. Javidan, P. W. Dorfman, and V. Gupta (Eds.), *Culture, leadership, and organizations: The GLOBE study of 62 societies* (pp. 564–601). Thousand Oaks, CA: Sage.

Kapsalis, A. (2012). Τα Ελληνικά συνδικάτα στο περιβάλλον της οικονομικής ύφεσης και κρίσης. [The Greek labour unions within the environment of recession and economic crisis]. Retrieved from http://rosalux.gr/sites/default/files/kapsalis_greekfinal_0.pdf.

Kouzis, G. (2007). Τα χαρακτηριστικά του ελληνικού συνδικαλιστικού κινήματος. [The characteristics of the Greek labour movement]. Αθήνα: Gutenberg.

Καθημέρινή (2013, Feb 26). Άγνωστος ο πραγματικός αριθμός των παράνομων μεταναστών στην Ελλάδα. [Unknown is the real number of illegal immigrants in Greece]. Retrieved from www.kathimerini.gr/29189/article/epikairothta/ellada/gnwstos-o-pragmatikos-ari8mos-twn-paranomwn-metanastwn-sthn-ellada.

Leymann, H. (1996). The content and development of mobbing at work. *European Journal of Work and Organizational Psychology, 5,* 165–84.

Loh, J., Restubog, S.L.D., and Zagenczyk, T. J. (2010). Consequences of workplace bullying on employee identification and satisfaction among Australians and Singaporeans. *Journal of Cross-Cultural Psychology, 41,* 236–52.

Mouzelis, N. (2012). Developments leading to the Greek crisis. Paper presented at the *Workshop on social change: Theory and applications (the case of the Greek society),* 9 March, London School of Economics, London, UK.

Neall, A. M., and Tuckey, M. R. (2014). A methodological review of research on the antecedents and consequences of workplace harassment. *Journal of Occupational and Organizational Psychology, 87,* 225–57.

Nielsen, M. B., Matthiesen, S. B., and Einarsen, S. (2010). The impact of methodological moderators on prevalence rates of workplace bullying: A meta-analysis. *Journal of Occupational and Organizational Psychology, 83,* 955–79.

Nielsen, M. B., Skogstad, A., Matthiesen, S. B., Glasø, L., Aasland, M. S., Notelaers, G., and Einarsen, S. (2009). Prevalence of workplace bullying in Norway: Comparisons across time and estimation methods. *European Journal of Work and Organizational Psychology, 18,* 81–101.

Ostvik, K., and Rudmin, F. (2001). Bullying and hazing among Norwegian army soldiers: Two studies of prevalence, context and cognition. *Military Psychology, 13,* 17–39.

Papastergiou, V., and Takou, E. (2014). Η μετανάστευση στην Ελλάδα: Έντεκα μύθοι και περισσότερες αλήθειες. [Immigration in Greece: Eleven myths and even more numerous truths]. Αθήνα: Ιδρυμα Ρόζα Λουξεμπουργκ.

Power, J., Brotheridge, S., Blenkinsopp, J., Bowes-Sperry, L., Bozionelos, N. Buzady, Z., Chuang, A., . . . , Nnedumm, A.U.O. (2013). Acceptability of workplace bullying: A comparative study on six continents. *Journal of Business Research, 66,* 374–80.

Robinson, S. L., and O'Leary-Kelly, A. M. (1998). Monkey see, monkey do: The influence of work groups on the antisocial behavior of employees. *Academy of Management Journal, 41,* 658–72.

Samnani, A.-K., and Singh, P. (2012). 20 years of workplace bullying research: A review of the antecedents and consequences of bullying in the workplace. *Aggression and Violent Behavior, 17,* 581–9.

Schein, E. (2004). *Organizational culture and leadership* (3rd ed.). San Francisco: Wiley & Sons.

Stratoudaki, H. (2008). Ερευνες για τους μετανάστες στην Ελλάδα: Ερευνητικές εμμονές και εκκρεμμότητες. [Research for the immigrants in Greece: Obsessions and pending issues]. Αθήνα: Εθνικό Κέντρο Κοινωνικών Ερευνών.

Tepper, B. J., and Henle, C. A. (2011). A case for recognizing distinctions among constructs that capture interpersonal mistreatment in work organizations. *Journal of Organizational Behavior, 32,* 487–98.

Thorpe, W. H. (1963). *Learning and instinct in animals.* London: Methuen.

Transparency International (2012). Corruption perceptions index. Retrieved from http://cpi.transparency.org/cpi2012/results/#myAnchor1.

Triandis, H. C., Vassiliou, V., and Nassiakou, M. (1968). Three cross-cultural studies of subjective culture. *Journal of Personality and Social Psychology Monograph Supplement, 8*(4), 1–42.

Trompenaars, F. (1993). *Riding the waves of culture: Understanding cultural diversity in business.* London: Nicholas Brealey Publishing.

Tsakiris, T. (2012, April 18). Το Ελληνικό συνδικαλιστικό κίνημα – μέρος 1. [The Greek labour movement – part 1]. *Working Greece: Sociology of work.* Retrieved from https://workingreece.wordpress.com/2012/04/18/.

Vassiliadis, S., and Vassiliadis, A. (2014). The Greek family businesses and the succession plan. *Procedia Economics and Finance, 9,* 242–7.

Voulgaris, G. (2006). Κράτος και κοινωνία πολιτών στην Ελλάδα: Μια σχέση προς επανεξέταση [State and society of citizens in Greece: A relationship under reconsideration]. *Ελληνική Επιθεώρηση Πολιτικής Επιστήμης, 28,* 5–33.

Workplace Bullying Institute (2013, December 11). Hazing in China, the same the world around. Retrieved from www.workplacebullying.org/2013/12/11/hazing-china/#more-14742.

8   Poland

One nation, one religion – tradition and change

Irena Pilch and Elżbieta Turska

Introduction

Poles are a European nation with a tempestuous and tragic history, one that is proud of their historical heritage but also one that was devoid of sovereignty in the past, for which they have fiercely fought. They were the first nation to free themselves from the bonds of communism, thus beginning the Autumn of Nations – the revolutions of 1989 in the communist states of Central and Eastern Europe. Poland is a country working its way up; rich among the poor and poor among the rich. Over the last 25 years, Poles have experienced unimaginable political and economic transformations. Despite the fact that Poles are a nationally and religiously homogeneous group, and a large part of the society still adhere to traditional values, a change towards adopting more modern values may be observed, although this is rather slow. This chapter will take a critical look at the predicament and culture of the country, looking for elements (having their source in tradition or resulting from transformations) which may be helpful in understanding the highly undesirable phenomenon of aggressive, harmful and unkind behaviours at work. Workplace bullying appears to be a significant social problem in Poland, and the measures taken to prevent it can be considered insufficient. The vast majority of Polish publications devoted to this subject concentrate on the experiences of other countries. That is why it is essential to take into consideration the factors specific to the Polish national culture when analysing bullying in Polish workplaces.

Poland as a part of Europe

The Republic of Poland is a medium-sized country in Central Europe, bordering Germany, the Czech Republic, Slovakia, Ukraine, Belarus, Lithuania and Russia. According to the estimates of the Polish Central Statistical Office (2015), Poland has a population of over 38 million people (48 per cent males, 52 per cent females), 61 per cent of whom live in urban areas. Poland is an ethnically (98.5 per cent Polish) and religiously (approximately 90 per cent Catholics) homogeneous country. As a democracy, it has representative bodies elected in general elections (*Sejm*, Senate, President and local self-government entities).

The labour force participation rate is 56 per cent (men 64 per cent, women 48 per cent), and the registered unemployment rate at the end of 2014 was over 11 per cent.

In the 18th century, the country lost its independence and its land was divided among the neighbouring states Austria, Prussia and Russia. Until regaining independence in 1918, the Polish people had been cultivating their national identity and organising against invaders. During World War II, Poland was occupied by Germany and the Soviet Union (USSR). After the war, it existed within new borders determined by the leaders of the winning coalition and remained under the influence of the USSR, adopting a 'peoples' democracy' system similar to the Soviet Union, with ruling communist Polish United Workers' Party in power. Changes were initiated by the formation of the national union movement 'Solidarity' (with Lech Walesa as its leader) in 1980, which fought both for employee rights and for the overthrow of the communist system. In 1989, an agreement between the authorities and the opposition (the Round Table) finally led to a partially free election won by Solidarity. A process of political and economic change began, involving a transition from communism and a centrally planned economy, to democracy and a free market economy. The economic reforms introduced in 1990 marked the end of the economic crisis and the start of a period of development. In 1999, Poland joined the North Atlantic Treaty Organization (NATO), and in 2004 became an associate member of the European Union (2003), thus accomplishing its ambitions to become an important player in Europe.

Polish society is strongly influenced by the Catholic Church, whose current position results from the role it used to play during the partition period and the communist reign. Historically, the Church served to strengthen cohesion and national identity. Catholicism is therefore thought to be an element of Polish national identity (a Pole = a Catholic; see Kloczowski 2000, Porter-Szűcs 2011). The Church supported the Solidarity movement, and during the martial law period (1981–3), many priests were engaged in opposition activity. Polish religiousness is folk and ritualistic in character (Gannon and Pillai 2013). The Polish Church influences political and social life (in matters such as sex education, abortion, in vitro fertilisation and partnerships). Believers, however, tend to apply the values and norms propagated by the Church in a selective way (Baniak 2007).

Polish national culture

The traditional image of a Pole includes qualities such as pride, obstinacy, generosity, hospitality, religious tolerance, patriotism, inclination to make sacrifices for the fatherland and aversion to compromise. During the communist period, many Poles were able to adjust to the two coexistent contradictory ideological systems. The traditional, Catholic/national system of values was dominant in the private sphere, while communist ideology was practised in public. This combination led to patriotism and religiousness creating a socially aware appreciation for equality and justice. Again in the 1990s, two systems of values were observed in Poland: the first, referring to this combination of patriotic/religious and egalitarian values, and the newly formed one, referring to individualistic, secular, rationalistic and materialistic attitudes. Currently in Poland, materialistic values (connected with the needs of survival and security) have been found to outweigh post-materialistic ones, connected with self-expression, self-fulfilment, the pursuit of happiness, tolerance and trust (Ziółkowski 2000, Jasińska-Kania 2012). The structure of values important for Poles has not changed much in the last ten years (Boguszewski 2013, Czapiński and Panek 2013). Family happiness and health are still of key importance. The role of religion, patriotism and wealth, however, is decreasing, while the value of respect for others and an honest life is on the increase.

Poland has been included in international projects comparing national cultures, the most significant of which are studies by Hofstede (Hofstede *et al.* 2010), Hall (2001) and the GLOBE Study (Koopman *et al.* 1999, Bakacsi *et al.* 2002, House *et al.* 2004). Unfortunately, the findings of these studies do not always provide consistent results. The power distance index in Poland is undoubtedly high, which is confirmed both by studies that apply the Hofstede model and those following GLOBE. Poles as a nation tend to accept differences in the distribution of power. According to Hofstede, another important feature of Polish culture is the high preference for avoiding uncertainty. This, combined with high power distance, creates the need for a supportive, autocratic leader and provides fertile ground for conservatism and moral rigour. Added to this is distrust and aversion to those representing different opinions, and a lack of tolerance for diversity. Data from the GLOBE project, however, show that Poland is characterised by low uncertainty avoidance, defined as seeking orderliness, formalised procedures and laws in everyday life. This result may not reflect a preference for unstructured situations, but rather show the post-communist society's aversion to observing top-down rules. In Poland, evading or bending rules is considered to be an effective way of coping and in many situations is not stigmatised by the community, so paradoxically it can help to reduce the unpredictability (i.e. to increase the chance of accomplishing one's goal).

Another important dimension of Polish culture, evaluated differently in different studies, is individualism versus collectivism. According to Hofstede and Hall, Polish culture is individualistic with some elements of collectivism, whereas in the GLOBE study, Poland is characterised by high group and family collectivism. Family is definitely very highly valued in Poland, but no similar principles apply to organisations as a whole, which is reflected in studies on family enterprises that clearly favour workers from the family at the expense of others (Marjański and Sułkowski 2009). As for the masculinity (Hofstede) and assertiveness (GLOBE) dimensions, Poland ranks medium to high. As the data from the GLOBE project show, Poland ranks low on the future, performance and humane orientations. Polish society, in accordance with Hall's concepts, is high-context and polychronic, reflecting ambiguity in the process of communication, and the need for strong leadership.

Global evaluations of national culture refer to mean values of dimensions which do not reflect the real diversification within a culture. In Poland, as a result of systemic and economic transformation, changes leading to culture elements resembling those of the dominant European models might be expected. These are, however, not clearly observed in study findings. In Poland, people attached to the traditional system of values react strongly to its modification. Modification, in turn, provides the basis for cultural change within a segment of the population. One can even speak of two 'Polands', or two tribes, as reflected by the media – the conservative newspapers, and the so-called mainstream (rather liberal) press. In the area of political attitudes, this duality may be represented as a liberal or conservative affiliation, and in the area of private life, it is correlated with attitudes to religion (see Cześnik and Kotnarowski 2011). The first Poland is more collectivistic; it appeals to traditional values such as the nation, religion or family, and affirms the traditional lifestyle. This Poland is an embodiment of tradition: the first of the elements included in the title of the chapter. The other Poland is more individualistic, concentrated on the needs of an individual, preferring autonomy, development, pluralism and tolerance. Its culture, however, also includes collectivistic elements, manifested in attributing high value to cooperation. This group, in turn, may be regarded as a seedbed of permanent cultural change. It is difficult for these two groups, pro-traditional and anti-traditional, to coexist on the basis of mutual tolerance and respect of the right to choose one's own way of life, which causes a split, or differentiation, in the seemingly homogeneous society. The above-mentioned differences may be a constant source of tension, although there are no studies available to determine their influence on workplace conflicts.

Polish people have a high level of trust in the private sphere (trust in family members and friends), and low in the social sphere (trust in institutions and people in general). Surveys show that around 75 per cent of Poles (including young ones) think that caution is necessary in contact with people, although this mostly refers to strangers (Czapiński and Panek 2013). This phenomenon is accompanied by a low tendency to establish or join associations, and the feeling that others will certainly prove to be abusers, which leads to the conclusion that while the nation and family are important for Poles, the community understood as common actions is non-existent (Czapiński 2006). Such an attitude must have a negative influence on the ability to cooperate.

Another typical feature of Polish culture is the tendency to express negative opinions on the social world publicly (referring to the world as unjust and harmful), and the tendency to complain (Wojciszke 2004). This, too, may emanate from the communist period, when boasting was regarded as conceit, whereas finding numerous obstacles and complaining was a form of protection

from failure. Even nowadays it is rather unpopular among Poles to show satisfaction with life, or to boast about accomplishments.

Organisational culture of Polish enterprises

During more than 40 years of an economy based on central planning, a set of
norms and values connected with the working environment (making a specific
organisational culture) developed in Poland (see Rapacki 1995, Sikorski 2012).
Conformism, passivity, obedience, loyalty, unobtrusiveness and change avoidance
were typical characteristics of employees, whereas managers were submissive
towards their superiors and directive towards subordinates. This produced a
sense of security connected with the permanence of employment. Innovation
and entrepreneurship were not required, since the economic calculation was not
the key principle in the operation of most enterprises. What was appreciated
were certain qualities (such as cunning and resourcefulness), and behaviours
('arranging' things – the ability to get things done, trying to find a way around
the regulations; see Gannon and Pillai 2013). An employee could achieve extra
profits or privileges without any labour expenditure, sometimes breaking the
rules or behaving unethically. There are still companies where this attitude is
visible. Despite the declared will to change, employees strive to maintain the
status quo and keep previous privileges (e.g. connected with the particular
industry); security of employment is one that is most important.

Conservatism, authoritarianism and elements of the masculine culture are
interrelated, making a coherent set of norms and values. The employees' low
tolerance of uncertainty, connected with the fear of innovation and change, and
the pursuit of security, enhances the need for a strong (authoritarian) leader.
Research confirms that the significant characteristics of Polish national culture
are transmitted into organisational culture. Comparative studies conducted in
the years 1996/97 and 2008/09 among Polish managers showed the intensification of tendencies dominant in Polish culture: higher power orientation,
masculinity and higher acceptance of the autocratic orientation were observed,
along with increasing collectivism (Mączyński *et al.* 2010). Another study (Sitko-
Lutek 2004) revealed that contemporary managers perceive Polish organisational
culture as still oriented toward tasks rather than people, and characterised by
high power distance, masculine models, passivity, high-context communication,
ascription status oriented, and having a polychronic approach to time, while
hoping for the reverse. This hope may be a harbinger of future change. Already,
high uncertainty avoidance and collectivism are accepted as culture characteristics.
Expatriate managers employed in Poland confirm that the most distinct feature
of Polish management culture is strong hierarchy, formality and status conscious-
ness (Brewster and Bennett 2010).

The organisational culture preferred in Poland is one that is bureaucratic and
associated with task orientation and high power distance; referred to as the
Eiffel Tower culture by Trompenaars and Hampden-Turner (2012). In Poland,
an important factor which results in increasing regulation is a lack of trust in

employees. Paradoxically, such behaviour seems justified, because the equally distrustful attitude of employees to the employer's or superior's intentions often leads to evading or breaking norms.

Strong family bonds, connected with the historically determined low esteem for state authorities, and the weakness of the civic society, may result in negative forms of familism – nepotism and inherited power and professional careers within companies and institutions (Marjański and Sułkowski 2009). A further manifestation of familism is the relatively high number of family enterprises; collectivism characterising such enterprises is usually limited to family members employed at the company.

An outline of mobbing in Poland

In Poland, just like in many other European countries (such as Germany, Austria and the Scandinavian countries), the phenomenon of workplace abuse, incivility and bullying is referred to as mobbing (Polish spelling: *mobbing*). This term is a legal concept and is used by scholars and associations helping victims; it has also become a part of everyday speech. Sometimes similar phenomena are studied as workplace violence, workplace aggression or under the collective name of unethical behaviour in the workplace. The concept of mobbing involves the relationship between the perpetrator(s) and the target. Most scholars are of the opinion that the terms 'bullying' and 'mobbing' refer to the same phenomenon (see Einarsen *et al.* 2011). Therefore, these two terms are used interchangeably below.

Studies on mobbing in Poland have been carried out since 2000. The scholars who analyse the phenomenon are influenced by Heinz Leymann (1990, 1996) and Marie-France Hirigoyen (2003). Polish scholars agree that mobbing is repeated, long-term violent behaviours (which may include economic, psychological or social violence) aimed at intimidating, weakening or humiliating the victim, producing negative results for the victim's emotions, health and professional status (Behowska-Gebhardt and Stalewski 2004, Kmiecik-Baran and Rybicki 2004). Research and diagnosis of the phenomenon in Poland is varied. It ranges from simple questions ("Have you been persecuted at work by your superior/ workmates within the last five years?"; Derczyński 2002, Omyła-Rudzka 2014), through to complex questionnaires: Polish versions of well-known instruments (Polish adaptation of NAQ – Negative Acts Questionnaire; Einarsen and Raknes 1997, Warszewska-Makuch 2007); instruments taking into consideration the specific Polish conditions (Multidimensional Questionnaire – MDM; Merecz-Kot and Cębrzyńska 2008); as well as interviews with targets (Chomczyński 2008).

The self-labelling method (Zapf and Einarsen 2003), where the respondents indicate whether or not they perceive themselves as targets of mobbing, is rarely used and the respondents are not usually made familiar with the definition of bullying (e.g. Derczyński 2002, Omyła-Rudzka 2014). The frequently used approach is the operational classification method (Leymann 1990). The respondents receive a set of items measuring exposure to specific kinds of mobbing behaviours. Each item is scored on frequency of occurrence. The frequency of mobbing is estimated on the basis of the responses. Particular studies differ in the number of acts included in the questionnaire, and in the criteria used to classify individuals as targets or non-targets of mobbing. Information on mobbing is usually received from the victims, less often from bystanders, and only occasionally from perpetrators (Pilch and Turska 2014). The studies have involved large groups representative of the general population, people working in selected industries, but also relatively small convenience groups.

Data concerning the rate of mobbing in Poland cover the period beginning in the year 2000. So far, the number of studies is limited. The first published data (Derczyński 2002) led to the conclusion that approximately 5 per cent of the respondents had experienced mobbing. Another study of that period showed that between 6.8 per cent and 47.2 per cent of the respondents had experienced particular mobbing activities (as listed by Leymann 1990, 1996; Delikowska 2004). Many studies were aimed at diagnosing the rate of mobbing in specific professional groups: nurses 18.6 per cent (Kunecka *et al.* 2008), teachers 9.7 per cent (Warszewska-Makuch 2008), and correctional officers 28.8 per cent (Merecz-Kot and Cębrzyńska 2008). In some studies much higher rates were observed due to less typical ways of operationalisation (61.5 per cent; Kmiecik-Baran and Rybicki 2004). Such discrepancies are, however, also observed in other countries (see Coyne *et al.* 2004). The most recent survey (Omyła-Rudzka 2014) shows that the scale of this phenomenon is not changing: approximately 28 per cent of employees have seen mobbing in their workplace, 19 per cent have experienced it, with a further 5 per cent having experienced it very often.

Some studies on mobbing give unexpected findings. The results of the European survey on working conditions (Parent-Thirion *et al.* 2007) allowed comparison of the rate of mobbing/bullying in Poland and other European countries. Only approximately 3 per cent of adult Poles gave a positive answer to a question on whether they had experienced bullying and/or harassment in the previous year, while the mean for EU countries was 5–6 per cent. In this study, other post-communist countries also registered low bullying rates. These results can be interpreted as an effect of lower cultural awareness and sensitivity to such behaviours. This interpretation is confirmed by the findings of a survey aimed at studying the acceptance of workplace bullying in 14 countries in six continents; Polish respondents demonstrated the highest acceptance of workplace bullying (Power *et al.* 2013).

In Poland, just like other EU countries, women (especially young ones) are more subject to mobbing behaviours than men (Parent-Thirion *et al.* 2007, Drabek and Merecz 2013). According to victims, superiors are usually the perpetrators (Kunecka *et al.* 2008, Omyła-Rudzka 2014). European studies have shown that the greatest number of mobbing acts are reported by employees of large establishments (Parent-Thirion *et al.* 2007). Such cases receive high levels of attention from the Polish media; however, it must be acknowledged that people employed in small, private enterprises are also exposed.

The frequent expressions of mobbing reported in Polish studies include: backstabbing, insulting, ignoring, treating others with contempt, unfavourable comments, unjustified criticism, questioning the target's opinions, intimidating, as well overloading with work, assigning tasks below one's qualifications, and lowering the employee's value (Merecz-Kot and Cębrzyńska 2008, Warszewska-Makuch 2008, Durniat 2012, Boguszewski 2013). Creating a negative atmosphere at the workplace by treating others unkindly is a very common form of inappropriate behaviour which can be referred to as workplace incivility. In a comparative study of 14 societies, Poles considered it less important to practice virtues such as kindness, helpfulness, empathy and friendship than did the representatives of other European countries (such as Austria, Germany or Norway; van Oudenhoven *et al.* 2014).

Legislative framework and workplace bullying prevention

The concept of mobbing was introduced into the Polish *Labour Code* in 2004. Mobbing is:

> any activities and behaviours concerning the employee or directed against them, consisting of persistent and long-term harassment or intimidation of the employee, resulting in the employee's understated assessment of professional fitness, resulting in or aimed at humiliation or embarrassment of the employee, their isolation or elimination from the team of co-workers.
>
> (*Labour Code*, Article 94(3), § 2)

The legislation obliges employers to counteract mobbing and makes them responsible for the actions of employees in the workplace. A victim of mobbing can claim compensation from the employer for work-related injury or illness. In Poland the *Labour Code* identifies two other pathological phenomena: harassment (one-time behaviour violating the employee's dignity), and discrimination (unfavourable treatment of the employee, connected with the conditions of employment).

The purpose of the *Code* is to bring about change in organisations to provide protection for employees; its effectiveness, however, seems to be limited. Although all employers have had the obligation to implement anti-mobbing policies, the general directive is not accompanied by any detailed regulations or guidelines. There are also no sanctions for failure to implement such actions, so in practice, each employer can decide whether to comply or not. Furthermore, taking legal action against an employer is difficult for targets as employees need to prove long-term persistent harassment and intimidation resulting in injury. Another difficulty is related to the interpretation of regulations, which do not determine precisely what is to be regarded as mobbing and what is not. Low perceived effectiveness of the legal system, high complexity and lengthiness of proceedings, as well as low compensation in the case of a positive result, discourage mobbing victims from pursuing their claims in court. In 2013, 734 court proceedings regarding mobbing were reported, with only 29 decided in favour of employees (Reference book of the Ministry of Justice, 2014).

The statutory obligation to cooperate with employers concerning mobbing prevention has been imposed on occupational health services and the National Labour Inspectorate (NLI). These institutions carry out educational activities; NLI also has inspection rights. Yet, diagnosing and planning interventions for specific organisations is not undertaken on a large scale (Mościcka 2010). Trade unions and employer organisations, operating together as so-called social partners, engage in popularisation and development of anti-mobbing procedures. This cooperation is the effect of the European framework agreement on harassment and violence at work, signed by the European social partners in 2007 and by Poland in 2008. Since 2000, anti-mobbing associations have been functioning in Poland, executing a number of preventative activities such as awareness raising, training sessions and projects, as well as providing legal and psychological assistance to victims. An employee who experiences mobbing may also turn to trade unions or the NLI. Knowledge on mobbing can be easily gained from widely available publications (such as monographs for professionals: managers, lawyers or social activists, and for employees subjected to bullying), as well as from online materials.

Initiatives taken in Poland with the support of the European Commission, which may contribute to reducing workplace mobbing and discrimination in the future, should not be disregarded. The Diversity Charter, an international initiative endorsed by the European Commission which promotes equality and workplace diversity management, has been implemented in Poland since 2012 (106 entities have signed so far; Responsible Business Forum 2013). Signing of the Charter by an employer is a voluntary commitment to implementation of anti-discriminatory and anti-mobbing policies; it allows for exchanging experiences with other entities involved, and ensures promotional benefits. For many years, Polish enterprises have been making attempts to implement the principles of Corporate Social Responsibility, a strategy of the European Commission (Williamson *et al.* 2014). One of its important elements is to influence organisational culture by the development of an organisational climate promoting the principles of fair play at work.

The stance of the Church towards mobbing is explicitly negative. Catholic social teaching emphasises the lack of consent to any kind of violence or injustice, and its doctrine stresses human's inviolable dignity and the need to build a "civilisation of love" (Pontifical Council for Justice and Peace 2004). Hence, it can be expected that in Catholic Poland the Church will be an important ally in the prevention of mobbing behaviours. Unfortunately, at present workplace bullying is not among the topics discussed in the context of Church teaching.

Although much is done for employers and managers to discern the threats connected with mobbing, the current effects of these actions appear to be insufficient. Little interest from employers in the problem of mobbing, and low motivation of people subjected to these behaviours to seek assistance, either from the organisation or national institutions, result from historical determinants, and the Polish national and organisational culture. Only some Polish organisations have implemented anti-mobbing policies and codes of ethics. The same applies to the institution of academic ombudsmen for universities. Poland has no mobbing prevention program at the national level, which means that no standard actions have been developed with consideration for the Polish social and cultural situation. The experiences of other European countries are frequently referred to, yet they may not be compatible with Polish conditions. This may be the reason why the activities aimed at promoting knowledge have not so far translated into measurable successes, such as increased individual and enterprise interest in reduced risk and mobbing prevention.

Mobbing, economy and culture: the causes of workplace abuse in Poland

Although the main object of interest is the relationship between workplace abuse and national and organisational culture, it seems appropriate to discuss other factors. One of these is the high unemployment rate. The labour market promotes a lack of respect for the employee, as it is easy to replace each employee with another, and therefore an employee who is afraid of losing their job is likely to tolerate improper behaviours. Especially difficult is the situation of employees with contracts for a specific period of time, usually with low pay. The high number of such workers in Poland is considered to be a social problem.

Some of the universal factors connected with changes in the working environment which foster the increase of bullying activities (Harvey *et al.* 2006) – the pressure of change, time pressure, or diversity in the workplace – seem to be especially pronounced in Poland. The global pressure of change (e.g. with globalisation, hyper-competition and technological change), which intensifies uncertainty and requires continuous adjustment, in Poland (and other post-communist countries) is accompanied by an even more dramatic change connected with the process of transformation of the economic system. For example, the restructuring of enterprises, usually connected with a reduction of employment and budget cuts, increases uncertainty and frustration among employees, evokes stress and a sense of helplessness, fosters internal competition, and lowers the aggression threshold, which in turn increases the probability of bullying (Salin 2003, Skogstad *et al.* 2007).

Forcing higher work rates can be justified in Poland if consideration is given to lower work productivity in comparison with the countries of 'old' Europe (such as Germany or France), an effect of decades of the communist planned economy. Working under constant time pressure may be unfamiliar, leading to unexpected results, so the manager may be more inclined to use unauthorised negative (abusive) ways of motivating subordinates, who in turn may resort to (reciprocal) bullying to keep their position in the company (Zapf 1999). The increase in diversity in the workplace may lead to the formation of lobby groups, and intensification of competition between and within the groups, and as a result, to workplace aggression (LaVan and Martin 2008).

Increased diversity in Poland is the result of the economic changes and also of changes in culture and in Poles' mentality. Contradictory systems of norms and values (traditional, conservative and collectivistic versus liberal and individualistic) occurring in a group of employees may be the cause of mutual adversity, conflicts and increased frequency of workplace violence. Such diversity is not accepted in Poland, maybe due to the beliefs, still common in the society, that Poland is a homogeneous nation, and to the general low tolerance for difference.

A new source of division may be employing foreigners. In Poland this factor will probably grow in importance in the future, along with the necessity to further open up the labour market to foreign workers. Mobbing directed at foreigners working in Poland is not considered a significant problem at the moment, mainly because of the relatively low number of such workers. On the other hand, there are situations, when a company is taken over by a foreign investor and conflict between the staff and the new management grows as the new managers try to introduce some elements of their own culture, which employees may view as mobbing.

In Polish national culture, and the organisational cultures based on it, mobbing may potentially be promoted by factors which: make it easier for the perpetrator to take actions harmful to the victim; increase the acceptance of such actions; and reduce the probability of the victims trying to defend themselves. What must also have influenced the situation is the history of the Polish nation, which has made Poles value resistance and fighting over the ability to compromise and solve conflicts peacefully. Informing the authorities of irregularities or improper conduct of third parties is not favoured; this is related to low respect for state institutions and their representatives (since in the times of partition and communism the State was the embodiment of the enemy) (Gannon and Pillai 2013). Expressing one's feelings at work is not recommended either (Trompenaars and Hampden-Turner 2002), so both victims and witnesses of mobbing may feel obliged to pretend that nothing has happened.

High power distance, a feature of Polish culture, is combined with a preference for an authoritarian form of exercising power. It is difficult to ensure the necessary control of those in authority as power is still often treated as primary to morality, and superiors have the tendency to be isolated from subordinates. The 'benevolent autocrat' is willingly accepted as the boss; however, in Poland moral standards are not something that leads to promotion. Wide powers of superiors and the passivity of subordinates can create a fertile ground for vertical (top down) mobbing (Einarsen 2000). Greater acceptance of this type of mobbing can also be expected – some behaviours may be regarded as normal expressions of power, thus reducing the victim's discomfort to a certain degree. The effects of such acts are still harmful to victims. Studies have supported the notion that bullying lowers job satisfaction and workgroup identification even in cultures with high power distance (Loh *et al.* 2010). Polish culture having more masculine than feminine features, may also promote authoritarianism; whenever subordinates demand some rights or autonomy, an authoritarian superior may respond with aggression.

Another characteristic of Polish culture which may potentially contribute to mobbing is the tendency to avoid uncertainty. This feature is connected with the lack of tolerance for diversity and a higher inclination to emotional aggressive behaviours (Hofstede 1980, Bergeron and Schneider 2005). High in-group collectivism, being the reflection of the tendency to favour the members of one's group at the expense of others, transfers this tendency to reference groups: the family and the social group. In family businesses, such collectivism may lead to so-called amoral familism, manifested in creating different rules for relatives and for employees from the outside. People who apply this attitude are altruistic and cooperative towards family members and at the same time egoistic, combative and parasitic towards other employees (Marjański and Sułkowski 2009). Collectivism combined with intolerance may foster aggression within an organisation – external, directed at 'strangers', or internal, directed at individuals who negate the common system of beliefs and thus are a threat for group coherence.

From the point of view of cultural determinants of mobbing in Poland, the position of Polish culture in the humane orientation dimension seems very important, with low significance attributed to such individual qualities as compassion, altruism, fairness, generosity and kindness. People with these traits will not get promoted or be valued as leaders, which may translate into disregard for the moral dimension of interpersonal contact, and into ordinary rudeness in daily situations. In addition, quite a high level of assertiveness, defined as the tendency to being confrontational and aggressive, may foster workplace incivility. As already mentioned, agreeableness, open-mindedness and kindness were not previously regarded as important in a society that was forced to fight for its independence. In Poland, kindness may be identified with weakness: children are supposed to be kind to adults, and younger people to older ones; it does not work the other way round. The little importance attached to kindness is also visible in political life, where hostile and rude behaviour towards political adversaries does not disqualify a politician, but to the contrary arouses the observers' interest.

High context Polish society (Hall 2001) may be connected with the possibility of a leader abusing power. Assuming that high context communication is effective if the parties have a common frame of reference, problems may arise in the interpretation of an ambiguous message, if it includes contents that are insulting for the other party. Some of the younger generation of Poles – not yet holding managerial positions – have exposure to low context Western cultures. This may lead to conflict when they become part of traditionally high context organisations.

A look ahead: creating a mobbing-free working environment

The title of this chapter stresses the contradiction between the widely held view of Polish society as homogeneous, and the reality. Modernisation processes are connected with an increase in a diversity of systems of beliefs, values, attitudes and lifestyles among Poles, as well as polarisation of the society, which is to a large extent based on the attitude to tradition and change. This division is a common source of emotions and the breeding ground for conflicts in Poland. Some of the cultural factors which increase the probability of mobbing stem from one or the other of these two variations of Polish national culture. The traditional culture is characterised by high power distance and a lack of tolerance for diversity. The modern culture values individualism and can increase competition, thus fostering mobbing aimed at weakening the competitor, and decreasing the sensitivity to injustice.

Other elements of Polish national and organisational culture which are the remains of the former political system, as well as a difficult labour market, may foster conflict, embolden perpetrators and discourage targets and bystanders from opposing mobbing. Relatively low tolerance for difference in Polish society means that diversity may become an excuse for attributing low value to a person and making them a sanctioned target (see Omari *et al.* 2014). Further work needs to be done to establish which of the potential dimensions of diversity are particularly related to workplace bullying in Poland.

An attempt has been made in this chapter to discuss the mobbing phenomenon in the context of Polish national culture. As has been mentioned earlier, mobbing in Poland is a relatively unexplored phenomenon. The few studies devoted to this problem are fragmentary and usually not grounded on profound methodological reflection, and diversified methodology makes it impossible to compare their results. These studies to date do not provide a comprehensive view of the phenomenon. Therefore, research on organisational causes and consequences of bullying in Poland is still lacking. Much of the Polish literature tends to focus on research from other countries, and best practice in prevention and intervention. Although it is beneficial to learn from the best, adapting anti-mobbing programs for Polish conditions seems to be essential.

As the number of Polish organisations introducing policies is currently growing, it is necessary to investigate the efficiency of different preventative measures and anti-mobbing interventions in Polish conditions. This is even more important because employers are sometimes accused of implementing policies which may be effective at face value, but result from the intent to protect themselves from perceptions of inaction, rather than from the belief that the problem is significant (Durniat 2012). Creating a positive atmosphere for the introduction of such programs, and convincing employers of the measurable benefits connected with them, seems to be one of the most important challenges for the future.

Gannon and Pillai (2013) use the village church metaphor for Poland: the nation has peasant roots which have shaped its traditional mentality. The nation is, however, becoming a modern one, active in Europe, well educated and more and more open to change. Thus, there is legitimate hope that despite the historical and cultural determinants, increasing public awareness of mobbing and its consequences, as well as efforts by numerous organisations and institutions, will give positive results in the future.

References

Bakacsi, G., Sandor T., Andras K., and Viktor I., 2002. Eastern European cluster: tradition and transition. *Journal of World Business*, 37 (1), 69–80.

Baniak, J., 2007. *Desakralizacja kultu religijnego i świąt religijnych w Polsce. Studium socjologiczne* [Desacralisation of worship and religious holidays in Poland. A sociological study study]. Kraków: Nomos.

Bechowska-Gebhardt, A., and Stalewski, T., 2004. *Mobbing. Patologia zarządzania personelem* [Mobbing. The pathology of staff management]. Warszawa: Difin.

Bergeron, N., and Schneider, B. H., 2005. Explaining cross-national differences in peer-directed aggression: A quantitative synthesis. *Aggressive Behavior*, 31 (2), 116–37.

Boguszewski, R., 2013. *Wartości i normy*. [Values and norms]. Research report BS/111/2013 [online]. Warszawa: Public Opinion Research Center. Available from: www.cbos.pl/SPISKOM.POL/2013/ K_111_13.PDF [Accessed 15 November 2014].

Brewster, C., and Bennett, C., 2010. Perceptions of business cultures in Eastern Europe and their implications for international HRM. *The International Journal of Human Resource Management*, 21 (14), 2568–88.

Chomczyński, P., 2008. *Mobbing w pracy z perspektywy interakcyjnej: proces stawania się ofiarą* [Workplace mobbing from the interactive perspective: The process of becoming a victim]. Łódź: Wydawnictwo Uniwersytetu Łódzkiego.

Coyne, I., Craig, J., and Smith-Lee Chong, P., 2004. Workplace bullying in a group context. *British Journal of Guidance and Counselling*, 32 (3), 301–17.

Czapiński, J., 2006. Polska – państwo bez społeczeństwa [Poland – The state without the society]. *Nauka*, 1, 7–26.

Czapiński. J., and Panek, T., eds., 2013. *Social diagnosis 2013. The objective and subjective quality of life in Poland. Report* [online]. Warsaw: The Council for Social Monitoring. Available from: www.diagnoza.com/data/report/report_2013.pdf [Accessed 15 November 2014].

Cześnik, M., and Kotnarowski, M., 2011. Nowy wymiar politycznego współzawodnictwa: Polska solidarna versus Polska liberalna [A new dimension of political competition. United Poland vs. liberal Poland]. *Studia Polityczne*, 27, 129–58.

Delikowska, K., 2004. Raport z badań na temat działań mobbingowych w miejscu pracy [Report from research on workplace mobbing activities]. *Społecznik*, 7, 5–31.

Derczyński, W., 2002. *Szykany w miejscu pracy* [Persecutions in the workplace]. Research report BS/107/2002 [online]. Warszawa: Public Opinion Research Center. Available from: www.cbos.pl/SPISKOM.POL/2002/K_107_02.PDF [Accessed 15 November 2014].

Drabek, M., and Merecz, D., 2013. Skala narażenia na agresję w miejscu pracy pracowników służby zdrowia i sektora usług [The rate of exposure to aggression at work among people working at health care institutions and in the services sector]. *Medycyna Pracy*, 64 (3), 283–96.

Durniat, K., 2012. Możliwości i ograniczenia diagnozowania mobbingu w miejscu pracy [The possibilities and limitations of diagnosing mobbing in the workplace]. *Czasopismo Psychologiczne*, 18 (2), 221–31.

Einarsen, S., 2000. Harassment and bullying at work: A review of the Scandinavian approach. *Aggression and violent behavior*, 5 (4), 379–401.

Einarsen, S., Hoel, H., Zapf, D., and Cooper, C., 2011. The concept of bullying and harassment at work: The European tradition. In: S. Einarsen, H. Hoel, D. Zapf, and C. Cooper, eds., *Bullying and harassment in the workplace: Developments in theory, research, and practice*, 2nd ed. Boca Raton, FL: CRC Press, 3–40.

Einarsen, S., and Raknes, B. I., 1997. Harassment in the workplace and the victimization of men. *Violence and Victims*, 12 (3), 247–63.

European Union, 2003. Council decision on the admission of ten states to the EU (14 April 2003). *Official Journal of the European Union, Legislation, L 236*, Vol. 46, 23 September. Available from: http://eur–lex.europa.eu/ [Accessed 15 January 2015].

Gannon, M. J., and Pillai, R., 2013. *Understanding global cultures. Metaphorical journeys through 31 nations, clusters of nations, continents, and diversity*, 5th ed. Los Angeles, CA: Sage.

Hall, E. T., 2001. *Poza kulturą* [Beyond the culture]. Warszawa: PWN.

Harvey, M. G., Heames, J. T., Richey, R. G., and Leonard, N., 2006. Bullying: From the playground to the boardroom. *Journal of Leadership and Organizational Studies*, 12 (4), 1–11.

Hirigoyen, M. F., 2003. *Molestowanie w pracy* [Harassment in the workplace]. Poznań: W drodze.

Hofstede, G., 1980. *Culture's consequences. International differences in work-related values*. Beverly Hills, CA: Sage.

Hofstede, G., Hofstede, G. J., and Minkov, M., 2010. *Cultures and organizations: Software of the mind*, 3rd ed. New York: McGraw-Hill.

House, R. J., Hanges, P. J., Javidan, M., Dorfman, P. W., and Gupta, V., 2004. *Culture, leadership, and organizations: The GLOBE study of 62 societies*. Thousand Oaks, CA: Sage.

Jasińska-Kania, A., ed., 2012. *Wartości i zmiany. Przemiany postaw Polaków w jednoczącej się Europie* [Values and changes. Transformations of attitudes of Poles in unifying Europe]. Warszawa: Scholar.

Kloczowski, J., 2000. *A history of Polish Christianity*. Cambridge: Cambridge University Press.

Kmiecik-Baran K., and Rybicki J., 2004. *Mobbing – zagrożenie współczesnego miejsca pracy* [Mobbing – A threat to the contemporary workplace]. Gdańsk: Pomorski Instytut Demokratyczny.

Koopman, P. L., Den Hartog, D. N., and Konrad, E., *et al.*, 1999. National culture and leadership profiles in Europe: Some results from the GLOBE study. *European Journal of Work and Organizational Psychology*, 8 (4), 503–20.

Kunecka, D., Kamińska, M., and Karakiewicz, B., 2008. Skala zjawiska mobbingu wśród pielęgniarek/pielęgniarzy zatrudnionych w szczecińskich szpitalach [The scale of mobbing among nurses employed in Szczecin hospitals]. *Medycyna Pracy*, 59 (3), 223–8.

LaVan, H., and Martin, W. M., 2008. Bullying in the US workplace: Normative and process-oriented ethical approaches. *Journal of Business Ethics*, 83 (2), 147–65.

Leymann, H., 1990. Mobbing and psychological terror at workplaces. *Violence and Victims*, 5 (2), 119–26.

Leymann, H., 1996. The content and development of mobbing at work. *European Journal of Work and Organizational Psychology*, 5 (2), 165–84.

Loh, J., Restubog, S.L.D., and Zagenczyk, T.J., 2010. Consequences of workplace bullying on employee identification and satisfaction among Australians and Singaporeans. *Journal of Cross-Cultural Psychology,* 41 (2), 236–52.

Mączyński, J., Łobodziński, A., Wyspiański, D., and Kwiatkowski, P., 2010. Differences on organizational practices and preferred leader attributes between Polish managers investigated in 1996/1997 and 2008/2009. *Polish Psychological Bulletin,* 41 (4), 127–32.

Marjański, A.J., and Sułkowski, Ł., 2009. *Firmy rodzinne, jak osiągnąć sukces w sztafecie pokoleń* [Family business: How to succeed as part of succession]. Warszawa: Poltex.

Merecz-Kot, D., and Cębrzyńska, J., 2008. Agresja i mobbing w służbie więziennej [Aggression and mobbing among correctional officers]. *Medycyna Pracy,* 59 (6), 443–51.

Mościcka, A., 2010. Opieka profilaktyczna dotycząca psychospołecznych zagrożeń w miejscu pracy [Prevention of psychosocial dangers at work]. *Medycyna Pracy,* 61 (1), 91–100.

Omari, M., Paull, M., D'Cruz, P., and Guneri-Cangarli, B., 2014. Fair game: The influence of cultural norms in creating sanctioned targets in the workplace. 9th International Conference on Workplace Bullying and Harassment, 17–21 June 2014, Milan, 1–13.

Omyła-Rudzka, M., 2014. *Szykany w miejscu pracy* [Persecutions in the workplace]. Research report 109/2014 [online]. Warszawa: Public Opinion Research Center. Available from: www.cbos.pl/SPISKOM.POL/2014/K_109_14.PDF [Accessed 15 November 2014].

Parent-Thirion, A., Fernández Macías, E., Hurley, J., and Vermeylen, G., 2007. *Fourth European working conditions survey.* Dublin: European Foundation for the Improvement of Living and Working Conditions.

Pilch, I., and Turska, E., 2014. Relationships between Machiavellianism, organizational culture, and workplace bullying: Emotional abuse from the target's and the perpetrator's perspective. *Journal of Business Ethics* [online]. Available from: http://link. springer.com/article/10.1007/s10551-014-2081-3 [Accessed 20 August 2014].

Polish Central Statistical Office, 2015. Information Portal, Basic data. Available from: http://stat.gov.pl/en/basic-data/ [Accessed 30 January 2015].

Pontifical Council for Justice and Peace, 2004. Compendium of the social doctrine of the Church. Vatican City: Libreria Editrice Vaticana [online]. Available from: www.vatican.va/roman_curia/pontifical_councils/justpeace/documents/ [Accessed 15 August 2014].

Porter-Szűcs, B., 2011. *Faith and fatherland: Catholicism, modernity, and Poland.* Oxford: Oxford University Press.

Power, J. L. *et al.,* 2013. Acceptability of workplace bullying: A comparative study on six continents. *Journal of Business Research,* 66 (3), 374–80.

Rapacki, R., ed., 1995. *Problemy kształtowania się kultury przedsiębiorstw w Polsce w okresie transformacji* [Problems of the development of Polish organisational culture in the time of transformation]. Warszawa: Oficyna Wydawnicza SGH.

Reference book of the Ministry of Justice, 2014. *Discrimination, mobbing and harassment in the workplace* [online]. Available from: http://isws.ms.gov.pl/pl/ bazastatystyczna/publikacje/ [Accessed 15 December 2014].

Responsible Business Forum 2013. Diversity unites us! A guide to the Polish Diversity Charter. Warsaw. Available from: http://odpowiedzialnybiznes.pl/wpcontent/

uploads/2014/04/ KARTA–R–Przewodnik–ANG–podglad–OST.pdf [Accessed 15 January 2015].

Salin, D., 2003. Ways of explaining workplace bullying: A review of enabling, motivating, and precipitating structures and processes in the work environment. *Human Relations,* 56 (10), 1213–32.

Sikorski, Cz., 2012. *Stereotypy samobójcze. Kulturowe czynniki agresji w życiu społecznym i w organizacji* [Suicide stereotypes. Cultural factors of aggression in social life and within organisations]. Warszawa: Difin.

Sitko-Lutek, A., 2004. *Kulturowe uwarunkowania doskonalenia menedżerów* [Cultural determinants of manager improvement]. Lublin: Wydawnictwo UMCS.

Skogstad, A., Matthiesen, S. B., and Einarsen, S., 2007. Organizational changes: A precursor of bullying at work? *International Journal of Organizational Theory and Behavior,* 10 (1), 58–94.

Trompenaars, F., and Hampden-Turner, C., 2002. *Siedem wymiarów kultury* [Seven dimensions of culture]. Kraków: Oficyna Ekonomiczna.

Trompenaars, F., and Hampden-Tuner, C., 2012. *Riding the waves of culture: Understanding diversity in global business,* 3rd edition. New York: McGraw-Hill.

Van Oudenhoven, J. P., de Raad, B., Askevis-Leherpeux, F., Boski, P., Brunborg, G. S., Carmona, C., Barelds, D., Hill, Ch. T., Mlačić, B., Motti, F., Rammstedt, B., and Woods, S., 2014. Are virtues national, supranational, or universal? *SpringerPlus* [online], 3 (223), 1–12. Available from: http://link.springer.com/journal/40064/3/1 [Accessed 20 May 2014].

Warszewska-Makuch, M., 2007. Polska adaptacja kwestionariusza NAQ do pomiaru mobbingu [Polish adaptation of the NAQ questionnaire for measuring mobbing at work]. *Bezpieczeństwo Pracy,* 12, 16–19.

Warszewska-Makuch, M., 2008. Zjawisko mobbingu wśród nauczycieli [Mobbing among teachers]. *Bezpieczeństwo Pracy,* 5, 6–9.

Williamson, N., Stampe-Knippel, A., and Weber, T., 2014. Corporate social responsibility. National public policies in the European Union. Compendium 2014. European Union. Available from: http://ec.europa.eu/social/main.jsp?catId=738andlangId=enandpubId=7726andvisible=1 [Accessed 15 January 2015].

Wojciszke, B., 2004. The negative social world: The Polish culture of complaining. *International Journal of Sociology,* 34 (4), 38–59.

Zapf, D., 1999. Organisational, work group related and personal causes of mobbing/bullying at work. *International Journal of Manpower,* 20 (1/2), 70–85.

Zapf, D., and Einarsen, S., 2003. Individual antecedents of bullying: Victims and perpetrators. In: S. Einarsen, H. Hoel, D. Zapf, and C. L. Cooper, eds. *Bullying and emotional abuse in the workplace. International perspectives in research and practice.* London: Taylor & Francis, 165–84.

Ziółkowski, M., 2000. *Przemiany interesów i wartości społeczeństwa polskiego: teorie, tendencje, interpretacje* [Transformations of interests and values of Polish society: theories, trends, interpretations]. Poznań: Wydawnictwo Fundacji Humaniora.

9 The Czech Republic

Workplace abuse in a post-transitional country[1]

Kateřina Zábrodská and Petr Květon

Introduction

This chapter addresses workplace abuse in the Czech Republic, a country undergoing significant transformation. The Czech Republic belongs to a cluster of post-communist countries in Central and Eastern Europe (CEE) whose development, until 1989, was hindered by four decades of authoritative communist regime under the influence of the Soviet Union. As the chapter discusses, this communist past has had a detrimental impact on the country's work environment and work-related values and practices. Additionally, since Czech research was isolated during the communist era (Hilpert and Smith 2012), there has been a similarly detrimental impact on research. The Czech Republic and other CEE countries began to be included in organisational cross-cultural studies only in the 1990s, and have been under-researched compared to other cultural clusters (Gupta and Hanges 2004). Even today, the Czech Republic lacks systematic research on its work environment to the extent typical for Western European and Anglo-American countries. To explore workplace abuse in the Czech Republic, the authors therefore drew on a variety of resources, including scholarly work, national and European surveys and statistics, and internet resources, as well as their own research on workplace abuse and their personal knowledge of Czech work environments. The chapter offers an amalgam of these diverse resources but is not, by any means, a complete picture.

The chapter is structured in the following manner: First, we present a brief historical profile of the country, highlighting the ways in which the current work environment in the Czech Republic has been shaped by the confluence – common to post-communist countries (e.g., Aligica and Evans 2009) – of the communist legacy with the recent shift towards neoliberalism. We follow this with a discussion of the country's cultural profile using the dimensions of power distance, individualism-collectivism, and particularism; we draw links between these dimensions and workplace abuse. The chapter then details current workplace abuse research in the Czech Republic and, at the same time, draws attention to how workplace abuse has been discursively constructed in public debates. Using a recent controversy about sexual harassment in academia, we explore the arguments used by some members of the Czech intelligentsia to devalue policies addressing this form of workplace abuse. In order to illustrate the country's complexities, we then present a case study of workplace abuse using our own research on workplace bullying in Czech academia. The chapter concludes with a discussion of the practical implications for organisations in the Czech Republic.

Country profile

The Czech Republic is a country located in Central Europe, bordering Germany, Poland, Slovakia, and Austria. The total population is 10.5 million, more than 1 million of whom live in the capital, Prague. The Czech Republic has been a member of the European Union since 2004 and is a member of other major international organisations, including the North Atlantic Treaty Organization (NATO) and the Organisation for Co-operation and Development (OECD). The official language is Czech, a West Slavic language. The population is nationally and ethnically homogenous, with the majority of inhabitants (95 per cent) being of Czech origin (Czech Statistical Office 2011).[2] This homogeneity is a relatively recent feature. Before WWII, the then Czechoslovak Republic was "a modern multi-ethnic state, an experiment of civic coexistence" (Klicperová-Baker 2008, p. 159) which included Czechs, Slovaks, Germans, Hungarians, and Poles, as well as other nationalities. The current homogeneity in the Czech Republic is a result of a variety of factors, including the genocide of the Czech Jewish and Roma populations during WWII, the post-war expatriation of Germans and Hungarians, and the homogenisation of the society during the communist era. Contrary to the country's multi-ethnic history, the current attitudes to multiculturalism held by Czechs are reserved, and Czechs have been criticised by the European Union for ethnic discrimination, particularly of the Roma minority (Amnesty International 2014).

The milestone in the constitution of the present-day Czech Republic was in 1918 when, at the end of WWI and with the dissolution of the Austro-Hungarian Empire of which it had been a part, the country (then called Czechoslovakia) gained independence. The First Czechoslovak Republic (1918–1938) was a period of intense development when Czechoslovakia was one of the ten most industrialised countries in the world (European Commission 2014). This booming era ended abruptly with Nazi occupation and WWII. Three years after the end of WWII, the communists took power and began 40 years of an authoritarian communist regime (1948–1989). During this period, the country was subjected to the bureaucratic centralism of the ruling Communist Party of Czechoslovakia, and to the ideological principles of Marxism-Leninism. Private ownership was eliminated and replaced by an ineffective and corrupt planned economy, drastically reducing labour productivity and the quality of products. Civil rights were repressed and opponents of the regime persecuted, commonly through imprisonment, forced labour in labour camps, and limitations on their and their family members' education and job prospects (Myck and Bohacek 2011).[3]

In 1989 Czechs reclaimed democracy with the nonviolent Velvet Revolution and, four years later, the Czech Republic became an independent state after Czechoslovakia split peacefully into two countries: the Czech Republic and Slovakia. The Czech Republic was internationally acclaimed for its peaceful transition to democracy and its playwright president, Václav Havel, who symbolised revolutionary zeal and vision. Today, however, the revolutionary optimism has cooled. Nowadays, many Czechs express scepticism about their political situation and public discourse is permeated with discussions about disillusionment and negative mood (cf. Klicperová-Baker and Košťál 2015). This negativist discourse, though, does not necessarily correspond to the country's relatively high level of development. For instance, the Czech Republic ranks 28th out of 187 countries on the Human Development Index (Human Development Reports 2014), which combines indicators of longevity, access to knowledge, and living standards; it is the second highest score from a post-communist country (after Slovenia). Within the European Union, the Czech Republic has one of the lowest unemployment rates (Eurostat 2015) and at-risk-of-poverty rates (Czech Statistical Office 2014). Dissatisfaction is relative and, in the case of the Czech Republic, it seems to be linked to its location midway between Western and Eastern Europe. While Czechs do well compared to Eastern Europe and other developing countries, development still lags behind advanced Western European and Anglo-American countries on a number of well-being indicators, including financial wealth (OECD 2014) and quality of psychosocial work environment (Niedhammer *et al.* 2012).

The Czech Republic is referred to as a "post-transitional" country, which reflects its recent transformation from a centrally-planned communist economy to an advanced, free-market economy (Danis *et al.* 2011, Montgomery 2013). Relatedly, key forces shaping the current Czech work environment are the legacy of the communist workplace culture and the recent expansion of capitalism and neoliberalism. In terms of the legacy of the communist era, studies indicate that many negative features characteristic of Czech organisations, such as autocratic leadership, favouritism, conservatism, and materialist work values, have their roots in communist organisational practices (Soulsby and Clark 1996, Smith *et al.* 1996, Suutari and Riusala 2001, Reber *et al.* 2004, True 2003, Borgulya and Hahn 2013). Of particular relevance for the discussion of workplace abuse is the prevalence of autocratic behaviour among Czech managers (Reber *et al.* 2004) and organisational cultures based on informality, which entails the downplaying of formal structures and rules, while emphasising flexibility, improvisation, and person-centred control (Nový and Schroll-Machl 2003 cited in Reber *et al.* 2004). Both features suggest a work environment susceptible to workplace discrimination and abuses of power, particularly from employees in supervisory positions. This historic legacy intersects with a recent shift towards neoliberalism across the CEE region (e.g., Aligica and Evans 2009, Glassner 2013), with varied effects on workplace environment. Studies have mostly pointed to a negative confluence of post-communism and neoliberalism, reflected, for instance, in the weak position of trade unions in defending employee rights and low levels of concern with occupational health and safety issues (Woolfson 2006, Glassner 2013, Lee and Trappmann 2014). Overall, the available evidence suggests that, when compared to Western Europe, Czech employees are exposed to a greater number of negative workplace factors (Niedhammer *et al.* 2012) and, at the same time, receive less protection and support.

Cultural profile

As noted above, the Czech Republic has been relatively under-studied in organisational cross-cultural research and, unlike many of the countries discussed in this book, is not one for which Gannon and Pillai (2013) have created a cultural metaphor. Nonetheless, the Czech Republic has been included in several major models of national cultures, including those of Hofstede (Hofstede and Hofstede 2005, Hofstede Center 2015), Trompenaars (Smith *et al.* 1996, Trompenaars and Hampden-Turner 2012), and Schwartz (Schwartz and Bardi 1997, Schwartz 2014). These frameworks place the Czech Republic in the Central and Eastern European (CEE) cluster, together with countries such as Slovakia, Poland, and Hungary, which share experience of a "long period of dependence on a centralised regime and socialist ideals" (Borgulya and Hahn 2013, p. 24) and of a subsequent transition towards capitalism. Despite recent profound transformation, CEE countries have retained cultural characteristics which differ significantly from those typical of developed Western democracies (e.g., Smith *et al.* 1996, Suutari and Riusala 2001, House *et al.* 2004). Notably, cultural characteristics identified in CEE countries – including hierarchical values, conservatism, and utilitarianism (Smith *et al.* 1996, Hofstede and Hofstede 2005) – correspond to those which presumably increase both the incidence and acceptance of workplace abuse.

In what follows, we discuss several cultural characteristics which are of arguably highest relevance to workplace abuse (see Jacobson *et al.* 2014), and which appear particularly relevant to a discussion of workplace abuse in the Czech Republic. We draw from Hofstede's model on power distance and individualism-collectivism; from Trompenaars and Hampden-Turner's (2012) model, we employ particularism as it has direct relevance to perceptions of morality and, consequently, to attitudes towards workplace abuse policies. In our analysis, we define the Czech Republic as a hierarchical, individualist, and particularistic society, with mid-high in-group collectivism and very low institutional collectivism.

Power distance and hierarchy values

Power distance in the Czech Republic is higher than in Western Europe, but lower than in Eastern European countries (Schwartz 2014). Nonetheless, with a score of 57 in Hofstede's study, the Czech Republic is considered a hierarchical society (Hofstede Center 2015). In the early post-transition period, Smith *et al.* (1996) found that all post-communist countries formed a distinct cluster defined by hierarchy values which contrasted with egalitarianism in Western

Europe. Acceptance of hierarchy has been explained by the extended experiences of paternalism and strict power structures which characterise communist regimes, despite their rhetoric of equality (Suutari and Riusala 2001). Relatively high power distance and hierarchy values mean that Czechs expect and accept unequal distribution of power (Hofstede and Hofstede 2005). Consistently, Czech employees have been found to be relatively accepting of autocratic leadership, paternalism, and the preferential treatment of associates (Reber *et al.* 2004). Acceptance of power inequalities is an important antecedent of workplace abuse (Escartín *et al.* 2011; Jacobson *et al.* 2014) and has presumably increased the prevalence and acceptability of workplace abuse in Czech society. In hierarchical societies, such as the Czech Republic, workplace abuse is used to express and maintain power asymmetries (Jacobson *et al.* 2014), particularly those based on formal hierarchies which are perceived as legitimate. Additionally, addressing workplace abuse in such societies is difficult, as the gap between subordinates and superiors is relatively large and subordinates may be hesitant to share their concerns with management.

Individualism-collectivism

The Czech Republic is considered to be an individualist society (Trompenaars and Hampden-Turner 2012, Hofstede Center 2015), although estimated levels of individualism differ across studies. In Trompenaars and Hampden-Turner's (2012) study, the Czech Republic, in attributing responsibility at work to individuals and believing that individuals rather than teams should take both credit and blame for job performance, was ranked among countries with the highest scores on individualism. Being an individualist society, Czechs primarily look after themselves and their immediate families, view themselves as independent of groups, prefer individual goals to group goals, and emphasise rationality (Gelfand *et al.* 2004). In discussing the relationship between individualism-collectivism and workplace abuse, Jacobson *et al.* (2014) suggest that individualist societies have a higher incidence of workplace abuse than collectivist societies because "collectivistic cultures tend to have a higher level of care and concern for others" (p. 57). Additionally, individualist societies are hypothesised to evince dyadic, supervisory workplace abuse rather than group-initiated abuse (Jacobson *et al.* 2014), a hypothesis that corresponds to the authors' findings on workplace bullying in Czech academia (Zábrodská and Květon 2012, 2013). Individualism in Czech society may also negatively impact the capacity of targeted employees to resist workplace abuse. Specifically, it may lead to perceptions of workplace abuse as an individual problem with blame directed at the targets, while diminishing the willingness of co-workers to provide support, as individuals are primarily expected to take care of themselves.

Complementing the individualistic character of Czech society, the Czech Republic has very low institutional collectivism. While data about the Czech Republic were excluded from the GLOBE study,[4] we can extrapolate from other post-communist countries, such as Hungary or East Germany, which have the lowest institutional collectivism in the GLOBE study (Gupta and Hanges 2004). Low institutional collectivism indicates that Czechs feel little loyalty to macro level laws and societal programs. This means that abiding by laws is not highly valued and transgressions are easily accepted. In fact, one's capacity to go around the law is typically praised by Czechs as a proof of cleverness. This is reflected in relatively high[5] levels of tax fraud and corruption in Czech society (e.g., Smith 2010), corruption being particularly rampant in public procurement. In international comparison, the Czech Republic ranks as 53rd out of 175 countries on the Corruption Perception Index (Transparency International 2014), far below Western European countries. While the situation may be improving following recent calls by the public and civil organisations for stricter punishment of corruption at the state level, the fact remains that many corrupt acts in everyday life are perceived as normal. It is not uncommon, for instance, to offer gifts to an official as *quid pro quo* for a favourable outcome. The authors' experiences suggest that many Czechs are reluctant to see such acts as corruption or bribery and insist on their acceptability.

Particularism

The lack of regard for societal laws resonates with the particularism of Czech society (Trompenaars and Hampden-Turner 2012): a tendency to base organisational behaviour on particular circumstances and social relations rather than on universal rules. In a conflict between loyalty to a friend and adherence to universal rules of conduct or organisational policy, 76 per cent of Czechs would choose the former (ibid.). This means that Czechs tend not to take laws, policies, and regulations seriously and breach them easily, particularly for their own benefit or the benefit of an in-group member. A popular saying, 'Rules exist to be broken', aptly captures this attitude. The tendency to circumvent inconvenient rules is not normally perceived as immoral behaviour but rather as a logical, common-sense way to achieve outcomes. The relative disregard for rules has negative implications for workplace abuse policies. For instance, officials in charge of the policies might feel obliged to do a favour for an in-group member rather than follow policy. Consequently, the management of workplace abuse complaints by officials might not be impartial or fair – a concern often voiced by targeted employees in our research on workplace bullying. In fact, in being from a particularistic culture, Czechs may feel that sharing information with an in-group member or applying policies differently based on changing circumstances (e.g., who is filing a complaint against whom) is more moral than taking a neutral position.

Legislative frameworks for workplace abuse in the Czech Republic

Similar to other EU countries, workplace abuse in the Czech Republic can be addressed via general laws, particularly those guaranteeing equal treatment which appear in the Constitution and the Labour Code. The major vehicle for addressing workplace abuse is the *Anti Discrimination Act* (The Act No. 198/2009 Coll.), which recognises discrimination based on race, ethnicity, nationality, gender, sexual orientation, age, disability, religion, belief, and world view. This Act provides the legal means of addressing some forms of workplace abuse, particularly sexual harassment and discrimination against those with protected status. The legislation is insufficient, however, with regard to workplace bullying, which is not recognised by the Czech legal system and which often either does not correspond to the listed discrimination reasons, or a correspondence cannot be proved. Additionally, although these legislative avenues exist, it is not clear to what extent they can be used to effectively resolve workplace abuse cases, the research in this area being practically non-existent. It is likely that Czech employees are reluctant to mobilise the law to address workplace abuse, due in large part to their distrust of the Czech legal system, a distrust reflected in public polls (e.g., Czech Statistical Office 2014), as well as to other concerns, such as financial costs. In our research on workplace bullying, none of the 46 interviewed targets used legislative means to resolve their situation, mostly because they did not consider such an option to be viable (Zábrodská 2012).

Workplace abuse research in the Czech Republic

Workplace abuse research has emerged relatively recently in the Czech social sciences. Following the transition of the Czech Republic to a democracy in 1989, Czech social science research remained impaired by the four decades of communist control which had isolated Czech researchers from research developments in Western Europe and the U.S. (Hilpert and Smith 2012). Thus, workplace abuse only begun to appear as a subject for research in the late 1990s and early 2000s. In the next section, we discuss two types of workplace abuse which have gained the most scholarly and public recognition in the Czech Republic: workplace bullying and sexual harassment.[6]

Workplace bullying

Terminology

Two terms are most frequently used in the Czech language to refer to workplace bullying: *šikana na pracovišti* (workplace bullying) and *mobbing* (mobbing). The term 'workplace bullying' is clearly intelligible in the Czech language and, as such, is preferred in some contexts (e.g., Bártlová and Hajduchová 2009, Zábrodská and Květon 2012). However, the term is problematic because bullying semantically connotes physical rather than psychological harm and, in lay discourse, is strongly associated with school and army bullying. Additionally, the term is emotionally charged and its use somewhat scandalises the problem. In contrast, 'mobbing' – a term adapted from the Swedish term "mobbning" (Leymann 1990) – is more neutral and clearly connotes psychological harm. Presumably because of this, mobbing has been favoured by many Czech researchers (e.g., Čech 2011, Wagnerová 2011, Zábrodská 2011, Chromý 2014, Harsa *et al*. 2014, Vitková and Zábrodská 2014) and is also frequently employed by state institutions, activists, and practitioners.[7] It should be noted, however, that the uses of mobbing are not necessarily consistent; the term has been used to refer to bullying by a group (e.g., Čech 2011) and to bullying by one or more individuals (e.g., Zábrodská 2011) as in Leymann's (1990) original definition.[8] In public documents (see, for instance, The Public Defender Office of the Czech Republic 2015) and organisational policies (when available),[9] the terms 'workplace bullying' and 'mobbing' are often used interchangeably. Additionally, some researchers and practitioners use the untranslated English terms 'bossing' and 'staffing' to refer to top-down and bottom-up bullying respectively (e.g., Čech 2011, Chromý 2014).

Prevalence and rate

Research into workplace bullying is still limited in the Czech Republic both in extent and quality. The first references to workplace bullying by Czech scholars, made in the mid-1990s (e.g., Šolcová 1995), were purely conceptual and no attempts were made to measure the concept empirically. It took two decades for the first empirical studies of workplace bullying to be published, for example, in education (Čech 2011, Zábrodská and Květon 2012, 2013) and healthcare (Bártlová and Hajduchová 2009).

So far, the largest study into workplace bullying has been conducted by Zábrodská and Květon (2012, 2013) on a sample of 1,533 university employees at three Czech public universities. The participants included all university employees, with the majority of the sample comprised of academics and doctoral candidates involved in teaching and research (82 per cent). The exposure to workplace bullying was measured with the Negative Acts Questionnaire-Revised (NAQ-R – Einarsen *et al*. 2009). The NAQ-R includes the operational approach measuring exposure to 22 negative acts, as well as a self-labelling approach asking respondents to estimate their exposure to workplace bullying based on a well-established definition. The results showed that 13.6 per cent of the respondents had been targets of bullying during the past 12 months based on an operational definition of bullying (weekly exposure to one negative act). Based on the self-labelling approach, 7.9 per cent of the respondents believed that they had been targets of occasional bullying during the previous year, and 0.7 per cent reported being bullied on a weekly basis. The authors concluded that these rates were relatively consistent with findings reported by studies conducted in Scandinavia which used either the NAQ-R (Nielsen *et al*. 2009) or similar measurements (e.g., Salin 2001). By contrast, the prevalence of bullying among Czech academics was lower than that reported in studies conducted in university environments in Anglo-American contexts. This, the authors suggested, could be attributed to differences in methodology, a higher acceptance of negative behaviour in the Czech sample, or national differences in academic systems and governance (for details, see Zábrodská and Květon 2013).

Another larger study was conducted on a sample of 1,103 elementary school teachers (Čech 2011). The study did not use a validated instrument to measure the incidence of workplace bullying, and comparison is therefore difficult. Drawing on the Leymann's (1990) six months definition of workplace bullying, the study found that 14.3 per cent of the respondents reported being bullied by superiors (referred to by the author as "bossing"), while 9.3 per cent of the respondents reported experiencing bullying from colleagues (referred to as "mobbing"). Overall, a total of 18.4 per cent of the respondents reported being targets of systematic bullying at some time during their careers as primary school teachers. In the healthcare sector, Bártlová and Hajduchová (2009) examined beliefs about the prevalence of workplace bullying and sexual harassment in a sample of doctors (N = 535) and nurses (N = 537). The study found surprisingly little evidence of either workplace bullying or sexual harassment. For example, only 3.7 per cent of doctors reportedly believed that workplace bullying occurred in their workplace. Since international research shows that workplace abuse is prominent in the healthcare sector, these findings are somewhat dubious. Given that the study focused primarily on beliefs about workplace abuse rather than participants' direct experience, it appeared to reflect a low awareness of the problem rather than low prevalence.

An estimate of the workplace bullying rate in the Czech Republic is provided by the European Working Conditions Surveys (EWCS) which, however, typically indicate a much lower prevalence than do national studies (Vartia-Väänänen 2013). In the European Working Conditions Survey (2010), only 2.3 per cent of Czechs reported being targets of bullying or harassment, a considerably lower number than that reported in most Western EU countries. EWCS uses a self-labelling approach without providing definitions of bullying or harassment and, as such, is prone to the under-reporting of workplace abuse in countries with low awareness of these phenomena (Vartia-Väänänen 2013). Relatedly, the EU Workplace Violence and Harassment Report (EU-OSHA 2010) shows that older EU member states with higher awareness and developed policies report significantly higher prevalence of workplace bullying than do new EU member states (including the Czech Republic), where the phenomenon is less understood and tends to be under-addressed. This suggests that the lower prevalence reported for the Czech Republic in the EWCS is most likely due to lack of knowledge of workplace bullying rather than low incidence. Overall, both national and European studies indicate that workplace bullying is a relevant, yet under-researched and under-reported problem in the Czech Republic.

Sexual harassment

Controversy about the concept

Compared to workplace bullying, the concept of sexual harassment is better known by the Czech general public, yet it is also more controversial. The term arrived in the Czech Republic in 1989 but has never gained wide acceptance.

Sexual harassment is generally translated into Czech as *sexuální obtěžování,* which is close in meaning to the English term. However, the ironic term *sexuální harašení,* consistent with the original English term, which can be translated as "sexual buzz or rumble" (True 2003, p. 91), has been used to devalue and ridicule the sexual harassment agenda. Writing about the 1990s, True (2003) described how opponents of the concept, mostly from the Czech male intelligentsia, publically condemned it as a Western import and a threat to 'natural' sexual relations. As can be seen in recent research, this attitude does not appear to have changed much since then. In 2008–2009, two studies of sexual harassment in universities were conducted and both found sexual harassment to be widespread (Smetáčková and Pavlík 2011, Vohlídalová 2011). In response, several male members of the Czech intelligentsia denounced this research in the Czech press; the critique targeted the associated manual for preventing sexual harassment in universities (Kolářová *et al.* 2009). One of the harshest critiques was published by two Czech researchers (Komárek and Havlíček 2010) who compared the manual to the "totalitarian thinking" (p. 10) of the communist era, and portrayed it as a profound threat to the individual freedom and rights regained by Czechs after 1989. The two researchers also appealed to the Czech public to defend itself against foreign influences and resist the implementation of U.S.-inspired harassment policies. The two researchers received considerable support from the Czech public, as reflected in the ensuing heated discussions in Czech social media (Zábrodská 2010).

Prevalence and rate

The extent and quality of research on sexual harassment has sound foundations due to the strong presence of Czech gender researchers working over the past decade (e.g., Křížková *et al.* 2006, Smetáčková and Pavlík 2011, Vohlídalová 2011). The position of these researchers, however, is complex, due to the lenient attitudes of many Czechs towards sexual harassment behaviours, documented across numerous studies (e.g., Fasting *et al.* 2011, Vohlídalová 2011). In fact, research describes "a certain tolerance of mild forms of sexual harassment as characteristic of Czech society" (Fasting *et al.* 2011, p. 79). As with other cultural characteristics, this tolerant attitude has been traced back to the communist era. Despite the official rhetoric of gender equality, sexual harassment was normalised during communism and "obscene jokes, suggestive remarks, unwelcome advances, gentle slaps were apparently all part of 'the culture' of communist workplaces" (True 2003, p. 90). A tolerant attitude continues to define Czechs' relation to sexual harassment even today, as illustrated by the recent studies, in which the majority of participating Czech university students reported that they did not consider sexist jokes degrading or harassing (Smetáčková and Pavlík 2011, Vohlídalová 2011).

The tolerant attitude towards sexual harassment is reflected in empirical findings on its prevalence. Typically, studies reveal a very high prevalence based on expert definitions of sexual harassment, but a very low prevalence based on participants' subjective definitions (Smetáčková and Pavlík 2011, Vohlídalová 2011). In their research among university students, Smetáčková and Pavlík (2011) found that 78 per cent of the participants experienced sexual harassment based on the expert definition, but only 3 per cent self-identified as targets of sexual harassment. It should be noted, though, that the discrepancy between expert and participant definitions of sexual harassment is not unique to the Czech Republic and has been discussed as one of the reasons for the failure of anti-harassment policies globally (Vohlídalová 2011). What seems to be more culturally specific to the Czech Republic is the level of hostility targeted at efforts to research and manage sexual harassment, evident in academic discussions (as reported by Stöckelová and Slačálek 2010) as well as social media (Zábrodská 2010). The hostility appears to be fuelled by a pronounced distrust towards gender research and feminism, as well as strong individualist sentiments. As True (2003, p. 93) commented more than a decade ago, the controversy around sexual harassment illustrates "Czech neoliberal scepticism towards legislating morality" as well as the boundary around private life which Czechs typically wish to defend. The more recent controversy about sexual harassment in universities has highlighted a similar trend, namely that a sizeable number of Czechs do not perceive policies addressing this form of workplace abuse as a form of protection, but rather as social control endangering their freedom and well-being at work.

Making sense of workplace abuse: a case study of Czech academia

In this section, we illustrate how the various factors operative in the country contribute to workplace abuse by presenting a case study in which we draw on our research into workplace bullying in Czech academia (Zábrodská and Květon 2012, 2013). By our choice of Czech academia, we do not wish to indicate that workplace abuse is particularly widespread in this sector. Rather, we chose Czech academia because it provides an excellent example of the interplay between national and organisational factors in producing workplace bullying. Specifically, this case study documents how workplace bullying is produced in some Czech academic departments through the intersection of national and cultural characteristics, academic governance, and work environment, as well as inadequate organisational and legislative frameworks to address workplace bullying.

As noted above, our research consisted of a questionnaire survey in a sample of 1,533 university employees (Zábrodská and Květon 2012, 2013) and subsequent qualitative interviews with targets of bullying. The survey examined the prevalence and forms of workplace bullying in three major Czech universities, using the Negative Acts Questionnaire-Revised (NAQ-R – Einarsen *et al.* 2009). The survey also included demographic and employment variables to identify at-risk groups, as well as additional questions regarding the experience of bullying. The first author then conducted in-depth interviews with 46 targets of bullying who had provided their e-mail contacts in the survey, of whom 26 had been targeted in Czech academia. The interviews were analysed using thematic analysis, a flexible method for identifying patterns (themes) across a data set (Braun and Clarke 2006). In the following case study, we integrate our findings from both the published survey and as-yet unpublished interview data.

The noted confluence of the communist legacy and an emerging neoliberalism is one of the key factors in bullying in Czech academia. Interviews with targeted academics showed that workplace bullying typically occurred in two contrasting types of academic departments. The first type, typically in the humanities, reproduced some aspects of communist workplace culture, in particular its apparent disregard for job performance, conservatism, and maintenance of strict formal power hierarchies. In these workplaces, power and status were established through personal connections, sometimes carried over from the former regime, rather than on the basis of quality performance. Targets of bullying were junior academics who reported being bullied because of transgressing the rigid social norms and hierarchies, for example, by being innovative or by displaying too much initiative. In a distinct contrast, departments constituting the second type of academic workplace with bullying problems were overly invested in recent global trends involving the marketisation of education and research (e.g., Canaan and Shumar 2008). These workplaces, typically in the natural and technical sciences, were highly concerned with performance and profit-making. Here, targeted academics perceived bullying as a managerial strategy to maximise their performance while reducing costs, a feature of market-driven academia frequently discussed in Anglo-American contexts (Twale and De Luca 2008, Zábrodská *et al.* 2011). These findings have indicated that both the legacy of the communist workplace culture and an excessive market orientation contribute to bullying in Czech academia, albeit for different reasons.

Power abuse by supervisors and the related organisational hierarchies are other vital factors in bullying among Czech academics. Our survey showed a high prevalence of dyadic supervisory bullying as opposed to colleague-initiated bullying, with 73.3 per cent of those targeted reporting being bullied by their superiors (Zábrodská and Květon 2013). These findings are consistent with the relatively high power distance and individualism of Czech society, cultural characteristics which have been hypothesised to be associated with dyadic supervisory bullying (Jacobson *et al.* 2014). Apart from hierarchical national values, power asymmetry in Czech academia is further increased by the hierarchy of academic ranks (compared by some of our male participants to an army) and 'academic oligarchy'. Academic oligarchy, a prevalent form of academic governance at Czech universities (Dobbins and Knill 2009), is defined by the strong autonomy of academics in university governance, with relatively little control by external actors, such as the state or businesses. While autonomy in academic governance is generally positive, it also gives considerable power to those academics in managerial positions and, relatedly, entails risks of their abuse of power. Interviews with participants suggested, in line with this, that supervisory bullying was used to maintain university power structures, "seeking to keep lower power individuals 'in their place' " (Jacobson *et al.* 2014, p. 58). Targets of bullying in our study included doctoral candidates who were bullied when their publications began to be more prestigious than those of their supervisors, thus transgressing the formal asymmetry. Other participants told stories of being bullied by department chairs when they were perceived as having leadership ambitions which posed a threat to the power held by their superiors.

While the enactors of bullying in Czech academia are typically senior academics, targets are mostly newly employed, young academics in junior positions. In fact, being young and/or newly employed were the two most significant factors in predicting victimisation in our study (Zábrodská and Květon 2013). This finding can be again linked to the relatively high power distance in Czech organisations, intensified by the hierarchical structures of the university. Additionally, our study findings support those of Danis *et al.* (2011), who found that pre- and post-transition generations of Czech employees had been socialised into profoundly different workplace cultures which created an inter-generational split in work values and practices. Several studies have noted a gap between pre-transition preferences for autocratic leadership, instrumentalism, and self-interest, and post-transition tendencies towards egalitarianism, openness to change, and self-enhancement (Reber *et al.* 2004, Danis *et al.* 2011, Borgulya and Hahn 2013). This inter-generational conflict was prominent in our interviews with young bullied academics who described their expectations for a democratic, transparent, performance-based management style as clashing with their superiors' actual management style, which was based on autocratic behaviour and "old boys' networks". Resisting these managerial practices ultimately led, these young academics believed, to their bullying and expulsion.

Cultural characteristics of Czech society, namely relatively high in-group collectivism and low institutional collectivism, also play a role in bullying in Czech academia. An in-group mentality is enhanced, particularly in the humanities and social sciences fields, by the fact that many academics spend most of their career at a single institution, causing members to perceive themselves as family. While this can contribute to a positive work environment and culture of collegiality, rigid social norms may also develop, with newcomers or innovators easily becoming targets of bullying. In one instance, an assistant professor was bullied after being hired as the only 'outsider' in a small department in which all other faculty had been university schoolmates and were close friends. In another instance, a number of participants were bullied when they returned to Czech academia after holding academic positions abroad. These academics reported a strong in-group ethos into which they were unable (and unwilling) to integrate. The bullying of out-group members is further enhanced by the culture of informality discussed above. Most targets in our study reported an absence of vital institutional rules and procedures in their departments, such as job descriptions, career plans, salary and remuneration plans, or examinations requirements for doctoral courses. This appears to reflect the low levels of professionalism of some departments, as well as the common cultural practice of informally negotiating employment issues based on specific circumstances and individual employee status. Because such negotiations are neither impartial nor transparent, the culture of informality allows for discrimination and bullying of those perceived as members of an out-group.

Finally, workplace bullying in Czech academia is affected by the absence of effective organisational policies to address workplace abuse. In our survey, the prevalent responses to bullying were informal discussions with colleagues and friends. By contrast, formal responses were rare; only 1.7 per cent of the bullied participants lodged a formal grievance (Zábrodská and Květon 2013). This reflects the fact that most universities have neither formal nor informal mechanisms to address workplace bullying (such as grievance mechanisms or ombudsman's offices), nor are there officials appointed to deal with workplace abuse complaints. Targeted academics in our study were reportedly unable to identify personnel responsible for bullying concerns, apart from their superiors who, however, were typically the instigators of the bullying. Additionally, some targets voiced scepticism about the effectiveness of institutional procedures, if these were available. They did not believe that civility could be formally enforceable and were distrustful of the procedures, as these were, they believed, controlled by powerful alliances of which the instigators were members. In this institutional and discursive context, participants typically perceived exit as the only viable solution.

Practical implications

Effective policies concerning workplace abuse, we believe, should respect the specificity of national and organisational cultures (see also Jacobson *et al.* 2014). Therefore, recommendations for organisations in the Czech Republic primarily require more workplace abuse research across the country to identify concerns specific to particular industries. For instance, our research in Czech academia indicated a need for specific preventative measures, such as mentoring programs for junior academics and the integration of the newly employed (Zábrodská and Květon 2013). There is little doubt, though, that Czech organisations in general would benefit from two types of action. First, organisations should provide employee awareness training to increase employee understanding of what constitutes workplace abuse. Among those bullied in Czech academia, for instance, many were unaware of the concept of workplace bullying until they had been targeted for extended periods of time. Second, Czech organisations should implement organisational policies and appoint officials responsible for handling complaints. Lacking such policies and procedures, organisations currently spend substantial time and resources dealing afresh with each case, as the authors have observed in Czech academia. By implementing explicit procedures, organisations can create a more transparent and structured space from which all parties in a conflict can benefit.

At the same time, it is interesting to speculate how Czech employees might respond to more robust policies and legislation for managing all forms of workplace abuse, given the country's history and cultural profile. In contrast to universalist countries, such as the U.S., the particularism of Czech society implies preferences for informal, flexible, and person-controlled responses to abuse at work, rather than formal procedures or legislation. In discussions on sexual harassment legislation, for instance, its opponents argued that it was incompatible with Czech views of morality and would be undermined by everyday practice (True 2003). Additionally, given the negative experience of Czechs with state power and state-enforced policies during the communist era, some Czechs may perceive formal policies as a threat to their autonomy at work, something that has clearly manifested in the sexual harassment debates. While we do not suggest that this should obviate the implementation of workplace abuse policies, it is plausible that these factors make Czech employees more reserved towards formal policies. Therefore, organisation-specific procedures characterised by informality and flexibility, such as an organisational ombudsman, are likely to be more acceptable and effective in the Czech context.

Notes

1 Acknowledgement: This work was supported by the Czech Science Foundation (GA14–02098S) and a Fulbright-Masaryk scholarship awarded to the first author. The Fulbright-Masaryk scholarship generously funded the first author's research stay at the University of North Carolina at Chapel Hill (UNC-CH), thus providing access to scholarly resources about the Czech society, many of which, ironically, are unavailable in the Czech Republic. The authors would also like to thank Martina Baker-Klicperová, Kateřina Machovcová, Libora Oates-Indruchová, Josef Švéda, and Marta Vohlídalová for their helpful suggestions on an earlier version of the chapter, and Constance Ellwood for editing the chapter.
2 This figure includes both Czechs and Moravians, the latter being an ethnic group from Moravia, a region of the Czech Republic.
3 The severity of the persecution varied in the different phases of communist rule, which in Czechoslovakia is typically divided into five phases: Stalinism, de-Stalinisation, thaw, Prague Spring and normalisation (Havelková and Oates-Indruchová 2014). The most brutal persecutions took place during the Stalinist period (1948–1953), during which many of the regime's opponents were executed or died as a consequence of imprisonment or incarceration in labour camps (Myck and Bohacek 2011).
4 Originally, the Czech Republic was included in the GLOBE project (House *et al.* 2004), but data were later excluded due to systematic bias (Gupta and Hanges 2004).
5 The authors here use "relatively" because, in comparison with EE post-communist countries, corruption in the Czech Republic is relatively low, which is true of all CEE countries (Holmes 2013). Corruption in the Czech Republic is high compared to Western European standards, however.
6 Other workplace abuse concepts, such as workplace violence, have been also recognised (e.g., Chromý 2014), but the published research in this area so far remains limited.
7 The term 'mobbing' is used, for instance, by the Czech Social Security Administration (www.cssz.cz/en/about-cssa/) and the "Anti-Mobbing Club" (http://anti-mobbing-club.cz), the latter being the first expert group on workplace bullying/mobbing in the Czech Republic.
8 "Psychical terror or mobbing in working life means hostile and unethical communication which is directed in a systematic way by one or a number of persons mainly toward one individual" (Leymann 1990, p. 120).
9 Given that the concept of workplace abuse has been recognised only recently in the Czech Republic, many Czech organisations lack workplace abuse policies and grievance procedures.

References

Aligica, P.D., and Evans, A.J., 2009. *The neoliberal revolution in Eastern Europe: Economic ideas in the transition from communism.* Cheltenham: Edward Elgar Publishing.

Amnesty International, 2014. *EU action against Czech Republic for discrimination in schools is a victory for rights, justice, and Roma.* Available from: www.amnesty. org/en/news/eu-action-against-czech-republic-discrimination-schools-victory-rights-justice-and-roma-2014-09.

Bártlová, S., and Hajduchová, H., 2009. Šikana a sexuální obtěžování na pracovišti z pohledu lékařů a sester. *Prevence úrazů, otrav a násilí,* 5, 128–39.

Borgulya, A., and Hahn, J., 2013. Changes in the importance of work-related values in Central and Eastern Europe: Slovenia and Hungary against the trend? *Journal of Arts and Humanities,* 2 (10), 24–36.

Braun, V., and Clarke, V., 2006. Using thematic analysis in psychology. *Qualitative research in psychology,* 3 (2), 77–101.

Canaan, J.E., and Shumar, W., 2008. *Structure and agency in the neoliberal university.* London: Routledge.

Čech, T., 2011. *Mobbing jako negativní fenomén v prostředí základních škol.* Brno: Masarykova univerzita.

Chromý, J., 2014. *Násilí na pracovišti.* Praha: Wolters Kluwer.

Czech Statistical Office (various years). Statistical yearbook for the Czech Republic. Available from: www.czso.cz/eng/redakce.nsf/i/home.

Danis, W.M., Liu, L.A., and Vacek, J., 2011. Values and upward influence strategies in transition: Evidence from the Czech Republic. *Journal of Cross-Cultural Psychology,* 42 (2), 288–306.

Dobbins, M., and Knill, C., 2009. Higher education policies in Central and Eastern Europe: Convergence toward a common model? *Governance,* 22, 397–430.

Einarsen, S., Hoel, H., and Notelaers, G., 2009. Measuring exposure to bullying and harassment at work: Validity, factor structure and psychometric properties of the Negative Acts Questionnaire-Revised. *Work & Stress,* 23 (1), 24–44.

Escartín, J., Zapf, D., Arrieta, C., and Rodriguez-Carballeira, A., 2011. Workers' perception of workplace bullying: A cross-cultural study. *European Journal of Work and Organizational Psychology,* 20 (2), 178–205.

EU-OSHA. European Agency for Safety and Health at Work, 2010. *Workplace violence and harassment: A European picture.* European Risk Observatory Report. Luxembourg: Publication Office for the European Union. Available from: https://osha.europa.eu/en/publications/reports/violence-harassment-TERO09010ENC.

European Commission, 2014. *Czech Republic: Country profile.* Available from: http://ec.europa.eu/enlargement/archives/enlargement_process/past_enlargements/eu10/czech_republic_en.htm.

European Working Conditions Survey, 2010. *Subjected to bullying or harassment at work.* Available from: www.eurofound.europa.eu/surveys/data-visualisation/european-working-conditions-survey-2010.

Eurostat, 2015. *Unemployment rates, seasonally adjusted, May 2015.* Available from: http://ec.europa.eu/eurostat/statistics-explained/index.php/Unemployment_statistics.

Fasting, K., Chroni, S., Hervik, S.E., and Knorre, N., 2011. Sexual harassment in sport toward females in three European countries. *International Review for the Sociology of Sport,* 46 (1), 76–89.

Gannon, M. J., and Pillai, R., 2013. *Understanding global cultures: Metaphorical journeys through 31 nationals, clusters of nations, continents, and diversity.* 5th ed. Thousand Oaks: Sage.

Gelfand, M., Bhawuk, D.P.S., Nishii, L. H., and Bechtold, D. J., 2004. Individualism and collectivism. *In:* R. J. House, P. J. Hanges, M. Javidan, P. W. Dorfman, and V. Gupta, eds., *Culture, leadership, and organizations: The GLOBE study of 62 societies.* Thousand Oaks: Sage, 437–512.

Glassner, V., 2013. Central and eastern European industrial relations in the crisis: National divergence and path-dependent change. *Transfer: European Review of Labour and Research,* 19 (2), 155–69.

Gupta, V., and Hanges, P. J., 2004. Regional and climate clustering of societal cultures. *In:* R. J. House, P. J. Hanges, M. Javidan, P. W. Dorfman, and V. Gupta, eds., *Culture, leadership, and organizations: The GLOBE study of 62 societies.* Thousand Oaks: Sage, 178–218.

Harsa, P., Macák, M. M., Kertészová, M. D., Chrenková, M. P., Michalec, M. J., Nechanická, M. N., Krupníková, H., and Bačkovská, M. S., 2014. Mobbing – vážné potíže v pracovním soužití s důrazem na problémy ve zdravotnickém prostředí. *Psychiatrická prax,* 15 (3), 110–13.

Havelková, H., and Oates-Indruchová, L., 2014. Expropriated voice: Transformation of gender culture under state socialism; Czech society, 1949–89. *In:* H. Havelková and L. Oates-Indruchová, eds., *The politics of gender culture under state socialism: An expropriated voice.* London: Routledge, 3–28.

Hilpert, U., and Smith, H. L., 2012. *Networking regionalised innovative labour markets.* New York: Routledge.

Hofstede, G., and Hofstede, G. J., 2005. *Cultures and organizations. Software of the mind.* New York: McGraw-Hill.

Hofstede Center, 2015. National cultural dimensions. Available from: http://geerthofstede.com/national-culture.html.

Holmes, L., 2013. Postcommunist transitions and corruption: Mapping patterns. *Social Research: An International Quarterly,* 80 (4), 1163–86.

House, R. J., Hanges, P. J., Javidan, M., Dorfman, P. W., and Gupta, V. (eds.), 2004. *Culture, leadership and organisations: The GLOBE study of 62 societies.* Thousand Oaks: Sage.

Human Development Reports, 2014. Czech Republic. Available from: http://hdr.undp.org/en/countries/profiles/CZE.

Jacobson, K. J., Hood, J. N. and Van Buren, H. J., 2014. Workplace bullying across cultures: A research agenda. *International Journal of Cross Cultural Management,* 14 (1), 47–65. Online First.

Klicperová-Baker, M., 2008. Education for citizenship and democracy: The case of the Czech Republic. *In:* J. Arthur, I. Davies, and C. Hahn, eds., *SAGE handbook of education for citizenship and democracy.* London: Sage, 158–74.

Klicperová-Baker, M., and Košťál, J., 2015. Non-democratic character in post-totalitarian societies and the "bad mood" or "blah mood" phenomenon. Presentation for the *Annual Meeting of the International Society of Political Psychology.* Omni, San Diego, July 3–6.

Kolářová, K., Pavlík, P., and Smetáčková, I., 2009. *Co je sexuální obtěžování a jak se mu bránit. Příručka pro studující vysokých škol.* Prague: Faculty of Humanities, Charles University in Prague.

Komárek, S., and Havlíček, J., 2010. Manuál moderního inkvizitora. *Hospodářské noviny*, 54 (35), 10.

Křížková, A., Maříková, H., and Uhde, Z., 2006. *Sexualizovaná realita pracovních vztahů. Analýza sexuálního obtěžování v České republice.* Praha: Sociologický ústav AV ČR.

Lee, A. S., and Trappmann, V., 2014. Overcoming post-communist labour weakness: Attritional and enabling effects of multinationals in Central and Eastern Europe. *European Journal of Industrial Relations*, 20, 113–29.

Leymann, H., 1990. Mobbing and psychological terror at workplaces. *Violence and Victims*, 5 (2), 119–26.

Montgomery, A., 2013. Culture and change in developing Western countries. *In:* H. S. Leonard, R. Lewis, A. M. Freedman, and J. Passmore, eds., *The Wiley-Blackwell handbook of the psychology of leadership, change, and organizational Development*, 357–77. Chichester: John Wiley & Sons. Available from: anthonyjmontgomery.com.

Myck, M., and Bohacek, R., 2011. Long shadows of history: Persecution in Central Europe and its labor market consequences. *IZA Working Paper 6130*, Institute for the Study of Labor (IZA).

Niedhammer, I., Sultan-Taïeb, H., Chastang, J. F., Vermeylen, G., and Parent-Thirion, A., 2012. Exposure to psychosocial work factors in 31 European countries. *Occupational Medicine*, 62 (3), 196–202.

Nielsen, M. B., Skogstad, A., Matthiesen, S. B., Glasø, L., Aasland, M. S., Notelaers, G., and Einarsen, S., 2009. Prevalence of workplace bullying in Norway: Comparisons across time and estimation methods. *European Journal of Work and Organizational Psychology*, 18 (1), 81–101.

OECD, 2014. Organisation for cooperation and development. Better life index. Available from: www.oecdbetterlifeindex.org/countries/czech-republic/.

Reber, G., Auer-Rizzi, W., and Malý, M., 2004. The behaviour of managers in Austria and the Czech Republic: An intercultural comparison based on the Vroom/Yetton model of leadership and decision making. *Journal for East European Management Studies*, 9 (4), 411–29.

Salin, D., 2001. Prevalence and forms of bullying among business professionals: A comparison of two different strategies for measuring bullying. *European Journal of Work and Organizational Psychology*, 10, 425–41.

Schwartz, S. H., 2014. National culture as value orientations: Consequences of value differences and cultural distance. *In:* V. A. Ginsburgh and D. Throsby, eds., *Handbook of the Economics of Art and Culture*. North Holland: Elsevier, 547–86.

Schwartz, S. H., and Bardi, A., 1997. Influences of adaptation to communist rule on value priorities in Eastern Europe. *Political Psychology*, 18 (2), 385–410.

Smetáčková, I., and Pavlík, P., 2011. Sexuální obtěžování na vysokých školách: Teoretické vymezení, metodologický přístup, výzkumné výsledky. *Sociologický časopis*, 47 (2), 361–87.

Smith, M. L., 2010. Perceived corruption, distributive justice, and the legitimacy of the system of social stratification in the Czech Republic. *Communist and Post-Communist Studies*, 43 (4), 439–51.

Smith, P. B., Dugan, S., and Trompenaars, F., 1996. National culture and the values of organizational employees. *Journal of Cross-Cultural Psychology*, 27 (2), 231–64.

Šolcová, I., 1995. Šikanování v zaměstnání: úvod do problému. *Československá psychologie*, 39 (5), 440–3.

Soulsby, A., and Clark, E., 1996. The emergence of post-communist management in the Czech Republic. *Organization Studies*, 17 (2), 227–47.

Stöckelová, T., and Slačálek, O., 2010. Studentky, co nosí v kabelce zrní. *A2* 6 (8), 38. Available from: www.advojka.cz/archiv/2010/8/studentky-co-nosi-v-kabelce-zrni.

Suutari, V., and Riusala, K., 2001. Leadership styles in Central Eastern Europe: Experiences of Finnish expatriates in the Czech Republic, Hungary and Poland. *Scandinavian Journal of Management*, 17 (2), 249–80.

The Public Defender Office of the Czech Republic, 2015. Emotional abuse at work: Mobbing, bossing and discrimination. Available from: www.ochrance.cz/en/complaints-about-authorities/do-you-wish-to-complain/problems-and-their-solution/emotional-abuse-at-work-mobbing-bossing-a-discrimination/.

Transparency International, 2014. Corruption by country: Czech Republic. Available from: www.transparency.org/country#CZE.

Trompenaars, F., and Hampden-Turner, C., 2012. *Riding the waves of culture: Understanding diversity in global business*. 3rd ed. London: Nicholas Brealey Publishing.

True, J., 2003. *Gender, globalization, and postsocialism: The Czech Republic after communism*. New York: Columbia University Press.

Twale, D. J., and De Luca, B. M., 2008. *Faculty incivility. The rise of the academic bully culture and what to do about it*. San Francisco: Jossey-Bass. A Wiley Imprint.

Vartia-Väänänen, M., 2013. Workplace bullying and harassment in the EU and Finland. *In:* K. Sugeno, ed., *Workplace bullying and harassment*. Tokyo: The Japan Institute for Labour Policy and Training, 1–22.

Vitková, M., and Zábrodská, K., 2014. Coping a rezistencia voci mobbingu v kontexte paradigmatického přístupu. *Československá Psychologie*, 58 (3), 254–69.

Vohlídalová, M., 2011. The perception and construction of sexual harassment by Czech university students. *Czech Sociological Review*, 47 (6), 1119–47.

Wagnerová, I., Hoskovcová-Horáková, S., Šírová-Bidlová, E., Kmoníčková, J., and Baarová, E., 2011. *Psychologie práce a organizace*. Praha: Grada.

Woolfson, C., 2006. Working environment and "soft law" in the post-communist New Member States. *JCMS: Journal of Common Market Studies*, 44 (1), 195–215.

Zábrodská, K., 2010. Agency and resistance to change in Czech public discourse: Examples from research on gender identity and gender-related bullying. Presentation for the *Psychology of Women Section Annual Conference*, BPS, Windsor, UK, July 14–16.

Zábrodská, K., 2011. Mobbing ve vysokoškolském prostředí: zkušenosti ze zahraničního výzkumu. *Československá psychologie*, 55 (4), 333–45.

Zábrodská, K., 2012. Forms of resistance to workplace bullying. Presentation for the *8th International Conference on Workplace Bullying and Harassment*, University of Copenhagen, Denmark, June 12–15.

Zábrodská, K., Linnell, S., Laws, C., and Davies, B., 2011. Bullying as intra-active process in neoliberal universities. *Qualitative Inquiry*, 17 (8), 709–19.

Zábrodská, K., and Květon, P., 2012. Šikana na pracovišti v prostředí českých univerzit: výskyt, formy a organizační souvislosti. *Sociologický časopis*, 48 (4), 641–68.

Zábrodská, K., and Květon, P., 2013. Prevalence and forms of workplace bullying among university employees. *Employee Responsibilities and Rights Journal*, 25 (2), 89–108.

10 Merlion

The influence of Singapore's cosmopolitan culture on workplace incivility

Jennifer (M.I.) Loh

Introduction

This chapter provides a picture of workplace incivility in Singapore. Most of the research conducted to date on workplace incivility has been in Western countries; there is a dearth of research in this area in Singapore. To overcome this challenge, the author will draw on her own knowledge of Singapore and her experience of the Singaporean workplace to enrich the narrative. The author grew up and attended primary and secondary schools in Singapore and has worked in a variety of private and public industries (e.g., shipping, sales and marketing, hospital, and tertiary institutions). It is acknowledged that while personal experiences may be perceived as subjective and interpretive, it is nonetheless important to recognise the role these play in the development of scientific knowledge (Kuhn 1970, Feyerabend 1981). Empirical studies conducted by researchers including the author on workplace incivility in Singapore are complemented by this personal perspective.

Workplace incivility

In recent years, workplace incivility has received much attention from organisational researchers (Andersson and Pearson 1999, Lim and Cortina 2005). The term has been defined as "low-intensity, disrespectful or rude deviant workplace behaviour with ambiguous intent to harm the target and is in violation of workplace norms for mutual respect" (Andersson and Pearson 1999, p. 457), characterised by rudeness and disregard for another's dignity (Kane and Montgomery 1998). These behaviours can include not saying thank you, rolling one's eyes at co-workers' suggestions, making derogatory comments, and ignoring or insulting colleagues (Pearson and Porath 2009).

Workplace incivility operates as a means of asserting social power (French and Raven 1959, Cortina *et al.* 2001), defined as the measure of influence an individual is able to assert over other people or outcomes (French and Raven 1959). Salin (2003) argued that workplace mistreatments such as bullying, harassment and incivility are unavoidable because power imbalances occur in organisations throughout the world. Cortina (2008) and Kabat-Farr and Cortina (2012) posit that incivility evolves out of old-fashioned discriminatory behaviours. Selective incivilities are evolved behaviours (e.g., sexism, racism) which have become more subtle and ambiguous in nature as a reaction to modern political correctness (Cortina 2008, Kabat-Farr and Cortina 2012). For example, instead of being blatantly racist or sexist towards a subordinate, a superior may undermine the credibility of the subordinate by ignoring any suggestion they may have, in front of others. Consequently, these behaviours may be misinterpreted by others as simply rude or discourteous.

Social Power and Selective Incivility theories provide an explanation as to why workplace incivility occurs in Western cultures; however, they do not adequately explain how the behaviour may be perceived or defined in the East. An understanding of incivility in Singapore is critical due to differences between Western and Eastern workplace cultures (Triandis 1994, Hofstede 2001). Culture may be described as representing a shared system of norms that guides beliefs, feelings and behaviours (Markus and Kitayama 1991). Perceived this way, culture plays a key role in regulating all human behaviours, including workplace incivility. This chapter sets out to examine whether certain cultural features (e.g., collectivism, Confucianism, power distance) make incivility more accepted in Singaporean workplaces. Furthermore, given the increased cultural exchanges between East and West, knowledge of workplace incivility is vital to help employers and employees better understand their workplaces (Pearson *et al.* 2000). Before discussing these cultural influences, the impact and prevalence of workplace incivility are discussed.

Prevalence of workplace incivility in the West

Evidence suggests that workplace incivility is on the rise and that it is a common occurrence in work settings in many developed countries including the US and Canada (Pearson and Porath 2009, Trudel 2009). For example, half of a sample of 125 white collar employees polled in Canada reported that they had experienced incivility from their co-workers at least once a week, and 99 per cent of these respondents had witnessed incivility in their workplace (Pearson and Porath 2004, Pearson and Porath 2009). In the Civility in America 2011 study, 43 per cent of respondents reported that they had experienced incivility at work, 38 per cent said the workplace is becoming more uncivil compared to a few years ago, 86 per cent said they are victims of incivility, and at the same time 59 per cent admitted that they have also been uncivil. These studies provide important evidence to suggest that workplace incivility is a prevalent and growing problem (Trudel 2009).

Impact of workplace incivility in the West

In terms of impact, research has found a positive association between workplace incivility and negative organisational outcomes such as work withdrawal (Lim *et al.* 2008; Pearson and Porath 2009), absenteeism, reduced job satisfaction and decreased work commitment (Andersson and Pearson 1999, Cortina *et al.* 2001, Miner-Rubino and Cortina 2004, Lim and Cortina 2005; Lim *et al.* 2008, Pearson and Porath 2009). A positive association has also been found between workplace incivility and poor psychological health (e.g., anxiety, depression, insomnia, stress) among victims (Cortina *et al.* 2001, Estes and Wang 2008). More seriously, workplace incivility can be a precursor to workplace aggression and workplace violence (Andersson and Pearson 1999, Pearson *et al.* 2000).

While workplace incivility has received much attention in Canada and the US, there have been very few studies in Singapore. To date, there are no reliable Singaporean statistics on workplace incivility; only two studies have been identified that have examined workplace incivility in this context.

Workplace incivility in Singapore

In a survey across six Asian countries – China, Hong Kong, India, Japan, Korea and Singapore – Yeung and Griffin (2008) found that 77 per cent of the 116,986 respondents reported that they had experienced workplace incivility. They also found that cultures with high performance and Confucian orientations (e.g., China, Singapore) were more accepting of work-related mistreatment such as bullying and incivility. Similarly, a recent survey of 180 employees from various organisations in Singapore found that workplace incivility is common, with 91 per cent of respondents reporting that they had experienced workplace incivility in the previous five years (Lim and Lee 2011). Lim and Lee (2011) also found that employees in Singapore experienced more incivility from their supervisors than from their co-workers or subordinates. They found, however, that Singaporean participants reacted differently to workplace incivility depending on who the perpetrators were. For example, participants experienced lower supervisor satisfaction and higher work-to-family conflict when the perpetrators were their supervisors. In contrast, participants experienced reduced co-worker satisfaction, higher depression and increased perception of unfair treatment when the perpetrators were their co-workers. Findings from the above studies suggest the importance of incorporating culture when investigating workplace incivility (Escartín *et al.* 2011; Lian *et al.* 2012). The country and cultural profile of Singapore are examined next.

Singapore's country profile

Singapore is a modern cosmopolitan city located at the southern tip of the Malay Peninsula, 137 kilometres (85 miles) north of the Equator. Covering an area of only 704 square kilometres, Singapore is geographically the smallest country in Southeast Asia. Singapore's original Malay name is Singapura, which means 'lion' (Singa) and 'city' (pura) in the Sanskrit language. According to the *Malay Annals*, Singapura was named by a fourteenth-century Sumatran prince named Sang Nila Utama, who spotted a lion-like auspicious animal not long after first coming ashore. Consequently, this island became known as

Singapura or 'Lion City'. Myth or not, the name 'Lion City' (Turnbull 2009) is popular with many locals and tourists.

In addition, the Merlion – a mythical creature with the head of a lion and the body of a fish – was adopted as a corporate logo by the Singapore Tourist Promotion Board in 1964 to promote Singapore as a tourist destination from 1966 to 1997 (Yong 2011). The Merlion is now regarded as a national icon of Singapore, and as an important symbol (Lee 2004). The fish body represents Singapore's origin as a fishing village when it was called Temasek or 'sea town' in Javanese (Yong 2011). The lion head is a reference to Singapore's original name. More recently, the Merlion was incarnated as a central character in the 1997 National Day musical, 'My Singapore, Our Future', and depicted the development of Singapore from its humble beginnings to a prosperous multi-cultural cosmopolitan city (Peterson 2001).

As of June 2014, Singapore had an estimated population of 5.47 million people (Singapore Bureau of Statistics [SBS] 2014). One of Singapore's key distinguishing features is its diversity. The country is home to four main ethnic groups: Chinese (74.3 per cent), Malay (13.3 per cent), Indian (9.1 per cent) and Eurasian (3.3 per cent). Singapore is also home to at least ten religions with Buddhism (33.9 per cent), Christianity (18.1 per cent), Islam (14.3 per cent) and Hinduism (5.2 per cent) as the four principal faiths. According to the *Republic of Singapore Independence Act 1965*, Singapore has four national languages: Mandarin, English, Malay and Tamil. The literacy level is high with 95.9 per cent of the population (aged 15 and over) being able to read and write (SBS 2014). Singapore does not possess any natural resources or major manufacturing industries. Despite this, the country has one of the highest per capita Gross Domestic Product (GDP) in the world (Friel 2014). In 2014, the US based research institute for Business Environment Risk Intelligence (BERI) ranked Singapore as the city with the best investment potential (Economic Board of Development [EBD] 2014).

Brief history of Singapore

According to historians Kelly (1993) and Turnbull (2009), Singapore was probably a trading outpost and supply point for Malay, Thai, Javanese, Chinese, Indian and Arab traders in the sixteenth century. It had a small population and was ruled by a succession of local emperors and Malayan sultans. Modern Singapore was founded by Sir Stamford Raffles in 1819 and became one of the British Straits Settlements in 1826. During World War II, Singapore was occupied by the Japanese (1942–1945) and reverted back to British control after the war. The country became independent from the United Kingdom and merged with the Federation of Malaya to form Malaysia in 1963. On 9th August 1965, social unrest and ethnic conflict led Singapore's ruling party, the People's Action Party (PAP), to separate Singapore from Malaysia to become an independent republic. Since then, the government and citizens have sought to maintain a culture built on high collectivism, Confucianism and cooperation amid great ethnic diversity (Gannon and Pillai 2010). The Singapore Government (1991) identifies that these cultural characteristics complement the national values of respect, tolerance and cooperation (Tan 2012) and are instrumental in shaping how many Singaporeans feel, think and behave.

Singapore's cultural profile

Culture refers to a set of ideas, behaviours, attitudes and traditions that exist within large groups and distinguish members of one group from another (Hofstede 1980; see also Omari and Sharma this volume). Culture is important as it not only guides the ethos of how 'things are done', but it also affects how people think and feel. According to Hofstede's cultural framework (The Hofstede Center n.d.), Singapore is classified as being collectivistic, high on power distance, low in uncertainty avoidance, moderately masculine and high in Confucianism. Hofstede's cultural framework complements research by Triandis and colleagues on individualism/collectivism and allocentrism/idiocentrism (Singelis *et al.* 1995, Triandis 1995). According to this cultural orientation, Singaporeans are said to have a vertical collectivist orientation where they emphasise hierarchy, and accept social order and inequality among individuals.

Collectivism

As a collectivist society, Singaporeans tend to prioritise group needs over personal needs. Individuals are integrated from birth into strong, cohesive in-groups which provide them with life-long protection (Hofstede 1991). Consequently, collectivism imposes certain expectations and obligations on individuals, such as deference and cooperation toward leaders (Hui and Triandis 1986, Hofstede 2001, Gannon and Pillai 2010). The problem many Singaporeans face today is an inability to critically evaluate an issue when in-groups are involved. The influence of in-groups is so strong that decisions usually revolve around in-group norms. Coupled with Singaporeans' passive-avoidant style of handling conflict and high vertical collectivism (Leung 1988, Triandis 1995, Yuen 1998), many workplace mistreatment issues are hidden away. For instance, during a recent academic trip to Singapore, the author spoke with a number of colleagues about whether any of them have experienced workplace incivility or workplace bullying. The responses were a resounding *yes* for both workplace bullying and workplace incivility. More importantly, many of the respondents believed that there is nothing they can do about workplace mistreatments, because they are an inherent part of the workplace culture in Singapore. As one colleague stated, "Why bother? If you bring the issue up, it will simply get swept under the carpet. This is how we [Singaporeans] handle conflict."

Power distance

Power distance refers to individuals' acceptance of the unequal distribution of power in societies and institutions (Hofstede 1991, 2001). Chinese Singaporeans are expected to know their place in a hierarchical social structure and respect those in authority (Loh *et al.* 2010). Relationships between superiors and subordinates are characterised by deference and formality. Elders in the community are to be treated with respect, care and consideration, as are superiors. This cultural dimension operationalises one of the key Confucian teachings, which advocates the importance of maintaining five basic relationships among people: emperor–subject; father–son; older brother–younger brother; husband–wife; and senior friend–junior friend (Waley 1938). Each of these relationships has its own rules and obligations. The Malays in Singapore also follow a strict code of conduct based on the *Adat Resam* or the Malay Customary Code of Conduct. Malay children and young adults are expected to obey their parents, elders and authoritative individuals. Similarly, Indian Singaporeans are expected to obey and respect their parents and elders. They also have to display respectful behaviour such as not shouting or talking too loudly when an elder is in the room. There is a level of uniformity across these different cultures with respect to behaviour towards elders and superiors.

Uncertainty avoidance

Singapore scores very low on the uncertainty avoidance dimension. Uncertainty avoidance indicates the "extent to which a society feels threatened by uncertain and ambiguous situations, and avoids these by providing greater career stability, establishing more formal rules, not tolerating deviant ideas and behaviours, and believing in absolute truths and the attainment of expertise" (Hofstede 1991, p. 45). Singapore is a rule-based society, not because of a lack of structure but because of high power distance – respect and acceptance for differential social power and authorities. Consequently, model Singaporeans of all ethnicities are expected to abide by the rules, laws and regulations ascribed to them by various institutions, agencies and authorities.

Assertiveness (masculinity)

Singapore scores moderately on the masculinity dimension. In other words, values such as modesty, sympathy, self-restraint and social harmony are strongly advocated by all the cultures in Singapore. This leads to actions in the workplace such as burying conflict in the interests of peace, and individuals not asserting their position in the interest of harmony.

Long versus short term orientation (Confucian dynamism)

Initially called Confucian dynamism by Hofstede and Bond (1988), long term versus short term orientation refers to the willingness to accept legitimate hierarchies, traditional and social obligations, as well as to preserve values such as perseverance, thrift, status and modesty (Hofstede 1991). One of the tenets of this cultural dimension is the need to be disciplined, efficient and productive. Singapore scores high on this dimension; the need for efficiency in the workplace can at times comes across as being uncivil or rude.

Indulgence versus restraint

The dimension of indulgence versus restraint relates to the extent to which people try to control their desires and impulses as they enjoy life (Hofstede *et al.* 2010); Singapore scores medium on this dimension. According to Gannon and Pillai (2010), the lives of Singaporeans revolve around work and there is hardly any time for leisure. This has created what one scholar referred to as work-life imbalance (Lim 2010). Consequently, many Singaporeans feel *rush* or stressed in their daily lives (Lim 2010).

As previously discussed, modern Singaporean society is an amalgamation of Asian and European cultures, influenced heavily by British, South and East Asian cultures (Turnbull 2009, Ti and Ti 2012); a cosmopolitan and multicultural city based on an ideology of racial and religious harmony. Gannon and Pillai (2010) use the metaphor "Hawker Centers" to describe Singapore and its culture. Hawker centres, which sell a variety of inexpensive cooked food, are places where Singaporeans from diverse ethnic backgrounds meet to eat, sit and talk to one another. An interesting feature of hawker centres is the ability for many stall owners to cooperate with one another even as they compete for customers (Gannon and Pillai 2010). This ethos encapsulates Singapore's national ideology of cooperation amidst great diversity.

Singaporeans are generally known to be kind, respectful, orderly, inquisitive, efficient and friendly. They can, however, also be competitive and territorial. Gannon and Pillai (2010) state that Singaporeans are competitive collectivists who can be paradoxically courteous and rude. For example, many Singaporeans will go out of their way to help a lost tourist, but they can also behave in a selfish or rude manner. The author experienced this on a train trip to Orchard Road, one of the main shopping districts in Singapore. Many of the passengers on a train pretended to sleep while sitting on reserved seating; however, they would miraculously 'wake up' when the train arrived at their destination stop.

Gannon and Pillai (2010) identified a Singaporean attitude called *Kiasu*. This refers to a grasping and selfish attitude where one is afraid of losing out (Oxford Dictionary n.d.). For example, piling up plates with food from a buffet or placing some inanimate object (e.g., packet of tissues or umbrella) on a seat to prevent other people from sitting on it. Another example relates to social hierarchy and status which also play an important role in the lives of many Singaporeans regardless of ethnicity: many Singaporeans jokingly refer to their desires for the 'five cs': car, condominium, credit card, club membership and career, important symbols of wealth and status.

The Singaporean workplace culture

The Singaporean workplace reflects the aforementioned complexities of its citizens. It is common to have multi-national, multi-cultural and multi-religion work places, especially in big corporations. Despite the influence of Western work cultures, workplaces in Singapore are dominated by traditional sociocultural patterns. Workplaces are generally fast, and for most, official working hours are 44 hours per week. Employees are scheduled to start work at 8 a.m. and finish at 5 p.m.; however, it is common for employees to spend an extra hour or so at work after close of business. Official communications are conducted mostly in English, although it is common to find Chinese workers using Mandarin, Malay workers using Malay, and Indian workers using Tamil in their communications with each other.

Work place relationships are generally professional in nature and it is uncommon for co-workers to socialise after work hours. People are friendly towards each other and many identify and cooperate with members from their company or from their in-group (Loh *et al.* 2010). Most traditional workplaces have strict hierarchical structures where employees are expected to accept the legitimate authority of supervisors. For instance, subordinates are expected to obey their superiors, and upward feedback is not welcome unless requested (Connor 1996). Despite the hierarchy, decisions in the workplace are usually reached by group consensus, and cooperation amongst group members is strongly encouraged to promote group harmony.

'Face – 臉, *liǎn*' and '*guanxi* – 关系' are important concepts in the Singaporean workplace. 'Face' can be conceptualised as a person's dignity, pride or social standing and is particularly important in hierarchical relationships (Ho 1976, Leung and Chan 2001). In Singapore, it is important to preserve one's face and that of others. For example, a subordinate must never openly point out his or her superior's mistakes, as this will cause the supervisor to lose 'face'. Subordinates are expected to accept and tolerate superior's misbehaviour even if it borders on being abusive. In addition to 'face', networking and personal relationships are vital in the Singaporean workplace. From a business perspective, *guanxi* can be conceptualised as a network of mutually beneficial relationships used to support personal and business agendas (Wang 2005; Wong *et al.* 2010). *Guanxi* entails mutual trust in exchange for favours, patience, respect, reciprocity and reliance (Wang 2005). More importantly, long-term reciprocity is central to the concept of g*uanxi* and can often replace conventional obligations. *Guanxi* is vital in the Singaporean workplace and it extends to all its citizens, including Chinese, Malay and Indian Singaporean workers.

When it comes to communication, Singapore falls within the high-context countries of Hall's taxonomy (Hall 1976). Singaporeans tend to use implicit communication styles (Hall 1976, Gudykunst and Nishida 1994), and this occurs when most of the information is contained in the physical context or internalised in the person. In contrast, explicit communication occurs when most of the information is expressed explicitly in a non-coded manner (Hall 1976). In the context of the Singaporean workplace, facial expression, tone of voice, silence, pause and posture are important non-verbal cues of communication. Singaporeans also tend to be subtle, indirect and implicit in their communication style. For example, rather than saying 'no', Singaporeans might say, 'I will see what I can do' or 'I will think about it.' They can also become curt in their communication. For example, individuals can actively discourage meaningless conversation (Gannon and Pillai 2010) especially when the response can be answered with a simple 'yes' or 'no'. The author had an experience of this during a visit to a hawker stall. She was in the midst of trying to order some food but was cut off by the stall owner and asked to indicate whether she would like lunch set A, B or C. The stall owner did not intend to be rude, he was simply seeking a quick response. Outsiders who are unaware of this communication style may find this exchange rude or uncivil.

Singaporeans are uncomfortable with conflict as they live in a culture dominated by the need to be consensual and harmonious (Leung 1988, Yuen 1998). As in many South East Asian countries, decisions on how best to resolve conflicts generally reside with individuals of high status and rank (e.g., supervisor, boss). This can become problematic if superiors take advantage of their position to demand obedience from their workers. If not handled carefully, this can quickly escalate into workplace mistreatment, including abuse, incivility and bullying

What is civil or uncivil depends on the sociocultural customs in a particular cultural setting. Ferriss (2002) argued that civility or incivility is mitigated or filtered through the lens of one's culture. Culture is important as it provides a reference point for analysing the interpersonal relations in all human interactions and behaviours. This chapter concludes by highlighting the need to incorporate culture when discussing or conducting research in workplace incivility in the Singaporean context.

Workplace incivility in Singapore

Singaporeans have been brought up to accept the existence of the unequal balance of power in their society. In such a society, employees accept that in turn there is a marked power imbalance in organisations. In a cross-cultural study, Loh *et al.* (2010) found that employees in low power distance cultures (e.g., Australia) were less accepting of the power imbalances in their organisation, and reacted more negatively to workplace mistreatment than employees from high power distance cultures (e.g., Singapore). Moreover, because of the Confucian emphasis on consensus and harmony in all interactions, Singaporeans were more inclined to tolerate workplace mistreatments than individuals from other cultures; a study by Power *et al.* (2013) concurred. In this large study of six continents, Power *et al.* (2013) found that individuals in Confucian Asia displayed a tendency to be more tolerant of workplace mistreatments when compared to workers from other cultures. Similarly, Escartín *et al.* (2011) found that culture moderated the relationships between workplace mistreatments and the way in which these were tolerated. Mistreatments were more accepted in Confucian Asian countries (e.g., China, Singapore) and less accepted in Anglo or Latin American cultures.

The legitimacy of power plays an important role in regulating people's behaviour and compliance levels. For instance, Lian *et al.* (2012) also found that in high power distance settings, subordinates were more tolerant of supervisory mistreatment. Similarly, Lim and Lee (2011) found that Singaporeans continued to perceive their superiors as being fair even when they were mistreated. Salin

(2003) argues that workplace mistreatments (e.g., bullying or incivility) will continue to exist in collectivist societies as long as they are used as legitimate forms of maintaining hierarchy and order. Finally, Ferriss (2002) argued that incivility represents a covert form of discrimination in modern society which allows one group, usually the powerful majority, to control another group, usually less powerful minorities.

Conclusions and future directions

The complexities of Singapore's sociocultural dynamics and its emphasis on the importance of in-groups make the sensitive topic of workplace mistreatment or incivility a challenge to research. To date, there has been scant attention paid to incivility research in Singapore. This chapter makes an attempt to bring together research in this area using empirical evidence, including the author's own research (Loh *et al.* 2010, Lim and Lee 2011, Power *et al.* 2013) and personal work experiences in Singapore.

As discussed in this chapter, the studies from Loh *et al.* (2010), Lim and Lee (2011), and Power *et al.* (2013) highlight the importance of incorporating culture into workplace incivility research. Increased awareness may assist individuals to avoid or minimise misunderstandings that can lead to conflict escalation (Pearson *et al.* 2000). The acceptance and tolerance of workplace incivility is closely linked to the dominant culture of a society. The collectivist strict adherence to social order and acceptance of social inequality may have made workplace mistreatments more acceptable, especially between those with power and those with less, in Singapore. Indeed, a number of past studies from a range of collectivist countries have found that many of the perpetrators of workplace mistreatments are superiors who perceive these mistreatments as legitimate forms of social control and order (Bairy *et al.* 2007, Ahmer *et al.* 2009, McCormack 2009).

The challenge for managers is in promoting a fair and safe workplace while taking into consideration the traditional workplace cultures of Singapore. Rather than accepting cultural relativism, managers should recognise that workplace incivility and other forms of workplace mistreatment can have detrimental individual and organisational outcomes (Andersson and Pearson 1999, Cortina *et al.* 2001, Lim and Cortina 2005, Cortina and Magley 2009, Estes and Wang 2008, Pearson and Porath 2009). It is important to ameliorate these negative workplace behaviours. Singaporean workers, including supervisors and managers, similar to their counterparts in other parts of the world, should be educated and trained about workplace mistreatments. This increased awareness will allow Singaporeans to become more active in identifying, preventing and reporting workplace mistreatments, including incivility.

References

Ahmer, S., Yousafzai, A., Siddiqi, M., Faruqui, R., Khan, R., and Zuberi, S., 2009. Bullying of trainee psychiatrists in Pakistan: a cross sectional questionnaire survey. *Academic Psychiatry,* 33 (4), 335–9.

Andersson, L. M., and Pearson, C. M., 1999. Tit for tat: the spiraling effect of incivility in the workplace. *The Academy of Management Review*, 24 (3), 452–71.

Bairy, K., Thirumalaikolundusubramanian, P., Sivagnanam, G., Saraswathi, S., Sachidananda, A., and Shalini, A., 2007. Bullying among trainee doctors in southern India: a questionnaire survey. *Journal of Postgraduate Medicine*, 53 (2), 87–90.

Connor, U., 1996. *Contrastive rhetoric: cross cultural aspects of language writing*. New York: Cambridge University Press.

Cortina, L. M., 2008. Unseen justice: incivility as modern discrimination in organisations. *Academy of Management Review*, 33 (1), 55–75.

Cortina, L. M., and Magley, V. J., 2009. Patterns and profiles of response to incivility in organizations. *Journal of Occupational Health Psychology*, 14, 272–88.

Cortina, L. M., Magley, V. J., Williams, J. H., and Langhout, R. D., 2001. Incivility in the workplace: incidence and impact. *Journal of Occupational Health Psychology*, 6 (1), 64–80.

Economic Board of Development, 2014. *Facts and rankings* [online]. Economic Board of Development. Available from: www.edb.gov.sg/content/edb/en/why-singapore/about-singapore/facts-and-rankings/rankings.html [Accessed 23 January 2015].

Escartín, J., Zapf, D., Arrieta, C., and Rodríguez-Carballeira, A., 2011. Workers' perception of workplace bullying: a cross-cultural study. *European Journal of Work and Organisational Psychology*, 20 (2), 178–205.

Estes, B., and Wang, J., 2008. Workplace incivility: impact on individual and organisational performance. *Human Resource Development Review*, 7 (2), 218–40.

Ferriss, A. C., 2002. Studying and measuring civility: a framework, trends and scale. *Sociological Inquiry*, 72 (3), 376–92.

Feyerabend, P., 1981. How to defend society against science. *In:* I. Hacking, ed., *Scientific revolutions*. Oxford: Oxford University Press, 156–67.

French, J.R.P. Jr., and Raven, B. H., 1959. The bases of social power. *In:* D. Cartwright, ed., *Studies in social power*. Ann Arbor: Institute of Social Research, 150–67.

Friel, D., 2014. *10 countries with the highest GDP per capita in the world* [online]. Available from: www.entrepreneurhandbook.co.uk/10-countries-with-the-highest-gdp-per-capita-in-the-world/ [Accessed 23 March 2015].

Gannon, M. J., and Pillai, R., 2010. *Understanding global cultures: metaphorical journeys through 29 countries, clusters of nations, continents, and diversity*. 4th ed. Thousand Oaks: Sage.

Gudykunst, W. B., and Nishida, T., 1994. *Bridging Japanese/North American differences*. Thousand Oaks: Sage.

Hall, E., 1976. *Beyond culture*. New York: Anchor Books.

Ho, D., 1976. On the concept of face. *American Journal of Sociology*, 81 (4), 867–84.

Hofstede, G., 1980. *Culture's consequences: international differences in work related values*. Beverly Hills: Sage.

Hofstede, G., 1991. Empirical models of cultural differences. *In:* N. Bleichrodt and P.J.D. Drenth, eds., *Contemporary issues in cross-cultural psychology*. Lisse: Swets & Zeitlinger Publishers, 4–20.

Hofstede, G., 2001. *Culture's consequences: comparing values, behaviours, institutions, and organisations across nations*. Beverly Hills: Sage.

Hofstede, G., and Bond, M. H., 1988. The Confucius connection: from cultural roots to economic growth. *Organisational Dynamics*, 16 (4), 4–21.

Hofstede, G., Hofstede, G. J., and Minkov, M. 2010. *Cultures and organisations: software of the mind.* 3rd ed. New York: McGraw-Hill.

Hui, C. H., and Triandis, H. C., 1986. Individualism-collectivism: a study of cross-cultural researchers. *Journal of Cross-Cultural Psychology,* 17 (2), 225–48.

Kabat-Farr, D., and Cortina, L. M., 2012. Selective incivility: gender, race, and the discriminatory workplace. *In:* S. Fox and T. Lituchy, eds., *Gender and the dysfunctional workplace.* Northhampton: Edward Elgar Publishing, 107–19.

Kane, K., and Montgomery, K., 1998. A framework for understanding disempowermentin organisations. *Human Resource Management,* 37 (3), 263–75.

Kelly, N., 1993. *History of Malaya and South East Asia.* Singapore: Heinemann Asia.

Kuhn, T. S., 1970. *The structure of scientific revolutions.* 2nd ed. Chicago: University of Chicago Press.

Lee, P., 2004. *Singapore, tourism and me.* Singapore: Pamelia Lee Pte Ltd.

Leung, K., 1988. Some determinants of conflict avoidance. *Journal of Cross Cultural Psychology,* 19 (1), 125–36.

Leung, T.K.P., and Chan, R., 2001. Face, favour and positioning: a Chinese power game. *European Journal of Marketing,* 37 (1), 1575–98.

Lian, H. W., Ferris, D. L., and Brown, D. J., 2012. Does power distance exacerbate or mitigate the effects of abusive supervision: it depends on the outcome. *Journal of Applied Psychology,* 97 (1), 107–23.

Lim, S., and Cortina, L. M., 2005. Interpersonal mistreatment in the workplace: the interface and impact of general incivility and sexual harassment. *Journal of Applied Psychology,* 90 (3), 483–96.

Lim, S., Cortina, L. M., and Magley, V. J., 2008. Personal and workgroup incivility: impact on work and health outcomes. *Journal of Applied Psychology,* 93 (1), 95–107.

Lim, S., and Lee, A., 2011. Work and non-work outcomes of workplace incivility: does family support help? *Journal of Occupational Health Psychology,* 16 (1), 95–111.

Lim, W. D., 2010. A culture of work-life imbalance in Singapore. *New Zealand Journal of Asian Studies,* 12 (2), 22–37.

Loh, M. I., Restubog, S.L.D., and Gallois, C., 2010. Attitudinal outcomes of boundary permeability: a comparison of Australian and Singaporean employees. *Cross Cultural Management: An International Journal,* 17 (2), 118–34.

Markus, H. R., and Kitayama, S., 1991. Culture and the self: implications for cognition, emotion and motivation. *Psychological Review,* 98 (2), 224–53.

McCormack, D., Casimir, G., Djurkovic, N., and Yang, L. 2009. Workplace bullying and intention to leave among school teachers in China: the mediating effect of affective commitment. *Journal of Applied Social Psychology,* 39 (9), 2106–27.

Miner-Rubino, K., and Cortina, L. M., 2004. Working in a context of hostility toward women: implications for employees' well-being. *Journal of Occupational Health Psychology,* 9 (2), 107–22.

Oxford Dictionary, n.d. Oxford Dictionaries [online]. Kiasu. Available from: www.oxforddictionaries.com/definition/english/kiasu [Accessed 16 September 2014].

Pearson, C. M., Andersson, L. M., and Porath, C. L., 2000. Assessing and attaching workplace incivility. *Organisational Dynamics,* 29 (1), 123–37.

Pearson, C. M., and Porath, C. L., 2004. On incivility, its impact, and directions for future research. *In:* R.W. Griffin and A. O'Leary-Kelly, eds., *The dark side of organisational behaviour.* San Francisco: Jossey-Bass Wiley, 131–58.

Pearson, C. M., and Porath, C. L., 2009. *The cost of bad behaviour: how incivility ruins your business and what you can do about it.* New York: Portfolio.

Peterson, W., 2001. *Theater and the politics of culture in contemporary Singapore.* Middleton: Wesleyan University Press.

Power, J. L. *et al.*, 2013. Acceptability of workplace bullying: a comparative study on six continents. *Journal of Business Research,* 66 (3), 374–80.

Republic of Singapore Independence Act 1965 (c. 9). Available from: http://statutes. agc.gov.sg/aol/search/display/view.w3p;page=0;query=DocId%3A%222cc15e67-cf27-44b1-a736-f28ab8190454%22%20Status%3Apublished%20Depth%3A0;rec=0 [Accessed 10 March 2015].

Salin, D., 2003. Ways of explaining workplace bullying: a review of enabling, motivating and precipitating structures and processes in the work environment. *Human Relations,* 56 (10), 1213–32.

Singapore Bureau of Statistics, 2014. *Population trends 2014.* Singapore: Singapore Bureau of Statistics.

Singapore Government, 1991. *Shared values.* Singapore: Singapore National Printers.

Singelis, T. M., Triandis, H. C., Bhawuk, D.P.S., and Gelfand, M. J., 1995. Horizontal and vertical dimensions of individualism and collectivism: a theoretical and measurement refinement. *Cross-Cultural Research,* 29 (3), 240–75

Tan, C., 2012. Our shared values in Singapore: a Confucian perspective. *Education Theory,* 62 (4), 449–63.

The Hofstede Center, n.d. Singapore, Central Intelligence Agency (CIA), Washington D.C., The United States of America. Available from: www.cia.gov/library/pub lications-world-factbook/geos/sn.html [Accessed 15 December 2014].

Ti, T. K., and Ti, E., 2012. *Singapore and Asia: celebrating globalisation and an emerging postmodern Asian civilisation.* Singapore: Xlibris.

Triandis, H. C., 1994. *Culture and social behaviour.* New York: McGraw-Hill.

Triandis, H. C., 1995. *Individualism and collectivism.* Boulder: Westview Press.

Trudel, J., 2009. *Workplace incivility: relationship with conflict management styles and impact on perceived job performance, organisational commitment and turnover.* Thesis (PhD). University of Louisville.

Turnbull, C. M., 2009. *A history of modern Singapore 1819–2005.* Singapore: National University of Singapore Press.

Waley, A., 1938. *The Analects of Confucius.* New York: Macmillan Publishers.

Wang, L. C., 2005. Guanxi vs. relationship marketing: exploring underlying differences. *Industrial Marketing Management,* 36 (1), 81–6.

Wong, Y. T., Wong, S. H., and Wong, Y. W., 2010. A study of subordinate-supervisor guanxi in Chinese joint ventures. *International Journal of Human Resource Management,* 21 (2), 2142–55.

Yeung, A., and Griffin, B., 2008. Workplace incivility: does it matter in Asia? *People and Strategy,* 31 (1), 14–19.

Yong, C. Y., 2011. *The Merlion* [online]. Singapore national library board: Singapore infopedia. Available from: http://infopedia.nl.sg/articles/SIP_938_2004–12–27. html [Assessed 13 April 2015].

Yuen, C. C., 1998. Social-cultural context of perceptions and approaches to conflict: the case of Singapore. *In:* L. Leung and D. Tjosvold, eds., *Conflict management in the Asia Pacific: assumptions and approaches in diverse cultures.* Singapore: John Wiley & Sons (Asia) Pte Ltd.

11 Israel

A land of contrasts – the contribution of attachment orientation, gender and ethical climate in the workplace to abusive supervision

Efrat Salton Meyer and Mario Mikulincer

Introduction

This chapter presents a description of abusive supervision – subordinates' perceptions of supervisor's sustained display of hostile behaviours toward them (Tepper 2000). The chapter starts by depicting characteristics of Israeli life and culture, while focusing on values and norms relevant to the workplace including low power distance and a typically suspicious view of authority. It continues with a review of research concerning abusive supervision around the world and in Israel in particular. Following this brief review is a description of a study conducted in Israel exploring the contribution of attachment orientations, gender, and ethical climate to abusive supervision in a mental healthcare organisation. The findings are discussed at the intrapersonal, interpersonal, and organisational levels in the context of Israeli culture, values, and norms relevant to the healthcare sector.

As described above, the current chapter focuses on abusive supervision. This term is related to bullying in many ways – both refer to a situation where individuals in organisations perceive themselves as receiving sustained negative actions which they feel difficulty in dealing with and protecting themselves from. Both terms relate to hostility while excluding physical violence. Abusive supervision focuses only on the interaction that occurs in the dyad of subordinate and direct supervisor. In this relationship, there are power differences between the parties due to the formal authority given to the supervisor by the organisation, which, in the case of abusive supervision, is used to the detriment of subordinates. Therefore, abusive supervision is regarded as abuse that is directed hierarchically downward, whereas in bullying this is not necessarily so. In addition, intent to cause harm is not necessary in the case of abusive supervision, contrary to many views of bullying (e.g., Tepper 2007).

Israel: geography and modern history

Israel is a small, densely populated, divided democracy in a constant state of war. It is geographically located on the eastern coast of the Mediterranean; its land area is about 21,500 square kilometres (excluding Israeli settlements in

Judea and Samaria), similar in size to Slovenia or New Jersey. Its population density is relatively high: around 360 people per square kilometre of land, similar to Japan (Israel Central Bureau of Statistics 2014a).

Israel shares borders with the Arab nations of Lebanon, Syria, Jordan, and Egypt. After a UN resolution in 1947 calling for the division of the land into two states, one Jewish and one Arab, the state of Israel was declared in 1948. Since then Israel has been in an almost constant state of war with its neighbouring Arab countries, and in violent clashes within Israel in the form of uprisings by Palestinians, including guerrilla warfare and suicide bombings.

Israel is a country of migrants; many of its incoming new Jewish citizens from all over the world were motivated by Zionism: the movement aimed at creating an independent state for the Jewish people in the land of Israel, their historic homeland (Gannon and Pillai 2013). The modern form of Hebrew is the official language of the country; Arabic is also an official language. Israel is a parliamentary democracy; its many subgroups are represented by numerous political parties in the elected parliament, and the government often consists of a coalition of different political parties.

Demographics, diversity, and the workforce in Israel

In 2013 Israel's population was over 8 million, about 75 per cent of its citizens were Jewish, 20 per cent Arab, and the rest consisted of other minorities. In addition, there were about 200,000 foreign workers in the country (Israel Central Bureau of Statistics 2014b). Although Jews are the majority of Israeli citizens, the nation is composed of different ethnic and religious subgroups divided by extremely different viewpoints and lifestyles. Israel is viewed as a cleft national culture, along with countries such as Belgium and Italy (Gannon and Pillai 2013). The current chapter refers mostly to the Jewish majority.

The majority of Israeli citizens are native Israelis; however, many have families that have resided in the country for only one or two generations. One prominent source of diversity within the Jewish population is country of origin. There is a distinction between Ashkenazi Jews (immigrants from Eastern and Western Europe, America, and Australia), and Sephardic Jews (who immigrated to Israel from the Middle East, North Africa, Spain, and Portugal); each comprise about half of the Jewish population. Although many of the Sephardic Jews prospered in Israel, a large number have not and a real socio-economic gap has emerged between the two groups (Gannon and Pillai 2013).

Another important source of diversity is the level of Jewish religiousness. At one extreme, many Israelis are secular or atheistic (42 per cent) and do not participate actively in Jewish rituals. At the other extreme, there are ultra-Orthodox Jews (8 per cent) who adhere to all Jewish rituals and commands, and believe that religious laws should be given precedence over the secular legal system (Gannon and Pillai 2013). The rest of the Jewish population lies between these two extremes. Rates of participation in the workforce differ greatly by level of religiousness, where ultra-Orthodox Jews' participation rates are relatively low compared to those of the general population (Israel Central Bureau of Statistics 2010).

In Israel, the workforce is relatively highly educated: twenty per cent are university graduates, second only to the United States. In comparison to other nations, Israel has the highest percentage of engineers, and is regarded a global leader in some areas, such as technology and science (Gannon and Pillai 2013).

Israel's cultural profile

Historically, at the time of the establishment of the state of Israel, there was a stronger emphasis on the needs of the group or society than on those of individuals, especially in the agricultural settlements of Kibbutzim. The private sector has grown since, so has Israeli participation in the global business world (the best example is the thriving Israeli hi-tech industry). Despite these economic structural trends promoting individualism and related values, individuals still sacrifice quite a lot for the collective as military service is mandatory, and taxes are extremely high. In Hofstede's (1991) study, Israel was in the middle of the individualism-collectivism dimension compared with other nations; however, over the years it seems that it has shifted towards individualism (House *et al.* 2004).

Israelis are 'doers', acting proactively to make progress, solve problems, and take control over situations. They take pride in their exceptional competence for improvising and providing creative solutions to both mundane as well as hopeless situations. This type of resourcefulness supports the development of innovation in different industries, such as the hi-tech sector that is ranked number one in the world after adjusting nations according to their population size (Gannon and Pillai 2013).

Israelis are often viewed as impolite, arrogant, and brash, and tend to improvise in their business and personal matters. This roughness is not directed only towards foreigners; rather it reflects the rules of conduct within Israel, and is regarded as a spillover of anxiety caused by constant external and internal strife (Gannon and Pillai 2013). Native Israelis are called Sabras, which is the name of a local wild cactus whose fruits have thorns on the outside and are sweet and delicate on the inside. This is a metaphor for Israelis, or how they view themselves: rough on the outside and friendly once one really gets to know them.

Israelis are also typically portrayed as getting quickly to the heart of matters in their discourse (Starr 1991). They speak their minds openly, are quick to criticise and to express their opinion overtly when they have a different point of view or think the other person is wrong (Starr 1991). Within Israeli society, this rule of conduct is viewed as an expression of openness, frankness, effectiveness, and supporting quick progress and problem solving. However, foreigners interpret this form of conduct as overly critical, disrespectful, and even aggressive.

Informality is the norm in conversation. For example, people talk to each other using first names regardless of status or rank; such is the case between children and their teachers, soldiers and their commanders, or subordinates and their managers. This results from Israelis' tendency to de-emphasise status differences, and their common impatience for rituals, formalities, protocol, and complicated bureaucratic procedures (Gannon and Pillai 2013). As a result, relationships of all kinds are relatively intimate in comparison to other countries, and are accompanied by a relatively strong sense of communion and togetherness.

In a study comparing cross-national cultural values (Hofstede 2001), Israel had the second lowest score in power distance, implying the relatively low cultural acceptance of inequality between members of society. Low power distance is a prominent value affecting behaviour in the workplace. One typical behavioural example is the common practice called 'open door' management, where subordinates feel free to initiate meetings with their supervisors without setting a time in advance, and often stepping into their manager's office and starting a conversation. Another example is the ease and openness with which Israeli employees often convey disagreement with their managers in public. Indications of low power distance also prevail in the Israeli military. For example, Elon (1971) described the minimal power distance that exists between soldiers and officers in the Israeli army, where officers have responsibilities with no benefits, and are mostly addressed by their surnames. As military service is mandatory at the age of 18 for both men and women, norms encountered in the army are often carried into the civilian workforce.

Another main characteristic of Israeli society is a typical disrespect for authority, probably related to a strong emphasis on egalitarianism. The origins of this emphasis may be tracked to the socialist ideas of the first pioneers who came to the country and established agricultural egalitarian settlements (Kibbutzim) in the beginning of the 20th century. In addition, the persistent oppression and persecution of Jews during 20 centuries has led to a typically suspicious view of power (Gannon and Pillai 2013). This culturally driven view of power and authority is especially relevant to our study in Israel, as our research focuses on abusive supervision, or what can be viewed as excessive use of power by supervisors as evaluated by their subordinates.

Workplace culture in Israel

Many of the values and rules of conduct described above influence culture in Israeli workplaces. Low power distance, common disrespect, and suspicion of authority figures have an impact on the leadership styles and managerial behaviours that are expected to be relatively influential in Israeli workplaces. In addition, action orientation, impatience for protocol and complex procedures, and the inclination to improvise have an impact on the manner in which assignments are performed. The tendency for relatively close relationships affects the way people interact, the type of working connections, and the degree of proximity that are commonly accepted between supervisors and their subordinates. The typical roughness and informality, and the tendency for overt expression of criticisms and challenging opinions, affect how people communicate with each other in organisations.

Organisations in different sectors have extremely different cultures that usually reflect the specific context in which they operate. For example, in banks, which are highly regulated, there is more emphasis on procedures, regulation, hierarchy, and formality than in hi-tech organisations, which emphasise creativity and flexibility. It is therefore important to keep in mind not only values that are typical to Israel, but also those that characterise a specific organisational sector in Israel.

The current research was conducted in an Israeli organisation providing mental health services. As part of the carry-over of a socialist system, the state provides mental healthcare services to those in need, either directly through its own medical institutions, or through contractors that receive payment from the state. Organisations in the mental healthcare sector encourage employees to empathise with and understand others, to be cooperative and sociable, to relate to others in a friendly and helpful manner, and to see the world in relatively flexible ways (Holland 1997). Many professional employees in this field are educated and trained in various professions, such as: social work, psychology, psychiatry, or nursing. Employees in these professions tend to be interested in working closely with people. They are trained to be empathetic, to care for the needs of others, to understand others' perspectives and needs, and to communicate effectively with others. Typical values in this field are caring for people and the community at large, adherence to legal and procedural requirements (due to regulation), and efficiency in terms of budgeting (for operations provided under tight government allocation); all these in an atmosphere of relatively high stress characteristic of the healthcare sector.

The contribution of attachment orientations, gender, and ethical climate to abusive supervision in the workplace

The main goal of the study in the Israeli mental healthcare sector was to examine the contributions of attachment orientations and gender of both supervisors and subordinates and the perceived ethical climate of the organisation to abusive supervision. Specifically, predictors of abusive supervision at the intrapersonal level (gender and attachment orientations of supervisors and subordinates), the interpersonal level (specific supervisor–subordinate interactions in the above individual-differences characteristics) and the organisational level (perceived ethical climate) were explored. In addition, how abusive supervision was associated with subordinates' reports of their emotions, attitudes, behavioural intentions and actual behaviours were assessed.

Abusive supervision: prevalence, antecedents, and consequences

Abusive supervision refers to subordinates' perceptions of the extent to which a supervisor engages in a sustained display of hostile verbal and nonverbal behaviours toward them (Tepper 2000). This includes behaviours such as rudeness, public ridiculing, angry outbursts, social isolation, scapegoating and humiliating subordinates, taking credit for subordinates' work, and blaming subordinates to avoid embarrassment. Tepper (2000) further conceptualises abusive supervision as a subordinate's subjective experience and evaluation; the same supervisor may be evaluated differently by different subordinates, and evaluation of the same supervisor by a single subordinate may vary in different situations depending on the subjective appraisal of the supervisor at a given moment. Unlike more explicit forms of aggression, abusive supervision does not necessarily involve hostility; it also refers to supervisor's expression of indifference toward a subordinate. In addition, it may not be considered deviant if it conforms to organisational policies, values, or norms (Yagil 2006).

In his review, Tepper (2007) estimated that 13.6 per cent of U.S. workers had experienced recurrent episodes of abusive supervision from a specific manager. Victims often report diminished well-being and quality of work life that can spill over to their lives away from work, negatively affect work attitudes, and lower job satisfaction and commitment (Schat *et al.* 2006). Tepper (2007) also reviewed studies assessing the cost of abusive supervision to U.S. corporations in terms of absenteeism, healthcare costs, and lost productivity, which has been estimated at US$23.8 billion annually. Additionally, Tepper (2007) described potential antecedents of abusive supervision, noting that this behaviour seems to be associated with supervisors' hostile attribution bias – the dispositional inclination to project hostile purpose onto others' behaviour (Tepper *et al.* 2006, Tepper 2007) – and subordinates' negative affectivity – a dispositional tendency to experience negative thoughts and emotions (Tepper *et al.* 2006).

Abusive supervision in Israel

In a study conducted in Israeli workplaces in a variety of sectors, Yagil (2006) revealed that supervisors' abusive behaviours were positively related to subordinates' burnout and their use of forceful upward influence tactics (e.g., threatening the supervisor and ceasing to cooperate with him/her). Whereas Israeli subordinates were willing to use unpleasant forceful tactics to influence their supervisor (Yagil 2006), research conducted in other countries indicated that the asymmetrical power relationship between supervisor and subordinate usually hinders responses such as subordinates' direct retaliation to abuse (Tepper *et al.* 2001). Due to the low power distance that characterises Israeli culture (Hofstede 2001), Yagil (2006) suggested that status differences could be less intimidating for Israeli workers than for workers in countries with higher power distance. In a more recent study, Yagil *et al.* (2011) revealed that Israeli subordinates relied on a variety of problem-focused and emotion-focused ways of coping for dealing with abusive supervision. Yagil *et al.* (2011), however, found that Israeli workers tended to avoid direct communication for coping with abusive supervision, which contradicts Israelis' cultural tendency to speak openly, criticise, and overtly confront another person when they think he or she is wrong (Starr 1991). These findings could be explained by subordinates' heightened sense of threat of further retaliation by an abusive supervisor, which can dramatically change the typical cultural communication style.

Findings from a recent study conducted by Peperman and Bar Zuri (2013) revealed that 55.4 per cent of Israeli employees encountered bullying or abuse in the workplace, and that 36.9 per cent reported being abused by managers. Findings also indicated that younger employees were more exposed to abusive supervision than older ones, probably because abuse and bullying are informally a part of common training and initiation processes within the rough Israeli culture. Additionally, contrary to findings in the U.S. (Zogby International 2010), Israeli men reported being exposed to more abusive supervision than women. Women's lower reported rates can result from enforcement of the sexual harassment prevention law, which can indirectly reduce other forms of harassment, including abusive supervision. Although the law relates to both men and women, men are often unaware of their rights with regard to this law and tend not to defend themselves accordingly. In terms of religiousness, religious employees reported higher levels of abusive supervision than did secular employees; this could have been explained as abuse directed toward minorities, however, this is not the case with Arabs, who also constitute a minority. The reported rates of bullying by managers are higher in organisations with over 100 employees than in those with less than 100. In addition, higher rates of bullying were reported by employees supervised by male managers than by those supervised by female managers (Peperman and Bar Zuri (2013, a finding that replicated those found in the U.S. (Zogby International 2010).

In a recent study of the consequences of managers' incivility (another form of abusive supervision), Itzkovich (2014) uncovered that perceived incivility frequency was higher in uncivil acts perpetrated by supervisors compared to those perpetrated by another worker. Moreover, workers reported more negative consequences from managerial incivility than incivility from another worker. Due to managers' central role in workplaces, it is reasonable to assume that many of their behaviours receive focal attention and have a relatively high impact on their employees' well-being and functioning. Moreover, in the context of Israeli culture, it is possible that Israelis' suspicious view of authority figures (Gannon and Pillai 2013) further focuses attention on incivility inflicted by managers.

Attachment orientations and abusive supervision

In the present study, the intention was to follow the above line of research assessing abusive supervision in Israeli workplaces, while at the same time examining potential characteristics in supervisors and subordinates, and in the organisational climate, that can contribute to abusive supervision. In this context, abusive supervision is conceptualised as a specific aggressive case of supervisor–subordinate interpersonal interaction, which can be affected by the way both parties perceive, evaluate, experience, and react to each other. In particular, mental perceptions of others, the tendency to experience interpersonal trust, and a sense of safety and emotional security in others' goodwill were assumed to be extremely significant in understanding the quality of interactions between supervisors and subordinates in general, and abusive supervision in particular. On this basis, Attachment Theory (Bowlby 1982) was used as a conceptual framework for understanding abusive supervision. This theory focuses on individual variations in representations of others, the sense of interpersonal trust and emotional security, and their effects on interpersonal behaviour relationship quality. Furthermore, the theory is highly relevant in explaining individual differences in hostility, aggression, and the use of power in relationships.

According to Attachment Theory (Bowlby 1982), human infants are born with a repertoire of behaviours *(attachment behaviours)* designed by evolution to assure proximity to supportive others *(attachment figures)* as a means of protecting them from physical and psychological threats and dangers. These security-seeking attachment behaviours are organised by an innate *attachment behavioural system*. This evolved because it increased the likelihood of survival and reproduction among social primates born with immature capacities for locomotion, feeding, and self-defence (Bowlby 1982). Although the attachment system is most important early in life, Bowlby (1988) claimed it is active over the entire human life span and is manifest in thoughts and behaviours related to proximity- and support-seeking in times of need.

Bowlby (1973) also discussed important individual differences in attachment-system functioning, which he attributed to reactions of relationship partners to one's bids for support in times of need. Interactions with attachment figures that are available, sensitive, and supportive at such times facilitate the smooth functioning of the attachment system, promote a sense of connectedness and security, and strengthen positive mental representations of self and others. When a person's attachment figures are not reliably available and supportive, however, a sense of security is not attained, worries about one's social value and others' intentions become ingrained, and strategies of affect regulation other than proximity-seeking are developed.

When studying individual differences in attachment-system functioning in adults, attachment research has focused on *attachment orientations* – patterns of relational expectations, emotions, and behaviours that result from internalising a particular history of attachment experiences (Mikulincer and Shaver 2007a). Research indicates that attachment orientations in adulthood can be located in a two-dimensional space defined by two roughly orthogonal dimensions: attachment-related anxiety, and attachment-related avoidance (Brennan *et al.* 1998). The avoidance dimension reflects the extent to which a person distrusts relationship partners' goodwill and defensively strives to maintain behavioural independence and emotional distance. The anxiety dimension reflects the extent to which a person worries that a partner will not be available in times of need, partly because of the person's self-doubts about his or her own love-worthiness. People who score low on both dimensions are said to be secure with respect to attachment. A person's location in the two-dimensional space can be measured with reliable and valid self-report scales, for example, the Experiences in Close

Relationships (ECR) scale (Brennan *et al.* 1998), and is associated in theoretically predictable ways with a wide variety of measures of relationship quality and psychological adjustment.

Although attachment orientations are initially formed in relationships with caregivers during childhood (Cassidy and Shaver 2008), Bowlby (1988) claimed that important interactions with later relationship partners can alter a person's working models and move him or her from one region of the two-dimensional (anxiety-by-avoidance) space to another. Moreover, although a person's attachment orientation is often conceptualised as a single global orientation toward relationships, it is actually an emergent property of a complex network of cognitive and affective processes and mental representations, which includes many episodic, context-specific, and relationship-anchored memories and schemas (Mikulincer and Shaver 2007a). Many studies indicate that a person's attachment orientation can change depending on current context and recent experiences (Mikulincer and Shaver 2007b), making it possible to study the effects of the extent to which specific interactions (e.g., supervisor–subordinate interaction) and contexts (e.g., organisational climate) elicit senses of security and insecurity.

Mikulincer and Shaver (2007a) proposed that a person's location in the two-dimensional anxiety-by-avoidance space reflects both his or her sense of attachment security, and the ways in which he or she deals with threats and stressors. People who score low on these dimensions are generally secure, hold positive mental representations of self and others, and tend to employ constructive and effective affect-regulation strategies. People who score high on attachment anxiety rely on hyper activating strategies – energetic attempts to achieve support and love combined with a lack of confidence that these resources will be provided, and with feelings of anger and despair when they are not. In contrast, people who score high on attachment-related avoidance tend to use deactivating strategies: trying not to seek proximity to others when threatened, denying vulnerability and needs for other people, and avoiding closeness and interdependence in relationships.

In a series of studies, Shaver *et al.* (2011) found that people differing in attachment orientations also differ in the way they experience having power over others. Specifically, when people were primed with a sense of power over others, more avoidant participants were more likely to objectify others, probably due to their tendency to use power as an opportunity to act on their preferences for autonomy and distance, their critical view of others, and their perception of others as objects to be used for their own need satisfaction. These findings further suggest that secure people (i.e., those low in insecure attachment orientations) may be able to maintain a sense of power without treating others as objects. Following this conclusion, findings of a second study showed that priming a sense of power over others reduced empathy toward others' needs and feelings only among insecurely attached people, but not among those who scored relatively low on attachment anxiety and avoidance; that is, more secure people (Mikulincer and Shaver 2011).

Following these findings, we hypothesised that more supervisors' attachment insecurities would be positively associated with the frequency of abusive supervision and its negative consequences. This hypothesis is further supported by findings from couple relationship studies showing that more anxiously attached individuals have the highest rates of violence in couples (Follingstad *et al.* 2002, Henderson *et al.* 2005), and more avoidant individuals are most hostile and devaluative towards relationship partners (Bartholomew and Allison 2006).

Gender and power in the workplace

In a review of gender and leadership style, findings reveal that female leaders tended to be more democratic (i.e., allowing subordinates to participate in decision-making), sharing, and caring, as opposed to male leaders whose styles tended to be more centralistic and autocratic (Eagly and Johnson 1990). Drory and Beaty (1991) also revealed gender differences in the way people evaluate power-related influence tactics of managers: as compared to women, men were more tolerant of managers' power-related behaviours and tended to downgrade their potential negative impact. In bullying-related studies, findings reveal that men were more often than women perpetrators of bullying at the workplace, and that they show a preference for same-gender harassment (Zogby International 2007). In addition, bullying most strongly affects women, who are targeted by bullies more frequently, especially by other women (Zogby International 2010). On this basis, we hypothesised that rates of abusive supervision would be higher among male supervisors than among female supervisors, and that these rates would be further higher in same-gender dyads than in different-gender dyads.

Ethical climate

Ethical climate has been found to be a meaningful factor in organisations and tends to contribute to workers' psychological well-being, organisational commitment, ethical behaviour, and job satisfaction (Johnson 2012). Organisations encounter different ethical challenges and develop a unique set of values and norms to address these issues. An ethical climate determines what members in the organisation believe to be right or wrong as well as their ethical decision-making and conduct. Kelley and Cullen (2006) portray five ethical climates. *Instrumental* climates typically hold norms and expectations that encourage ethical decision-making from an egotistic perspective while serving the individual, his or her immediate group, and organisation to the potential detriment of others. In *caring* climates, individuals perceive that decision policies and strategy are based on concern for the well-being of members of the organisation, as well as society at large. This climate has been found to be employees' most preferred work climate. In *independence* climates, decisions with moral consequences emphasise personal moral beliefs with little regard for external influence. *Law and code* climates support decision-making based on external codes, such as the law and professional codes of conduct. In *rules* climates, organisational decisions are perceived to be guided by rules, standards, and procedures developed within the organisation. In research conducted in Israeli schools, findings revealed that the caring, law and code, and rules ethical climates are the most predominant (Rosenblatt and Peled 2002).

In a review of studies using the above climate types (Johnson 2012), findings reveal that ratings of immoral and unethical behaviours are highest in work units and organisations with instrumental climates. In addition, members of these groups are less committed to their organisations. Caring climates were positively related to employee loyalty, whereas rules climates were negatively related to ethical misbehaviour and attachment to the organisation. Job satisfaction and psychological well-being were found positively related to laws and codes climates. From an attachment perspective, we view ethical climate as a contextual organisational activating factor of attachment orientations, with caring ethical climates being expected to contextually activate the sense of attachment security. In this climate, employees feel that their own well-being, as well as that of others, is considered a central factor in decision-making processes, that managers care about them, and that they can feel safe in their organisation. On the other hand, in instrumental ethical climates employees feel they are not cared for as people, that they are out for themselves, and that the only thing that matters is the organisation's interests. Therefore, this climate is expected to activate more insecure attachment orientations. In addition, we hypothesised that lower rates of abusive supervision would be found in caring climates, which emphasise caring for subordinates' well-being, than in other climates.

The current study

Based on the reviewed literature, attachment orientations, gender, and ethical climates were expected to be predictors of abusive supervision and its consequences. Specifically, the following hypotheses were proposed: (1) The higher the attachment insecurities of supervisors and subordinates, the higher the levels of abusive supervision and its negative consequences. (2) Male supervisors will show higher levels of abusive supervision than female supervisors, female subordinates will be recipients of higher levels of abusive supervision than male subordinates, and same-gender dyads of supervisor and subordinates will show higher levels of abusive supervision than different-gender dyads. (3) The higher the ratings of a caring ethical climate, the lower the attachment insecurity of supervisors and subordinates, and the lower the frequency of abusive supervision.

The study was undertaken in 31 teams working in geographically distributed units of an organisation providing mental healthcare services in Israel. The questionnaires were completed by 235 subordinates and 31 supervisors comprising dyads of male and female subordinates and supervisors. The questionnaire administered to supervisors included self-report scales assessing attachment orientation (ECR; Brennan *et al.* 1998) and organisational ethical climate

(Victor and Cullen 1988). The questionnaire administered to subordinates included the same scales on attachment orientations and organisational ethical climate, as well as scales tapping frequency of abusive supervision (Tepper 2000), well-being (a short version of the Mental Health Inventory, MHI; Florian and Drory 1990), burnout (Malach-Pines 2005), job satisfaction (Wanous *et al.* 1997) and questions about intentions to quit and absenteeism.

A series of Hierarchical Linear Models (HLMs) were conducted in order to examine the contribution of supervisors' and subordinates' attachment orientations (anxiety and avoidance) to subordinates' perceptions of abusive supervision and its consequences (well-being, distress, burnout, job satisfaction, intentions to quit, and absenteeism). Findings indicated that the higher the subordinates' attachment anxiety, the higher the reported frequency of abusive supervision, the lower their well-being and the higher their burnout (γs ranging from -0.23 to 0.33, all ps $< .05$). Although subordinates' attachment avoidance was associated with lower well-being and higher burnout scores, it showed no significant association with reported frequency of abusive supervision. Supervisors' attachment orientations were not significantly associated with subordinates' reports of abusive supervision.

In addition, the links between subordinates' attachment orientations and well-being were moderated by their supervisors' attachment orientations. The negative association between subordinates' attachment anxiety and well-being was significant only when supervisors scored relatively high on attachment avoidance (γs $= -0.34$, $p < 0.001$) but not when supervisors scored lower on this attachment scale (more secure supervisors). In addition, the negative association between subordinates' attachment avoidance and well-being was significant only when supervisors scored relatively high on attachment anxiety (γs $= -0.29$, $p < 0.01$), but not when supervisors scored lower on this attachment scale (more secure supervisors).

Overall, findings indicated that subordinates' evaluations of abusive supervision were positively related to their anxious attachment. Anxious individuals' chronic worries and anxieties with regard to relationship partners are possibly transferred into their relationship with a supervisor. As a result, their excessive expectations for attention and care, and reassurance-seeking from a manager, who is usually preoccupied with a group of subordinates and many other instrumental tasks and goals, may lead to inevitable relational tension and disappointment, negative feelings towards the supervisor, and potential conflicts with him or her. It is possible that all this relational mismatch is experienced by anxious subordinates as an abusive relationship, or that they may become a target for abusive supervision from a frustrated and tense supervisor who cannot empathise and effectively respond to the anxious demands for reassurance.

The hypothesised association between supervisor's attachment orientations and abusive supervision was not confirmed. It is possible that supervisors whose attachment orientation was insecure would have naturally tended to behave more abusively towards their employees. However, professional training, regulations, rules, and controls, as well as organisational culture and its enforcement, could have shaped managers' actual conduct in the workplace, resulting in behavioural adherence to organisationally expected managerial behaviour rather than to personal psychological dispositions.

An additional series of HLMs examined the contribution of supervisors' and subordinates' perceptions of ethical climate (instrumental, formal, independence, caring) to subordinates' attachment orientations (anxiety and avoidance). Findings indicated that the higher the subordinates' perceptions of instrumental or independence ethical climates, the higher their attachment anxiety. With respect to supervisors' perceptions of ethical climate, findings revealed that the higher their perceptions of formal ethical climate, the higher the subordinates' attachment anxiety ($\gamma = 0.43$, $p < 0.05$). Subordinates' attachment avoidance was not significantly linked with either subordinates' or supervisors' perceptions of ethical climate (γs ranging from -0.09 to 0.09, all ps > 0.05).

Findings from HLMs examining the contribution of supervisors' and subordinates' perceptions of ethical climate to subordinates' perceptions of abusive supervision and its consequences, indicated that the higher the subordinates' perceptions of a caring ethical climate, the higher their well-being and job satisfaction, and the lower their perceptions of abusive supervision and burnout (γs ranging from -0.51 to 15.86, all ps < 0.05). Regarding supervisors' perceptions of ethical climate, the analyses revealed that the higher their perceptions of instrumental ethical climate, the lower the subordinates' well-being and the higher their perceptions of abusive supervision.

The finding that higher subordinates' perceptions of formal ethical climate were associated with higher well-being is quite surprising. As described earlier in this chapter, in formal ethical climates, decision-making is based on the law, professional codes of conduct, standards, and procedures. While describing Israeli culture and typical Israeli personal style, we portrayed that informality is the norm in Israel, and that there is a low level of tolerance for formalities, protocol, and procedures. Therefore it may have been reasonable to expect that formal ethical climate would be negatively related to positive emotional consequences; however, a positive relationship was found between these variables. One possible explanation is that although Israelis tend to dislike formalities, such as rules and procedures, in the context of workplaces these provide employees a sense of security regarding their roles and terms of their employment. This is especially meaningful due to the trend of privatisation in the country, often accompanied with layoffs and employees' sense that they are on their own to fend for themselves.

With respect to supervisors' perceptions of ethical climate, the analyses revealed that the higher their perceptions of formal ethical climate, the higher subordinates' attachment anxiety. This finding is in accordance with the Israeli typical cultural inclination for informality and expectations for close relationships. When supervisors perceived the organisations' ethical climate as formal, and presumably behaved accordingly, subordinates whose expectations were probably for proximity, flexibility, and informality in their relationship with their manager, in accordance with Israeli culture, portrayed more attachment anxiety.

With regard to the contribution of supervisors' and subordinates' gender to subordinates' perceptions of abusive supervision, HLMs revealed that supervisors' and subordinates' gender had no significant effect on subordinates' perceptions of abusive supervision. This contradicts previous findings in the U.S. It is possible that the effects of professional expertise may supersede previously found gender-related differences in abusive supervision. The majority of supervisors in our study were social workers, and their professional education and training emphasises the development of skills for building effective, caring, and supportive relationships, and being empathetic and responsive to others' needs. People who choose social work as their profession often have effective interpersonal competencies and are interested in relationships in general and caring ones in particular (Holland 1997). Therefore, these capabilities and interests of social workers as well as their professional training may have blurred the previously found gender differences in abusive supervision. It is possible that when effective selection processes and training in the area of human relationships are conducted, gender differences of supervisors in abusive supervision are nullified.

Conclusions

In this chapter we discussed abusive supervision in the context of Israeli culture, reviewed findings of international as well as local research, and described our study in this field in an Israeli organisation in the mental healthcare sector. In this section we conclude with some directions for future research as well as practical implications.

Many findings in recent studies of abusive supervision and related terms that were performed in Israel could be expected in other cultures as well. For example our results on the positive association between subordinates' attachment anxiety and their evaluations of abusive supervision could be expected in other countries. However, as discussed throughout parts of this chapter, some unique results have been revealed as well, and those can often be explained in the context of national, organisational, or professional cultures. For example, the specific interpersonal conditions in which subordinates' anxiety would prosper may differ between cultures and organisations. It is also possible that ethical climates that foster meaningful deviations from cultural norms related to interpersonal interactions could elicit attachment anxiety, consequently leading to higher evaluations of abusive supervision. Therefore, replicating our study in additional cultural contexts would increase the validity and generalisability of our findings.

Some of the unexpected findings in our study may reflect the effect of organisational and professional norms on the expression of abusive supervision, suggesting the potentially influential role workplaces could take in the prevention of abusive supervision. This leads to possible practical implications. Organisations may be able to lower the frequency of abusive supervision by providing supervisors with training aimed at the development of interpersonal skills that support effective relationship management with subordinates, by developing and enforcing ethical climates in which both subordinates and supervisors feel secure, and by implementing effective selection and promotion processes that take into account human relation capabilities of candidates for supervisor positions.

References

Bartholomew, K., and Allison, C.J. 2006. An attachment perspective on abusive dynamics in intimate relationships. In: M. Mikulincer and G.S. Goodman, eds., *Dynamics of romantic love*. New York: Guilford Press, 102–27.

Bowlby, J. 1969/1982. *Attachment and loss: Vol. 1. Attachment*. 2nd ed. New York: Basic Books.

Bowlby, J. 1973. *Attachment and loss: Vol. 2. Separation: Anxiety and anger*. New York: Basic Books.

Bowlby, J. 1988. *A secure base: Clinical applications of attachment theory*. London: Routledge.

Brennan, K.A., Clark, C.L., and Shaver, P.R. 1998. Self-report measurement of adult romantic attachment: An integrative overview. In: J.A. Simpson and W.S. Rholes, eds., *Attachment theory and close relationships*. New York: Guilford Press, 46–76.

Cassidy, J., and Shaver, P.R., eds., 2008. *Handbook of attachment: Theory, research, and clinical applications*. 2nd ed. New York: Guilford Press.

Drory, A., and Beaty, D. 1991. Gender differences in the perception of organizational influence tactics. *Journal of Organizational Behavior*, 12 (3), 249–58.

Eagly, A.H., and Johnson, B.T. 1990. Gender and leadership style: A meta-analysis. *Psychological Bulletin*, 108 (2), 233–56.

Elon, A. 1971. *The Israelis*. New York: Penguin.

Florian, V., and Drory, Y. 1990. Mental Health Inventory (MHI) – Psychometric properties and normative data in the Israeli population. *Psychologia: Israel Journal of Psychology*, 2 (1), 26–35.

Follingstad, D.R., Bradley, R.G., Helff, C.M., and Laughlin, J.E. 2002. A model for predicting dating violence: Anxious attachment, angry temperament, and need for relationship control. *Violence and Victims*, 17 (1), 35–47.

Gannon, M., and Pillai, R. 2013. The Israeli Kibbutzim and Moshavim. In: *Understanding global cultures: Metaphorical journeys through 31 nations, continents, and diversity*. 5th ed. Los Angeles, CA: Sage, 332–53.

Henderson, A.J.Z., Bartholomew, K., Trinke, S., and Kwong, M.J. 2005. When loving means hurting: An exploration of attachment and intimate abuse in a community sample. *Journal of Family Violence*, 20, 219–30.

Hofstede, G.H. 1991. *Cultures and organizations: Software of the mind*. New York: McGraw-Hill.

Hofstede, G.H. 2001. *Culture's consequences: Comparing values, behaviors, institutions and organizations across nations*. 2nd ed. Thousand Oaks, CA: Sage.

Holland, J.L. 1997. *Making vocational choices: A theory of vocational personalities and work environments*. 3rd ed. Odessa, FL: Psychological Assessment Resources.

House, R.J., Hanges, P.J., Javidan, M., Dorfman, P.W., and Gupta, V. 2004. *Culture, leadership and organizations: The GLOBE study of 62 societies*. Thousand Oaks, CA: Sage.

Israel Central Bureau of Statistics. 2010. Social survey 2009 – Religiosity in Israel – Characteristics of different groups. Available from: www.cbs.gov.il/hodaot2010n/ 19_10_101b.pdf [Accessed 6 January 2015].

Israel Central Bureau of Statistics. 2014a. Statistical abstract of Israel international comparisons land area, population and population density, average 2013. Available from: www.cbs.gov.il/reader/shnaton/templ_shnaton.html?num_tab=st02_28& CYear=2014 [Accessed 6 January 2015].

Israel Central Bureau of Statistics. 2014b. Statistical abstract of Israel population by population group. Available from: www.cbs.gov.il/reader/shnaton/templ_shna ton.html?num_tab=st02_01&CYear=2014 [Accessed 6 January 2015].

Itzkovich, Y. 2014. Incivility: The moderating effect of hierarchical status does a manager inflict more damage? *Journal of Management Research,* 6 (3), 86–98.

Johnson, C. E. 2012. *Meeting the ethical challenges of leadership casting light or shadow.* 4th ed. Thousand Oaks, CA: Sage.

Kelly, D. M., and Cullen, J. B. 2006. Continuities and extensions of ethical climate theory: A meta analytic review. *Journal of Business Ethics,* 69, 175–94.

Malach-Pines, A. 2005. The burnout measure, short version. *International Journal of Stress Management,* 12 (1), 78–88.

Mikulincer, M., and Shaver, P. R. 2007a. *Attachment in adulthood: Structure, dynamics, and change.* New York: Guilford Press.

Mikulincer, M., and Shaver, P. R. 2007b. Boosting attachment security to promote mental health, prosocial values, and inter-group tolerance. *Psychological Inquiry,* 18, 139–56.

Mikulincer, M., and Shaver, P. R. 2011. Attachment, anger, and aggression. In: P. R. Shaver and M. Mikulincer, eds., *Human aggression and violence: Causes, manifestations, and consequences.* Washington, DC: American Psychological Association, 241–57.

Peperman, B., and Bar Zuri, R. 2013. Bullying and abuse in the workplace [online]. Israel Ministry of Industry Trade and Labour Research and Economy. Available from: www.tamas.gov.il/NR/rdonlyres/D3B1D180-B3A1–44C4-B10C-4132A1D5C90C/0/X12124.pdf [Accessed 3 December 2014].

Rosenblatt, Z., and Peled, D. 2002. School ethical climate and parental involvement. *Journal of Educational Administration,* 40 (4), 349–67.

Schat, A.C.H., Frone, M. R., and Kelloway, E. K. 2006. Prevalence of workplace aggression in the U.S. workforce: Findings from a national study. In: E. K. Kelloway, J. Barling, and J. J. Hurrell, eds., *Handbook of workplace violence.* Thousand Oaks, CA: Sage, 47–89.

Shaver, P. R., Segev, M., and Mikulincer, M. 2011. A behavioral systems perspective on power and aggression. In: P. R. Shaver and M. Mikulincer, eds., *Human aggression and violence: Causes, manifestations, and consequences.* Washington, DC: American Psychological Association, 71–87.

Starr, J. R. 1991. *Kissing through glass: The invisible shield between Americans and Israelis.* Chicago, IL: McGraw-Hill.

Tepper, B. J. 2000. Consequences of abusive supervision. *Academy of Management Journal,* 43 (2), 178–90.

Tepper, B. J. 2007. Abusive supervision in work organizations: Review, synthesis, and research agenda. *Journal of Management,* 33 (3), 261–89.

Tepper, B. J., Duffy, M. K., Henle, C. A., and Lambert, L. S. 2006. Procedural injustice, victim precipitation and abusive supervision. *Personnel Psychology,* 59 (1), 101–23.

Tepper, B.J., Duffy, M.K., and Shaw, J.D. 2001. Personality moderators of the relationship between abusive supervision and subordinates' resistance. *Journal of Applied Psychology*, 86 (5), 974–83.

Victor, B., and Cullen, J.B. 1988. The organizational bases of ethical work climates. *Administrative Science Quarterly*, 33 (1), 101–25.

Wanous, J.P., Reichers, A.E., and Hudy, M.J. 1997. Overall job satisfaction: How good are single-item measures? *Journal of Applied Psychology*, 82 (2), 247–52.

Yagil, D. 2006. The relationship of abusive and supportive workplace supervision to employee burnout and upward influence tactics. *Journal of Emotional Abuse*, 6 (1), 49–65.

Yagil, D., Ben-Zur, H., and Tamir, I. 2011. Do employees cope effectively with abusive supervision at work? An exploratory study. *International Journal of Stress Management*, 18 (1), 5–23.

Zogby International. 2007. *U.S. workplace bullying survey*. Bellingham, WA: Workplace Bullying Institute.

Zogby International. 2010. *The WBI U.S. workplace bullying survey*. Bellingham, WA: Workplace Bullying Institute.

12 Workplace bullying in New Zealand

'She'll be right?'

Bevan Catley, Kate Blackwood,
Darryl Forsyth and David Tappin

Introduction

'She'll be right' expresses the sentiment that 'everything will be fine' and 'there will be a happy outcome' (Cryer 2006, p. 148). Yet, it is a phrase that can convey both optimism and apathy. In a positive tone, 'she'll be right' expresses confidence in the outcome typically in an against-the-odds context. Conversely, it can also express a disengaged indifference that 'whatever happens, will happen'. As a deeply embedded New Zealand cultural value, the 'she'll be right' attitude is a source of both inspiration and frustration.

The attitude of 'she'll be right' has served New Zealanders admirably in a number of contexts. On the battlefield, the farm and the sports field especially, the positivity of the idiom manifests as resilience, determination, adaptability and innovation. It is arguably the attitudinal driving force behind the No. 8 wire mentality.[1] In other contexts, 'she'll be right' manifests as a lackadaisical, apathetic or even gung-ho attitude that can have severe negative and dangerous outcomes. Workplace health and safety is one such context where the consequences of a 'she'll be right' attitude can be disastrous.

Workplace bullying is a health and safety issue that has recently captured the attention of the media, scholars and regulatory agencies. Research indicates that workplace bullying is a significant problem in many New Zealand workplaces. In response, New Zealand regulators have framed workplace bullying as a hazard, bringing it within a health and safety management framework. More generally, the November 2010 disaster at the Pike River Coal mine, in which 29 miners lost their lives, has brought sharp scrutiny to New Zealand's workplace health and safety practices.

In response to the Pike River disaster, the government convened the Independent Taskforce on Workplace Health and Safety to "research and evaluate critically the workplace health and safety system in New Zealand" (Independent Taskforce on Workplace Health and Safety 2013, p. 6). Their report condemned New Zealand's poor record of health and safety and the commonplace work-related injuries and deaths. While the Taskforce concluded there was no one single critical factor, it did identify prevailing norms and values in New Zealand's national culture as one key factor undermining efforts to improve health and safety. The complacency associated with a 'she'll be right' attitude was one of the values identified as inhibiting employee health and safety (Independent Taskforce on Workplace Health and Safety 2013).

With this report as the departure point, this chapter suggests that deeply held cultural values may be contributing to the prevalence of workplace bullying in New Zealand. The chapter explores the dynamics of workplace bullying in the New Zealand context and the regulatory response to dismiss any notion that employers can take a lackadaisical 'she'll be right' attitude towards its management. The chapter next describes the profile of New Zealand's national culture as depicted in the cultural frameworks of Geert Hofstede (Hofstede *et al.* 2010) and the GLOBE project (House *et al.* 2004). The chapter concludes by speculating on how New Zealand's positioning on various cultural dimensions may inhibit or facilitate workplace bullying.

New Zealand: beginnings of a nation

While the exact date is unknown and subject to conjecture, evidence points to New Zealand first being settled in the thirteenth century (King 2007). In his history of New Zealand, Michael King writes that it seems most likely that New Zealand was settled as a result of deliberate voyages of discovery and colonisation during the great period of Polynesian ocean voyaging. From an initial 100–200 founding settlers, the population grew to around 100,000 by the turn of the eighteenth century (King 2007). The local population – Māori – would remain undisturbed until the first ripples of European expansion began to touch the shores of New Zealand in the middle of the seventeenth century (King 2007).

The Dutch explorer Abel Janszoon Tasman is credited with being the first Pākehā (non-Māori, typically of European descent) to sight New Zealand on the 13th of December 1642 (King 2007). Tasman, on a two-ship exploration on behalf of the Dutch East India Company, sighted the west coast of the South Island and sailed north before anchoring (King 2007). Tasman's anchorage proved violent and, in a brief skirmish with local iwi (tribe), four of his crew were killed along with one Māori. Tasman headed north charting the coast but not landing. He labelled the land he had seen Staten Land but over time it would eventually appear on European maps as New Zealand (King 2007). It would take 126 years for the next ripple of European expansion to reach the country.

In October 1769, the British Royal Navy's Lieutenant James Cook sighted the east coast of the North Island. Over the next six months, Cook circumnavigated the country and ultimately produced a highly accurate map (King 2007). In all, Cook made three voyages and was followed by other European explorers, which would place New Zealand firmly in the European conscience (King 2007). Commercial imperatives would drive the next more substantial ripple. Demand for seals, whales, timber and flax encouraged commercial expeditions to a country rich in such commodities (King 2007). The trade in fur seals drove the first European settlements in the South Island around the turn of nineteenth century; later whaling, timber and flax would be far greater drivers of European settlement throughout the country (King 2007).

From the 1830s, a number of factors encouraged the British government to step up its influence over the territory: a growing European population with a large British percentage; a territory renowned for its lawlessness and related concerns about the welfare of British citizens and local Māori; protection of an increasingly lucrative trade with the Australian colonies; and appeals from local iwi for British protection (King 2007). In May 1833, James Busby arrived in the Bay of Islands to take up the office of British Resident, and to act in effect as the representative of the British Government (King 2007). Over the next few years, Busby made requests of the British Government to intervene more strongly, and in 1839 a naval officer, William Hobson, was dispatched from London with orders, as King (2007, p. 138) describes it, "to negotiate the voluntary transfer of sovereignty from Māori to the British Crown."

In February 1840 at Waitangi in the Bay of Islands, a treaty between the British Crown and local iwi was signed that allowed the British to proclaim sovereignty over the country, and bring it into the fold of the British empire (King 2007). The Treaty was drafted quickly by Hobson, his secretary and Busby, none of whom had a legal background and with no draft provided by London for guidance (King 2007). Realising that Māori would not be able to understand or debate an English only version, the document was hastily translated into Māori in a classic 'night before' job. The result was a treaty with two official versions – Māori and English – and containing just a preamble and three short articles. While perhaps not the country's first DIY (do-it-yourself) job, it is arguably one of the most important. The haste in drafting the document, the manner in which it was signed and explained, and the differences in interpretation means that the Treaty remains controversial to this day. As King (2007, p. 138) writes, while the signing of the Treaty of Waitangi is regarded as "the most important chapter in the country's history", it would also turn out to be "the most contentious and problematic ingredient in New Zealand's national life."

While the Treaty provides the framework for formal relations between Māori and the Crown, and its principles are referred to in all Acts of Parliament, social New Zealand reflects a broad mix of influences. War and sport are typically listed as key influences in shaping New Zealand's national identity and cultural values. In particular, the exploits of New Zealand soldiers at Gallipoli during the First World War, the All Black rugby teams of the early twentieth century (the 1905 'Originals' and 1924 'Invincibles') and Sir Edmund Hillary's conquest of Mt Everest in 1953 have achieved almost mythical status to exemplify the values of mateship, determination and a 'can-do' attitude. These sorts of events, along with growing political independence from Britain, helped shape national culture and identity.

Contemporary New Zealand

In the years since 1840, New Zealand has grown into a relatively prosperous, stable, independent and democratic nation. It is a small island nation located in the South Pacific. The country consists of three main islands – the North Island (Te Ika-a-Māui), South Island (Te Waipounamu) and Stewart Island (Rakiura). At 269,652 sq km, the total land area of New Zealand is comparable to the United Kingdom or the Philippines (Statistics New Zealand – Tatauranga Aotearoa 2014b). As an island nation, New Zealand has a diverse geography ranging from the almost subtropical climes of the North Island to the alpine areas of the South Island; no place is more that 130km from the sea (Statistics New Zealand – Tatauranga Aotearoa 2014b). Located on the Pacific Rim's 'ring of fire', New Zealand is also well known for its earthquakes and volcanoes.

At just over 4.5 million people, the modern day population of New Zealand is similar to that of Ireland, Singapore or Norway (Statistics New Zealand – Tatauranga Aotearoa 2014b). By 2025, the population is projected to increase to around 4.9–5.1 million people (Statistics New Zealand – Tatauranga Aotearoa 2014a). Like many Western nations, New Zealand's population will continue to age as a result of lower birth rates and lower death rates (Statistics New Zealand – Tatauranga Aotearoa 2014a). The median age in 1970 was 25.6 years and by 2014 had risen to 37.5 years with a median age of 40 likely to be reached in the 2030s (Statistics New Zealand – Tatauranga Aotearoa 2014a).

At the most recent census (2013), 74 per cent of respondents identified themselves as being of European ethnicity, 14.9 per cent Māori, 11.8 per cent Asian and 7.4 per cent Pacific Peoples (Statistics New Zealand – Tatauranga Aotearoa 2013b). New Zealand's population is concentrated in the North Island and further concentrated in the Auckland region. Just over 1.4 million people live in the Auckland area, or 33.4 per cent of New Zealand's total population (Statistics New Zealand – Tatauranga Aotearoa 2013a). Most New Zealander's live in urban rather than rural areas and own their home (64.8 per cent) rather than rent (Statistics New Zealand – Tatauranga Aotearoa 2013a).

New Zealand has three official languages: English, te reo Māori and NZ Sign language. English is the dominant language and the principle language of government, business, education and the media. New Zealand has a strong Christian tradition, but there is no official religion. When reporting religious affiliation, census data reports that 48.9 per cent of New Zealanders indicated an affiliation to a Christian religion. However, 41.9 per cent indicated an affiliation to no religion, a figure that has been steadily increasing in recent years up from 29.6 per cent in 2001 (Statistics New Zealand – Tatauranga Aotearoa 2014b).

As explained on the New Zealand Government website (2014), the country is a constitutional monarchy with a parliamentary system of government. The head of state is Queen Elizabeth II, who is represented in New Zealand by the Governor-General. Members of Parliament are elected to the House of Representatives using the Mixed Member Proportional System. The government can only comprise of Ministers elected to the House of Representatives, and stays in office so long as it has the majority of members in the House. There is no upper house of parliament. The New Zealand system of government consists of three separate branches: the legislature (parliament), the executive and the judiciary.

Almost throughout its history, the New Zealand government has provided a wide range of benefits and services to its citizens. There is government provision for primary and secondary education, and an extensive public health system. A universal superannuation scheme operates for those New Zealanders over 65 years of age. Other government benefits and services, such as housing, and various forms of income support are provided on the basis of need. Social welfare and a generally socially progressive attitude are considered hallmarks of New Zealand governments, and mooted changes often become political flashpoints.

New Zealand's economy is relatively small by international standards and runs largely on free market principles. In the last 30 years, the New Zealand economy has undergone significant structural change as successive governments have moved to deregulate what was once a heavily regulated economy. Historically, agriculture formed New Zealand's economic base, but today's economy also consists of sizeable manufacturing and services sectors and a growing high-tech sector (The Treasury 2014). Exports are a key part of the economy and account for around 30 per cent of GDP, with Australia, China, North America, the European Union, Japan and South Korea the leading export markets (The Treasury 2014). The New Zealand economy proved largely resilient in the face of the Global Financial Crisis, experiencing only a relatively shallow recession between March 2008 and June 2009. Since the March 2010 quarter, the New Zealand economy has averaged an annual growth of 2.3 per cent (The Treasury 2014).

The labour market has been a sector of the economy that has undergone significant restructuring. Legislative change in 1991 set out to promote a free-market, individualised, employment system that reversed nearly a century of traditional roles and practices (Wilson 2010). The new legislation – *The Employment Contracts Act* – de-emphasised collective bargaining, industry awards and unions generally in favour of individual and enterprise bargaining as the means for promoting an efficient and flexible labour market. While this legislation has since been repealed, the emphasis on individual and enterprise bargaining has remained essentially unchanged. Largely as a result, union membership has steadily fallen both in absolute terms and as a percentage of the workforce. Union membership peaked in the post World War II period at around 60 per cent and held relatively steady through until the introduction of *The Employment Contracts Act* in 1991 (Ellem and Franks 2008). Today, union membership represents about 16 per cent of the employed labour force (Companies Office 2014).

Social and cultural New Zealand

A number of frameworks have attempted to categorise and compare national cultures according to a series of essential cultural values. Several of these cultural comparisons have included New Zealand. Given the strong historical links with

Great Britain, for many New Zealanders – especially Pākehā – Great Britain was the social and cultural reference point. Belich (2001, p. 21) writes that early colonial Pākehā saw themselves as "Britons of the South", an identification that would last until deep into the twentieth century. It is therefore understandable that in major frameworks comparing national cultures (e.g. Hofstede and GLOBE), New Zealand is often classified as part of the Anglo world; however, this and the homogeneity of New Zealand culture should not be overstated. Surges in immigration have given cities, like Auckland in particular, a strong cosmopolitan feel. Rather than 'Britain but with more sheep', New Zealand is a diverse Pacific nation that has built strong international relations with a number of countries.

Hofstede's framework

Hofstede's (1980) original framework categorised national cultures according to four dimensions – power distance, individualism-collectivism, masculinity-femininity and uncertainty avoidance. As recounted in Hofstede *et al.* (2010), further research yielded the inclusion of two additional dimensions: pragmatism and indulgence. Hofstede's (1980) original data set contained the responses of employees working at IBM from 40 different countries, including New Zealand. As the project expanded, the database grew to include data from 107 countries or regions, which was presented in the various editions of *Cultures and Organizations* (Hofstede *et al.* 2010).

The power distance dimension captures the extent to which the less powerful members expect and accept that power is distributed unequally (Hofstede *et al.* 2010). New Zealand scores very low on this dimension relative to others and below the other Anglo countries (Australia, Canada, Great Britain and the United States). New Zealand also scores low on the dimension of pragmatism – indicating a preference for traditions and norms while viewing societal change with suspicion (The Hofstede Centre 2015). On the dimension of individualism, New Zealand scores relatively highly and comparable to Canada and Great Britain, but lower than Australia and the United States. A relatively high score indicates a preference for the individual over the collective, and an emphasis on self-reliance. New Zealand also scores relatively highly on the indulgence dimension, indicating a preference for the gratification of basic desires to enjoy life and have fun (Hofstede *et al.* 2010). New Zealand's score tips it just over to the masculine side of the continuum, indicating a slight preference for ambition and achievement over caring and quality of life (Hofstede *et al.* 2010). In terms of uncertainty avoidance, New Zealand's score is intermediate with no preference for the need to reduce uncertainty and produce stability (Hofstede *et al.* 2010).

The GLOBE study

Similar to Hofstede's work, the GLOBE (Global Leadership and Organizational Behavior Effectiveness) project utilised cultural dimensions to compare societies.

Led by Robert House, GLOBE compared 62 societies along nine cultural dimensions using data from around 17,000 managers (House *et al.* 2004). The first six dimensions are similar to those found in Hofstede's work along with the additional dimensions of future orientation, performance orientation and humane orientation (House *et al.* 2004). As explained by House *et al.* (2004), future orientation is the extent to which societies engage in planning and investing in the future, and delaying individual and collective gratification; performance orientation is the extent to which group members are rewarded and encouraged for performance improvement and excellence; and humane orientation is the extent to which individuals are rewarded and encouraged for being fair, altruistic, caring and generous.

According to the GLOBE project (House *et al.* 2004), New Zealand ranked very low in societal assertiveness with only Sweden ranked lower, indicating that individuals are less likely to be confrontational and aggressive in their relationships with others. On the two collectivism scales, New Zealand scored very highly for societal institutional collectivism and higher than other Anglo countries, and very low for societal in-group collectivism, but comparable with other Anglo countries. This would indicate a preference for *some* forms of collectivism (e.g. rewarding and encouraging the collective distribution of resources and collective action), but not a preference for expressing pride, loyalty or cohesiveness in the family or organisation.

In terms of power distance, New Zealand was ranked relatively low compared to others but still in the second top band of countries (House *et al.* 2004). Thus, there is some expectation that power will be distributed unequally, but less of an expectation relative to a number of other nations. On the dimension of uncertainty avoidance, New Zealand ranked relatively highly indicating some focus on norms, rules and procedures to reduce the uncertainty of future events. For humane orientation, New Zealand was ranked in the second top band of countries, indicating some preference for caring and altruistic behaviours towards others. New Zealand was ranked very highly for performance orientation, placing it in the top band of countries. This ranking indicates an expectation that performance improvement and excellence will be encouraged and rewarded. On the dimension of gender egalitarianism, the country holds a middling ranking relative to others and a value that indicates a degree of male domination. New Zealand was ranked the lowest of the Anglo countries for future orientation, with a value that indicated a slight focus toward immediate issues.

New Zealand workplaces

Accordingly, cultural insights provided by the likes of Hofstede (Hofstede 1980, Hofstede *et al.* 2010) and the GLOBE project (House *et al.* 2004) can be used to produce a sort of 'profile' of the New Zealand workplace relative to others (see The Hofstede Centre 2015 for an example). This is not to suggest that all New Zealand organisations or any one organisation fit this profile. There will be significant variations between industries and between organisations within a given industry sector. Rather, the profile provides a "rough approximation" of a New Zealand workplace comparative to others (Thomas and Peterson 2015, p. 64).

New Zealand employees and managers are likely to consider themselves relatively equal as people, with the organisational hierarchy an expression of the inequality of roles. Employees are expected to be self-reliant, display initiative and a 'can-do' attitude. Managers and superiors are relatively accessible to employees, while employees are relied on for their experience and expertise. All employees are expected to work to their potential, achieve individual successes and 'win' (The Hofstede Centre 2015). Training and development opportunities are expected and valued. The acquisition of skills and experience that lead to performance provide the basis for career progression to a more senior role (House *et al.* 2004).

Organisational and individual performance is results-orientated, with bonuses and financial rewards linked to their achievement. However, for both managers and employees, the emphasis is likely to be on achieving relatively quick results and rewards (The Hofstede Centre 2015). Promotion to management roles is based on merit but 'technical skills' are likely to be emphasised over 'interpersonal skills'. Dependent on industry, many of the managerial roles and senior positions are likely to filled by men (House *et al.* 2004). Yet, there is also likely to be an emphasis on developing women for senior roles, and encouraging women to enter 'traditionally male' industries (e.g. agriculture, engineering, IT). Explicit exclusion from the workforce, or from a specific job on the basis of gender, ethnicity, sexual orientation, age, political affiliation and other non-work related factors is legally prohibited.

Intra-organisational communication is more informal, direct and participative. However, organisational roles will be formalised through written contracts along with formal policies to cover a wide range of organisational interactions. Dependent on the industry, employees are unlikely to belong to a union, with the union seen as not integral to the employment relationship. Gathering facts and figures and establishing their validity is an important part of decision-making (The Hofstede Centre 2015).

Norms of organisational conduct are likely to emphasise reserved interpersonal behaviours coupled with detached, largely unemotive responses to situations (The Hofstede Centre 2015). Corporate attire is relatively conservative for men and women. Individuals who display overly expressive, interpersonal behaviours that reveal thoughts and feelings, or flamboyant attire at work are likely to be treated with suspicion or ridicule. Norms are also likely to reinforce group or sub-group loyalty, experience and a cooperative spirit (House *et al.* 2004). An attitude of 'don't rock the boat' may be common amongst employees and management. Developing positive workplace relationships is seen as valued, as is not publically highlighting the deficiencies or errors of immediate peers and superiors. In this respect, there may be a degree of ambiguity and subtlety in language as a means of 'saving face' for a colleague.

For many, a 'work hard, play hard' ethos prevails and enjoying life outside work is considered important (The Hofstede Centre 2015). Career success is used to finance an enhanced lifestyle (e.g. holiday home, boat, overseas travel). However, successes must be tempered with humility and modesty (House *et al.* 2004). The accumulation of material gains is not to be 'thrust in people's faces', otherwise an individual risks being labelled as 'arrogant', 'brash' or worse. Individuals who brag about individual success or engage in ostentatious displays of wealth will be frowned upon or experience the "tall poppy syndrome".[2]

Workplace bullying in New Zealand

Relative to other nations New Zealand is mostly peaceful. The 2014 Global Peace Index ranks New Zealand 4th most peaceful from 162 countries (Institute for Economics and Peace 2014), while Transparency International (2014) ranked New Zealand second least corrupt on its 2014 Corruption Perceptions Index. New Zealand workplaces experience relatively few serious acts of physical workplace violence (Bentley *et al.* 2014), while industrial disputes rarely result in this. However, New Zealand compares unfavourably in terms of occupational fatal injuries (Lilley *et al.* 2013), and work-related injuries are common with approximately 1 in 10 workers harmed each year (Independent Taskforce on Workplace Health and Safety 2013).

Workplace bullying is a form of workplace ill treatment that has only recently come to the attention of New Zealand academics and regulators. Instead, it has been practitioners who have done much to bring workplace bullying to mainstream attention. Researchers and regulators are only just catching up. Arguably, it was practitioner Andrea Needham who first championed the cause for workplace bullying to be 'taken seriously'. The publication of *Workplace Bullying: The Costly Business Secret* (Needham 2003) drew on Needham's experience as both a human resources consultant and a target to describe workplace bullying and its consequences.

The impact of Needham's book and her associated training workshops was considerable, giving people the confidence and tools to label their experience and to take action. Hayden Olsen is another practitioner who has done much to raise the profile of workplace bullying as an unacceptable workplace behaviour. In his work, *Workplace Bullying and Harassment,* Olsen (2010) outlined the dynamics and consequences of workplace bullying along with practical suggestions and tools for how managers and supervisors could respond to the problem. Responses to the publicising of this 'new' workplace phenomenon were not universally popular. One senior manager was heard to complain that Needham's book had "brought nothing but trouble" (Swanwick 2004, p. 46). Needham responded that she was providing a label for the problem, not creating it. It was management who were contributing to the problem by closing ranks, or being unable to manage workplace bullying because they were poorly equipped in conflict management skills (Swanwick 2004).

Early academic research examining workplace bullying focused on the health sector. Small scale prevalence studies conducted by Foster *et al.* (2004) and Scott *et al.* (2008) indicated that workplace bullying was a problem for nursing students and for junior doctors. The first large scale study of the prevalence of workplace bullying was conducted by Bentley and colleagues in 2009 (Bentley *et al.* 2009). Using an internationally comparable measurement tool (Negative Acts Questionnaire), the study surveyed over 1,700 employees across 36 organisations drawn from the Health, Education, Hospitality and Tourism sectors (Bentley *et al.* 2009, O'Driscoll *et al.* 2011). The study reported an overall prevalence of 17.8 per cent with slightly higher rates reported for the Education (22.4 per cent) and Health (18.4 per cent) sectors, and slightly lower rates reported for the Hospitality (15.0 per cent) and Travel (11.4 per cent) sectors (Bentley *et al.* 2009). Nielsen's (2010) meta-analysis of international studies, which used a similar methodological approach, estimated a prevalence rate of 14.8 per cent.

Further evidence of the widespread nature of workplace bullying among New Zealand organisations was provided by Catley *et al.* (2012). Examining health and safety practitioners' perceptions about the extent and nature of workplace bullying, 70 per cent of the 252 respondents reported being aware of cases of bullying in their organisation within the last two years. A sizeable number of respondents (29 per cent) believed that bullying was a problem in their organisation. Yet, only 27 per cent believed that their organisation understood the problem of workplace bullying well enough to respond effectively, while only 41 per cent indicated that organisational leaders where prepared to confront bullies.

In terms of who does the bullying, the practitioners in Catley *et al.*'s (2012) study indicated bullying of staff by managers to be of most concern. Bullying of managers by staff was perceived to be of least concern. O'Driscoll *et al.* (2011) asked those who reported experiencing bullying behaviours to indicate who they believed was the source of the negative behaviour. Respondents reported bullying was experienced from a wide variety of sources, indicating it to be a '360 degree' problem. Bullying was reported from various levels of management: their employer (31.6 per cent), senior manager (36.9 per cent), middle manager (32.8 per cent), or immediate supervisor (36.4 per cent). Bullying was also experienced from subordinates (19.5 per cent), and clients or customers (26.9 per cent). However, bullying from colleagues (56.15 per cent) was the source most reported. Worryingly, the indication of multiple sources suggests that once a person is targeted for bullying it provides a 'license' for others to join in.

The damage done to targets from bullying is well documented in the research literature (for an overview see, for example, Hogh *et al.* 2011). Importantly, researchers (e.g. Vartia 2001, Lutgen-Sandvik *et al.* 2007, Paull *et al.* 2012) have also established that those who observe bullying in their workplace report many of the same negative consequences. Cooper-Thomas *et al.* (2014) provided a detailed analysis of the impact of bullying on observers and targets, drawn from a sample of New Zealand employees. Results indicated that observers of workplace bullying did experience a poorer workplace environment than non-bullied employees, but not as bad as targets. Successively greater exposure to bullying was also associated with poorer outcomes. Thus, observing workplace bullying was associated with poorer outcomes in terms of wellbeing, strain, affective commitment, perceived performance and intentions to leave the organisation, than for non-bullied employees. Targets of workplace bullying reported worse outcomes than for those who were only exposed as an observer. Being both a target and observer had a compounding effect in terms of wellbeing and strain, but not in terms of affective commitment, perceived performance or intentions to leave (Cooper-Thomas *et al.* 2014). These findings support the notion of workplace bullying having a 'ripple effect' (Lutgen-Sandvik *et al.* 2007) whereby the negative effects extend well beyond the immediate target.

Regulatory responses to workplace bullying

While the empirical picture of the nature and dynamics of workplace bullying in New Zealand is relatively incomplete, the available evidence does indicate a significant problem. As O'Driscoll *et al.* (2011, p. 402) write, if the sample used in their study is typical of New Zealand organisations, then the results "suggest that bullying may be somewhat more prevalent in New Zealand than in other countries." The growing evidence base of the prevalence and negative impact of bullying coupled with increasing media coverage of cases has arguably focused attention on the regulatory response. How have regulatory agencies responded?

At this point, there has been no change in New Zealand law to address workplace bullying explicitly. Employees who have been the target of workplace bullying who wish to seek legal redress can potentially do so via one of three legislative routes. One of those routes – *The Human Rights Act 1993* – has its emphasis on sexual and racial discrimination. Workplace bullying situations typically lack such a basis (Needham 2003), while the anti-discrimination procedures are repeated in *The Employment Relations Act* (2000). *The Health and Safety in Employment Act* (1992) enables claims to be brought against organisations or individuals for a breach of duty via a failure to take all practicable steps to ensure the safety of employees while at work. The Act was amended in 2002 to include physical and mental harm caused by work-related stress.

While health and safety legislation would seem best suited to handle psychosocial hazards such as bullying, the practicalities of filing such a complaint make this route difficult. WorkSafe New Zealand (WorkSafe) is the government agency responsible for administering and enforcing *The Health and Safety in Employment Act*. Before pursuing prosecution, WorkSafe is required to ensure that the case satisfies the threshold set by two tests: an evidential test and a public interest test. Broadly, these two tests consider the likelihood of a conviction, the gravity of the offence, and the seriousness of the harm (WorkSafe New Zealand 2014b). Thus, it is likely that only the most serious and flagrant cases of workplace bullying would satisfy WorkSafe's threshold.

Claims of workplace bullying are therefore most typically lodged via employment legislation as a personal grievance under *The Employment Relations Act*

(2002). An individual who believes they have experienced workplace bullying, or has been accused of it, can lodge a personal grievance under Section 103(b) of the Act on the grounds they were disadvantaged by some unjustifiable action by the employer. Should the individual no longer be employed, they can lodge a personal grievance on the grounds of having been unjustifiably dismissed (s103(a)). A number of remedies are available including reinstatement, reimbursement of wages and compensation for humiliation, injury or loss of dignity (Rudman 2014).

While prosecution is the most serious form of action to enforce compliance, WorkSafe also operates to educate employers and employees about their responsibilities and engage them to take action to reduce harm. As part of these latter efforts, WorkSafe (2014a) developed and released in February 2014 a set of best practice guidelines entitled *Preventing and Responding to Workplace Bullying*. In its media release, WorkSafe describes the guidelines as a "big step forward in support and guidance for business and individuals about what is a prevalent workplace hazard" (WorkSafe New Zealand 2014c). The aim of the guidelines is to provide employers and employees with examples of how to prevent and manage workplace bullying. In particular, the guidelines are intended to provide 'self-help' to individuals so that they can take action before seeking assistance from WorkSafe or other agencies. WorkSafe characterises the guidelines as encouraging people to "deal proactively with the issue themselves and to promote healthy work cultures" (WorkSafe New Zealand 2014c). Thus, the guidelines focus on trying to achieve workplace-based solutions to situations before they further escalate.

The guidelines are built on the premise that bullying is a hazard that manifests in specific behaviours that can, and should, be managed. The opening sentences of the guidelines make this clear:

> Bullying is a significant workplace hazard that affects employee health and business productivity. Employers have a duty to control all workplace hazards, including bullying and other undesirable behaviour.
>
> (WorkSafe New Zealand 2014a, p. 5)

The opening chapter of the guidelines provides a definition of workplace bullying, and discusses the types of bullying behaviours, bullies and bullying situations. The core definition of bullying is adopted from Safe Work Australia:

> Workplace bullying is repeated and unreasonable behaviour directed towards a worker or a group of workers that creates a risk to health and safety.
>
> • Repeated behaviour is persistent and can involve a range of actions over time.
> • Unreasonable behaviour means actions that a reasonable person in the same circumstances would see as unreasonable. It includes victimising, humiliating, intimidating or threatening a person.

A single incident of unreasonable behaviour is not considered workplace bullying, but it could escalate and should not be ignored.

(WorkSafe New Zealand 2014a, p. 6)

A section also clarifies that workplace bullying is not workplace conflict or reasonable management actions. WorkSafe describes the material in this chapter as contributing to taking the issue of workplace bullying "out of the too-hard basket" for employers and employees (WorkSafe New Zealand 2014c). The remaining chapters provide specific advice for employers and employees on how to respond to workplace bullying situations and guidance for managers on how to prevent bullying and build a respectful workplace environment. Several online tools are also provided to help manage and prevent workplace bullying. Importantly, however, WorkSafe's guidelines are not mandatory. Organisations are free to develop their own policies and practices for preventing and managing workplace bullying. However, the guidelines do have evidentiary status and will, over time, become incorporated into New Zealand's case law.

Workplace bullying: will she be right?

Within New Zealand workplaces the responsibility for preventing and resolving workplace bullying lies with the employer. Good faith in all aspects of the employment relationship is the central tenet of current employment legislation. Employers are also legally required to identify and control hazards that could harm their employees, with workplace bullying viewed as a hazard. WorkSafe's guidelines emphasise workplace-based solutions that aim to prevent the situation escalating so as to require regulatory intervention. Such a stance is consistent with the mainstream view that workplace factors, more so than interpersonal factors, are the leading antecedents of workplace bullying, and that management of workplace factors can prevent bullying from becoming embedded in an organisation. This view is underpinned by the findings of researchers who have invested considerable energy into investigating the role of workplace contextual factors contributing to bullying (for an overview see, for example, Salin and Hoel 2011). This investigation has extended to the role these contextual factors play in the efficacy of workplace bullying interventions (e.g. Fox and Cowan 2014, Woodrow and Guest 2014).

So, why does workplace bullying appear to flourish in New Zealand workplaces? A large part of the answer will lie in the interplay between interpersonal, task, organisational and industry factors. Additionally, the broader societal context has been posited as contributing to the prevalence of bullying (e.g. Hoel *et al.* 2001). The impact of national culture, however, has been less well articulated with little research conducted in the New Zealand context. Yet, given that national culture is seen to have a broad influence on organisational members' interpretations, expectations and interactions (e.g. House *et al.* 2004, Hofstede *et al.* 2010), and that organisational culture is viewed as an important moderator of bullying (e.g. Salin 2003, Baillien *et al.* 2009), we can surmise that national culture is likely to play a role.

Indeed, the recent report of the Independent Taskforce on Workplace Health and Safety acknowledged New Zealand's national culture as a key contributor to the country's poor health and safety performance (Independent Taskforce on Workplace Health and Safety 2013). The report laments a national culture that it views as having a high level of tolerance for risk, and a negative attitude towards health and safety generally. In particular, the report identified stoicism, deference to authority, laid-back complacency and suspicion of red tape as key cultural barriers to workplace health and safety systems. The Taskforce identified derivatives of 'she'll be right' – 'it won't happen to me', 'it's only minor' and 'it's all part of the work we do' – as examples of key contributors to poor health and safety (Independent Taskforce on Workplace Health and Safety 2013).

Returning to the New Zealand workplace 'profile' outlined previously, we can couple these insights to those of the Taskforce to speculate on how national culture might influence the prevalence of workplace bullying. On the positive side, the low power distance is likely to create the expectation for many employees that their manager – especially their immediate manager – treat them more like a colleague than a subordinate. That is, there is an expectation of being treated with respect and civility with managers not expected to act as dictators who rule over employees. This reflects broader societal expectations of politeness and civility to all, particularly to those individuals who are not personally known to you, or those you have a formal relationship with. National culture may therefore provide some protection from bullying with deviations considered unreasonable behaviour.

Unfortunately, other elements of national culture are likely to counter these protective effects. The Taskforce condemned the productivity-focused 'No. 8 wire', 'get on with it' mentality as producing "haste before care" (Independent Taskforce on Workplace Health and Safety 2013, p. 32). Although this comment was made with physical safety in mind, we would contend that the statement applies equally to an employee's emotional safety. The works of both Hofstede (2010) and the GLOBE project (House *et al.* 2004) indicate a preference for ambition, achievement and the pursuit of excellence over caring and quality of life, although this is tempered by a relatively strong humane orientation. A focus on short-term results and an emphasis on competition may translate into an attitude of no time to worry about people's feelings. Managing bullying is incidental or a distraction to the 'real job' of meeting performance targets.

Relatedly, the emphasis on technical skills as a prerequisite for management may lead many first-line managers to be ill prepared to manage a bullying situation. Research by Massey *et al.* (2005) gives some indication of the skills managers are developing – especially in small businesses. Massey *et al.* (2005) reported that management training providers were focusing on improving business capability, that is providing task orientated skills and knowledge. The Taskforce was damning of the low health and safety capabilities within many businesses: "management awareness, capabilities and training in health and safety are limited and variable" (Independent Taskforce on Workplace Health and Safety 2013, p. 26).

Thus, managers may see expending time and resources on managing workplace bullying as a low priority as they perceive little link between expending effort and improving short-term results. In fact, managers may conclude that taking action against a bully can even be detrimental to performance. Research has suggested that managers may be prepared to tolerate the behaviour of an alleged bully because of the seniority or their value as a 'star-performer' (Harrington *et al.* 2014). Additionally, the focus on developing and mastering task-based skills may see managers less inclined to want to take on complicated workplace relationship problems. In a British study, Woodrow and Guest (2014) identified time and confidence as being two of the key reasons why managers failed to act on a workplace bullying situation.

The GLOBE project's relatively low ranking for New Zealand in terms of social assertiveness may also play a role. A low ranking indicates the likelihood that people will be less confrontational and aggressive in their relationships with others. Managers and colleagues may find direct confrontation with others uncomfortable or be concerned that 'clear the air' conversations will be perceived as too threatening. The result may be the use of more subtle and passive forms of communication that could easily descend into actual or perceived bullying. Equally, an individual who perceives they are experiencing unreasonable behaviour may shun directly confronting the individual about their behaviour and instead look to other ways of coping.

Furthermore, if New Zealand culture emphasises relatively reserved and conservative conduct, then any perceived deviations from those norms may make an individual prone to bullying. Individuals who are perceived to be more flamboyant, or 'emotional', may be seen as having broken basic norms that mark them as a potential target. Being perceived as overly competent or highly conscientious may also be seen as another cultural transgression, particularly if the individual is perceived arrogant. Such transgression exemplifies the potential cultural contradiction of emphasising individual achievement but also being modest and humble.

From the target's perspective national culture may send strong signals that bullying is something to be endured. An emphasis on loyalty to the sub-group and cooperative loyalty often manifests in a strong value being placed on 'mateship'. From an early age, children are encouraged to 'not tell tales' about their peers, and to 'sort out' their own problems, reflecting perhaps a suspicion of having 'authority' intervene. In the workplace, such conditioning can only encourage a non-reporting culture towards workplace bullying. An emphasis on stoicism means that asking for help or talking about being bullied could be perceived as a sign of weakness. The management response may be to encourage employees to 'toughen up' and build resilience rather than address the more fundamental issues. In the health sector, for example, national, occupational and industry values congeal to form a strong norm of tolerating workplace bullying in the nursing profession which, in turn, discourages reporting (Carter *et al.* 2013). Nurses are encouraged and expected to 'deal with' what is typically a stressful and resource stretched work environment (Huntington *et al.* 2011).

With what appears to be little incentive for management to take action against workplace bullying and prevailing norms against reporting, employees are essentially left on their own to manage the problem. Low union membership may potentially compound the issue with non-union members having one less reporting channel and source of support. It is little wonder therefore, that Needham (2008) professes courage as a quality essential to combating workplace bullying: courage from managers to take action; courage from targets to bring the issue to management's attention; and courage from colleagues not to be mere bystanders.

Conclusion

The available evidence suggests that workplace bullying is a significant problem in many New Zealand workplaces. Workplace bullying cannot be dismissed as a bit of 'harmless fun'. Local and international research has provided compelling evidence of the damage done to targets and to those who witness bullying. Workplace bullying is toxic for individuals and corrosive to organisational performance. Consequently, the human, economic and legal costs of workplace bullying mean there is no place for a complacent 'she'll be right' attitude.

While the dynamics of workplace bullying are complicated and a number of interpersonal and workplace factors act as antecedents, it is likely that national culture also has a bearing. While attempts to profile national cultures are not intended to directly translate into how a given individual from that culture behaves, they can provide insight into the likelihood of how groups might respond on a comparative basis. Thus, while New Zealand may share many similarities with other Anglo countries, there are also important distinctions.

With research having broadly established the extent of the problem in New Zealand, attention now needs to be turned to prevention and management. While regulatory agencies provide the basic framework, the main thrust for prevention and management will need to be organisation based and tailored to meet specific circumstances. Effective responses to workplace bullying will therefore require the dynamics and context to be well understood if tailored intervention initiatives are to stand a chance of success. This will include understanding how deep cultural values shape both the problem of workplace bullying and its potential management. In this regard there is much further research to be done.

But no worries, she'll be right!

Notes

1   For many years the favoured wire for constructing farm fences in New Zealand was 'No. 8' because it was strong and widely available. Because it was often used for fixing other things on the farm, No. 8 wire became a catch-phrase for an ingenious repair using materials close at hand (Cryer 2002). In more recent times, 'No. 8 wire' has also come to mean a sort of short-hand for an innovative (and often simple and low-cost) solution to a problem.

2 Originally an Australian expression but widely used in New Zealand, the term in this context means to 'cut somebody down to size' and reflects an Australasian disdain and suspicion for individuals who are perceived to be overly successful or prominent (Cryer 2002).

References

Baillien, E., Neyens, I., De Witte, H. and De Cuyper, N., 2009. A qualitative study on the development of workplace bullying: Towards a three way model. *Journal of Community & Applied Social Psychology,* 19, 1–16.

Belich, J., 2001. *Paradise reforged: A history of the New Zealanders from the 1880s to the year 2000.* Auckland: Allen Lane The Penguin Press.

Bentley, T.A., Catley, B., Forsyth, D. and Tappin, D., 2014. Understanding workplace violence: The value of a systems perspective. *Applied Ergonomics,* 45 (4), 839–48.

Bentley, T.A., Catley, B., Gardner, D., O'Driscoll, M., Trenberth, L. and Cooper-Thomas, H., 2009. *Understanding stress and bullying in New Zealand workplaces. Final report to OH&S steering committee.* Auckland Massey University.

Carter, M., Thompson, N., Crampton, P., Morrow, G., Burford, B., Gray, C. and Illing, J. 2013. Workplace bullying in the UK NHS: A questionnaire and interview study on prevalence, impact and barriers to reporting. *BMJ Open,* 3 (6). doi:10.1136/bmjopen-2013-002628.

Catley, B., Bentley, T.A., Forsyth, D., Cooper-Thomas, H., Gardner, D. and O'Driscoll, M.P., 2012. Managing workplace bullying in New Zealand: Perspectives from occupational safety and health practitioners. *Journal of Management and Organization,* 19 (5), 598–612.

Companies Office, 2014. *Union membership return report 2014* [online]. Available from: www.societies.govt.nz/cms/registered-unions/annual-return-membership-reports/2014 [Accessed 2 February 2015].

Cooper-Thomas, H., Bentley, T.A., Catley, B., Gardner, D., O'Driscoll, M. and Trenberth, L., 2014. The impact of bullying on observers and targets. *New Zealand Journal of Human Resource Management,* 14 (2), 82–95.

Cryer, M., 2002. *Curious kiwi words.* Auckland: HarperCollins.

Cryer, M., 2006. *The godzone dictionary of favourite New Zealand words and phrases.* Auckland: Exisle Publishing.

Ellem, B. and Franks, P., 2008. Trade union structure and politics in Australia and New Zealand. *Labour History,* 95, 43–67.

Foster, B., Mackie, B. and Barnett, N., 2004. Bullying in the health sector: A study of bullying of nursing students. *New Zealand Journal of Employment Relations,* 29 (2), 67–83.

Fox, S. and Cowan, R.L., 2014. Revision of the workplace bullying checklist: The importance of human resource management's role in defining and addressing workplace bullying. *Human Resource Management Journal,* 25 (1), 116–30.

Harrington, S., Warren, S. and Rayner, C., 2014. Human resource management practitioner's responses to workplace bullying: Cycles of symbolic violence. *Organization,* 22 (3), 392–408.

Hoel, H., Cooper, C.L. and Faragher, B., 2001. The experience of bullying in Great Britain: The impact of organizational status. *European Journal of Work & Organizational Psychology,* 10 (4), 443–65.

Hofstede, G.H., 1980. *Culture's consequences: International differences in work-related values.* Beverly Hills: Sage.

Hofstede, G. H., Hofstede, G. J. and Minkov, M., 2010. *Cultures and organizations: Software of the mind: Intercultural cooperation and its importance for survival.* 3rd ed. New York: McGraw-Hill.

Hogh, A., Gemzøe Mikkelsen, E. and Hansen, Å.M., 2011. Individual consequences of bullying/mobbing. *In:* Einarsen, S., Hoel, H., Zapf, D. and Cooper, C. L., eds., *Bullying and harassment in the workplace: Developments in theory, research, and practice.* 2nd ed. Baca Raton: CRC Press, 107–28.

House, R. J., Hanges, P. J., Javidan, M., Dorfman, P. W. and Gupta, V., 2004. *Culture, leadership, and organizations: The GLOBE study of 62 societies.* Thousand Oaks: Sage.

Huntington, A., Gilmour, J., Tuckett, A., Neville, S., Wilson, D. and Turner, C., 2011. Is anybody listening? A qualitative study of nurses' reflections on practice. *Journal of Clinical Nursing,* 20 (9–10), 1413–22.

Independent Taskforce on Workplace Health and Safety, 2013. *The report of the independent taskforce on workplace health and safety.* Wellington: Independent Taskforce on Workplace Health and Safety.

Institute for Economcs and Peace, 2014. *Global peace index 2014: Measuring peace and assessing country risk.* Sydney: Institute for Economics and Peace.

King, M., 2007. *The Penguin history of New Zealand illustrated.* Auckland: Penguin.

Lilley, R., Samaranayaka, A. and Weiss, H., 2013. *International comparison of international labour organisation published occupational fatal injury rates.* Dunedin: Injury Prevention Unit, University of Otago.

Lutgen-Sandvik, P., Tracy, S. J. and Alberts, J. K., 2007. Burned by bullying in the American workplace: Prevalence, perception, degree and impact. *Journal of Management Studies,* 44 (6), 837–62.

Massey, C., Gawith, A., Perry, M., Ruth, D. and Wilson, M., 2005. *Building management capability in New Zealand.* Wellington: New Zealand Centre for SME Research, Massey University.

Needham, A. W., 2003. *Workplace bullying: The costly business secret.* Auckland: Penguin Books.

Needham, A. W., 2008. *Courage at the top: Igniting the leadership fire.* Auckland: Penguin.

New Zealand Government, 2014. *How government works* [online]. Available from: www.govt.nz/browse/parliament-and-politics/parliament/government-in-new-zealand [15 accessed Janurary 2015].

Nielsen, M. B., Matthiesen, S. B. and Einarsen, S., 2010. The impact of methodological moderators on prevalence rates of workplace bullying. A meta-analysis. *Journal of Occupational and Organizational Psychology,* 83 (4), 955–79.

O'Driscoll, M. P., Cooper-Thomas, H., Bentley, T. A., Catley, B., Gardner, D. and Trenberth, L., 2011. Workplace bullying in New Zealand: A survey of employee perceptions and attitudes. *Asia Pacific Journal of Human Resources,* 49 (4), 390–408.

Olsen, H., 2010. *Workplace bullying and harassment: A toolbox for managers and supervisors.* 2nd ed. Auckland: CCH New Zealand.

Paull, M., Omari, M. and Standen, P., 2012. When is a bystander not a bystander? A typology of the roles of bystanders in workplace bullying. *Asia Pacific Journal of Human Resources,* 50 (3), 351–66.

Rudman, R., 2014. *New Zealand employment law guide: 2014 edition.* Auckland: CCH New Zealand.

Salin, D. M. 2003. Ways of explaining workplace bullying: A review of enabling, motivating and precipitating structures and processes in the work environment. *Human Performance,* 56 (10), 1213–32.

Salin, D. M. and Hoel, H., 2011. Organisational causes of workplace bullying. *In:* Einarsen, S., Hoel, H., Zapf, D. and Cooper, C. L., eds., *Bullying and harassment in the workplace: Developments in theory, research, and practice.* 2nd ed. Boca Raton, FL: CRC Press, 227–43.

Scott, J., Blanshard, C. and Child, S., 2008. Workplace bullying of junior doctors: A cross-sectional questionnaire survey. *The New Zealand Medical Journal,* 121 (1282), 10–14.

Statistics New Zealand – Tatauranga Aotearoa, 2013a. *2013 census quickstats: About Auckland region.* Wellington: Statistics New Zealand – Tatauranga Aotearoa.

Statistics New Zealand – Tatauranga Aotearoa, 2013b. *2013 census quickstats: About national highlights.* Wellington: Statistics New Zealand – Tatauranga Aotearoa.

Statistics New Zealand – Tatauranga Aotearoa, 2014a. *National population projections: 2014–2068.* Wellington: Statistics New Zealand – Tatauranga Aotearoa.

Statistics New Zealand – Tatauranga Aotearoa, 2014b. *New Zealand in profile 2014: An overview of New Zealand's people, economy, and environment.* Wellington: Statistics New Zealand – Tatauranga Aotearoa.

Swanwick, D., 2004. How to beat the workplace bully. *New Zealand Management,* (June), 45–6.

The Hofstede Centre, 2015. *The Hofstede Centre* [online]. Available from: http://geert-hofstede.com [19 Accessed January 2015].

The Treasury, 2014. *New Zealand economic and finacial overview 2014.* Wellington: The Treasury, New Zealand Government.

Thomas, D. C. and Peterson, M. F., 2015. *Cross-cultural management: Essential concepts.* 3rd ed. Thousand Oaks: Sage.

Transparency International, 2014. Corruption perceptions index. Berlin: Transparency Interantional.

Vartia, M., 2001. Consequences of workplace bullying with respect to the well-being of its targets and the observers of bullying. *Scandinavian Journal of Work, Environment & Health,* 27 (1), 63–9.

Wilson, M., 2010. A struggle between competing ideologies. *In:* Rasmussen, E., ed., *Employment relationships: Workers, unions and employers in New Zealand.* New Edition. Auckland: Auckland University Press.

Woodrow, C. and Guest, D. E., 2014. When good HR gets bad results: Exploring the challenge of HR implementation in the case of workplace bullying. *Human Resource Management Journal,* 24 (1), 38–56.

WorkSafe New Zealand, 2014a. *Preventing and responding to workplace bullying.* Wellington: WorkSafe New Zealand.

WorkSafe New Zealand, 2014b. *WorkSafe New Zealand prosecution policy* [online]. Available from: www.business.govt.nz/worksafe/information-guidance/legal-framework/worksafe-new-zealand-prosecution-policy [Accessed 22 January 2015].

WorkSafe New Zealand, 2014c. *WorkSafe New Zealand releases guidelines for managing workplace bullying* [online]. Available from: www.business.govt.nz/worksafe/news/releases/2014/worksafe-new-zealand-releases-guidelines-for-managing-workplace-bullying/ [Accessed 22 January 2015].

13 Australia

The 'fair go' multicultural continent nation

Megan Paull and Maryam Omari

Introduction

For those far away, the image of Australia is one of contrasts: sun, sand, surf, blue skies, deserts, rainforests, and remarkably unique flora and fauna. Australian people are equally diverse, from the original Indigenous inhabitants to the British settlers, and the subsequent migrants from Europe, and more recently Asia, the Middle East and Africa. Qualities often associated with Australians include the notions of 'mateship', being 'down to earth', equality and freedom. Australians have prided themselves on a 'fair go' for all, while at the same time not necessarily always welcoming each new wave of migrants. Workplaces in Australia are multicultural; characterised by diverse value systems, providing different lenses through which interpersonal interactions are experienced, perceived and interpreted. This diversity at times leads to dissonance and conflict at work. Australian research on workplace abuse, incivility and bullying is fragmented. Recent findings from empirical work conducted in a variety of different sectors in Australia leads to the conclusion that there are inherent abuse, incivility and bullying issues in Australian workplaces needing attention. This chapter will provide a snapshot of Australia as a country, its cultural context, and findings to date relating to negative behaviours in the workplace.

Country profile

As at September 2014, Australia was estimated to have a population of just over 23.5 million people (The Australian Bureau of Statistics – ABS 2015); a small population for a country almost as large as the United States in land area. Australia is vast but sparsely populated, with most of its inhabitants living in cities and along the coastline. While English is the official language, and most Australians are Caucasian, there are an increasing number of languages spoken by Australians, including: Mandarin, 1.6 per cent; Italian, 1.4 per cent; Arabic, 1.3 per cent; Greek, 1.2 per cent; Cantonese, 1.2 per cent; and Vietnamese 1.1 per cent; with the ethnic groups divided into: 92 per cent white, 7 per cent Asian, 1 per cent Aboriginal and other (Central Intelligence Agency 2014). The Indigenous populations of the country (the Aboriginal and

Torres Strait Islander people) have to cope with many issues including: literacy, poverty, alcohol abuse, isolation and violence. Although constituting only around 1 per cent of the population, 27 per cent of the inmates in Australian prisons identify as being Indigenous (ABS 2014).

School attendance is compulsory until the age of 15, or older in some states, and the majority of the population attend government funded free schools. Despite curriculum requirements for languages other than English to be taught in schools, the evidence is that the native English speakers rarely speak a language other than English (ABS 2012). Australia has relatively low rates of tertiary education compared to many European countries, and despite a 30-year period of university tuition being free, only 24 per cent of 16 to 64 year olds hold a bachelor's degree or above (ABS 2012). The education sector (mostly at the tertiary level) is a significant income generator. The majority of the Australian universities (37 of 39) are publicly funded, with all being placed in the 10 per cent of the tertiary educational institutions in the world (Hare 2014). High demand from the rising, mainly Chinese and Indian, middle classes has been responsible for large numbers of international students. These students have limited work rights in Australia, and many of them take up these rights in order to fund their study. The continuous waves of migrants, along with international students having work rights, has resulted in significant diversity in Australian workplaces.

Most (61.2 per cent) of the Australian population identify with the different denominations of the Christian faith: Protestant, 28.8 per cent; Catholic, 25.3 per cent; Eastern Orthodox, 2.6 per cent; other Christian, 4.5 per cent; with a minority of other religions being practised, including: Buddhism, 2.5 per cent; Islam, 2.2 per cent; Hinduism, 1.3 per cent. Around 22 per cent of the population identify with having no religion (Central Intelligence Agency 2014). The Australian population, like most of the developed world, is ageing quickly; this, along with a slowing of birth rates, is placing significant pressures on the healthcare and taxation systems. There are many, including economists and politicians, who have expressed the view that to maintain the current high standards of living, Australia needs to open its door to migration as a strategy for influx of wealth and working age people (Kell *et al.* 2014).

Australia's 200 year history of European settlement, British colonial roots, and a migration record which included over 70 years of the White Australia policy, has influenced the composition of the dominant, mainly white, Christian population of the country. Many of the people who have come to Australia since 1945 were motivated by a commitment to family, or a desire to escape poverty, war or persecution. The first waves of postwar migrants and refugees came mostly from Europe (including significant populations of Greeks and Italians), with subsequent waves originating from the Eastern Europe, Asia–Pacific region, the Middle East and Africa (DFAT 2012). Specific migration schemes, including those which have attracted new migrants to the country, often take up employment in industries where the command of the English language is poor (Kell *et al.* 2014). Australia has also been a destination for refugees, both lawful and unlawful, an area of political debate (Phillips and Spinks 2013).

Due to geographic separation, Australia has unique flora and fauna, making it interesting and different to outsiders. The country's Mediterranean climate in coastal settled regions results in the population spending much time outdoors, at beaches, in the countryside or on sporting fields as either participants or spectators. Gannon and Pillai's (2013, p. 586) metaphor for Australia is "Australian outdoor recreational activities". The climate, geography and lifestyle have formed the basis for migration and tourism campaigns designed to attract the rest of the world to Australia.

Australians are generally liked and found to be interesting and different by others around the world. During a recent trip to Italy, the second author of this chapter had an experience that reinforced this contention. She was at a public venue speaking English to another person. An Italian child asked his father (within earshot) where the author was from, and the father replied *Americano* rather indifferently. The author upon hearing this, and being struck by the attitude of the father, politely corrected the father by looking at both and saying "Australian". An extremely big smile suddenly appeared on the father's face, he acknowledged the response happily with a nod of the head and replied *bene*.

Australia is known as the 'lucky country' (Horne 1964; DFAT 2012), with vast natural resources and huge potential. The country escaped the Global Financial Crisis of 2007–2008 almost unscathed on the back of its mining resources boom (commencing around 2003 and going strong until 2013) (OECD 2014). The resources boom riding on the back of significant exports to Asia brought with it significant labour shortages which resulted in opening up the labour market to overseas workers. Some '457 visa holders'[1] were able to demand extremely high salaries and good working conditions due to their value to the economy. This, however, resulted in some resentment on the part of workers who disputed the necessity of 'importing workers' and 'Australian jobs going to foreigners' (Kell *et al.* 2014). There were also instances of companies allegedly exploiting migrant workers by offering them lower conditions than their Australian counterparts, further increasing resentment (Fair Work 2013). The economy has, however, started to slow down and with it, the competition for jobs has been on the increase. Resentment towards others in the workplace, however, is not new, with history recording antagonism towards Chinese immigrants in the late nineteenth century (Lake 2013), and towards migrant workers on projects such as the Snowy River Scheme in the immediate postwar period (McGowan 2004).

Cultural profile

Gannon and Pillai's (2013) metaphors may not be universally accepted but are useful in providing descriptions relating to underlying values, attitudes and resulting behaviours. These metaphors have been built on dominant experiences in a society relating to: religion; early socialisation and family structure; small-group behaviour including leisure pursuits and interests; lifestyle; roles and status of different members of society; greeting behaviour; humour; sport as a reflection of cultural values; political structure; traditions; history; food and eating behaviour; class structure; organisation; and perspectives of work (Gannon and Pillai 2013, p. 15). This chapter will draw upon many of these indicators to help draw meaning and explain the possible root causes of negative behaviours at work in Australia.

Hofstede's framework (The Hofstede Centre n.d.) classifies Australia as being individualistic, having a masculine orientation, low power distance, being mid-range on uncertainty avoidance, low in pragmatism and high in indulgence (see Omari and Sharma this volume). This framework is indicative of communities which take care of themselves and their families, are competitive, focused on quick results and the 'here and now', enjoy life and have fun, are optimistic and spend money for interests and leisure. Australia demonstrates many of the characteristics of low-context countries in Hall's (1966) taxonomy. Australians are fairly direct (Gannon and Pillai 2013), indicating that, in the main, the spoken word is more important than other non-verbal cues in communication. The Steers *et al.* (2013) model categorises Australia as individualistic, rule-based, egalitarian, mastery-oriented and monochronic. The GLOBE classification (Center for Creative Leadership 2012) places Australia in the Anglo cluster countries, which are high in performance orientation and low in in-group collectivism. Finally, in Trompenaars and Hampden-Turner's (2012, p. 82) framework, Australia is seen as: universalist, individualist, specific, midway between neutral and affective, achievement oriented, having a sequential approach to time and controlling of the environment (see Omari and Sharma this volume).

Caution should be exercised in generalising about Australians given the multicultural nature of the nation. Power distance orientation, for example, is socially determined but there is evidence that some cultural groups' values are more consistent with those of their country of ethnic origin. Home culture and ethnicity influence the values of migrants and their families, and are also likely to influence adaptation to a new culture with some cultures becoming acculturated more easily than others (Sivasubramaniam and Goodman-Delahunty 2014).

History and culture

Australia's colonial past, convict heritage, class struggle, harsh climate and conditions are synonymous with its 'battler' mentality, which is well established in its culture of siding with the 'underdog', working against the unjust, and a 'fair go' for all. 'Mateship' is valued above all else, and is an unwritten code relating to egalitarian values and friendship (DFAT 2012). Russell Ward's book *The Australian Legend* (1958) suggests that this was forged in the Australian 'bush', came of age in the late nineteenth century and manifested itself in the 'Australian digger' during World Wars I and II. The word 'mate' is used often in conversation as a sign of belonging and affection. In Australia, self-promotion and arrogance is not looked at favourably, being seen as tasteless. Humility and casualness, on the other hand, are valued, and in-group out-group behaviour is often openly displayed, especially amongst boys and men, by using nicknames or shortening them; for example, John to Jonno or Steve to Stevo. Other nicknames are less obvious with redheads being referred to as 'Bluey', with even derogatory names being seen as a sign of affection and inclusion.

Australians are generally laid back, informal, open, direct, outgoing and casual when meeting new people; there is not much physical contact (hugs and kisses) at a first meeting other than a handshake in office-based work environments (a sign of equality, rather than bowing in some cultures – for example, in Japan – which demonstrates hierarchy). Colloquialisms, sarcasm, irony, jokes, dry wit and self-mockery are used as part of normal conversation. For those with English as a second language, who would literally translate what was being said, communication although understandable may be difficult to grasp in terms of context and actual meaning. This was the focus of a very successful series of comic novels (e.g. *They're a Weird Mob*) by author John O'Grady in the late 1950s and 1960s which emphasised the ability of Australians to laugh at themselves, but also highlighted some of the difficulties faced by immigrants. In the 1980s and 1990s a series of Australian comedies about migrant communities written for stage and television had similar success (e.g. *Wogs Out of Work* and a spin off *Acropolis Now*). Australian humour has been found to be consistent with the in-group collectivism of 'mateship'.

More than 80 per cent of Australians live within 50 kilometres of the coast; 'the beach' has therefore become an integral part the Australian lifestyle (Tourism Australia 2014). As the beach culture is often casual, this translates to the standards of dress and behaviour. For example, it is not unusual to see men in boardshorts *(boardies)* and no top, or women in their bathing suits with either a sarong or a short thin linen shirt covering their bathing suits in public places. As the standard of dress is casual there is often no visible distinction between people of different economic standing. The second author of this chapter had an interesting discussion with a student some years back. The Arab student from a very wealthy background was extremely perplexed, indicating that Australia is a very confusing place. He said: "You never know who has money and who doesn't here as everyone dresses the same." For the student, coming from a status oriented culture where one would socialise with like others, not knowing or seeing any overt signs of class and economic standing in the society was an issue. He did not know where he 'belonged', and who his 'like' others were.

Barbecues *(barbies)* are another symbol of the Australian lifestyle, and are the central to the metaphor ascribed to Australia by Gannon and Pillai (2013). They are outdoors and casual, and attendees are usually asked to bring along 'a plate' (i.e. a dish of food to share). Many a new migrant has been dismayed by this request, interpreted it literally, and brought along their own (empty) plate to eat from. The term BYO – bring-your-own – is applied to food and alcohol at many social occasions, although the next generation of migrant families can find themselves caught between the culture of their families and the 'Aussie' way of doing things.

The outdoor lifestyle also translates to sport having a significant place in Australian society, in, for example, language and interests. Inclusion can mean being able to join conversations about football or cricket. Despite competition being an inherent nature of sport, in Australia fairness is a highly prized value in sport with many awards being given in different sports for 'fairest and best'.

More than 6.5 million migrants have settled in Australia since 1945 (DFAT 2012). These migrants have brought with them their own culture and heritage and have enriched many aspects of Australian life from business, to food, entertainment, science, sport and the arts. The new arrivals, many from hierarchical or collectivist cultures, have in turn had to adapt to Australia's informal and broadly egalitarian society. There are many subcultures and ethnically homogenous neighbourhoods in Australia, such as: Melbourne having the second largest population of Greeks in a city outside Greece; Sydney having large neighbourhoods of Lebanese and Vietnamese migrants; and Perth the same with South African, British and South East Asian arrivals. Large subcultures can be important in providing social support, especially at the early stages of migration; however, they can also impede assimilation, and fuel perceptions of the 'other'.

Recent politics

The influx of asylum seekers through Australian waters has been a contentious issue for many years. Often referred to as 'boat people' since the time of the Australian involvement in the Vietnam War, many come from war torn countries such as Afghanistan, Iraq, Pakistan, Iran and Sri Lanka. There is indignation at 'queue jumping', people not waiting their turn – relating to the mainly monochronic time orientation of the nation and to the Australian notion of the 'fair go' being available to those who take their turn. Officially known as irregular maritime arrivals, the numbers making their way to Australia are far less than to other countries (Phillips and Spinks 2013), but the distances travelled and the political and media mileage obtained from their arrivals has further fuelled fears associated with difference.

The Australian Department of Foreign Affairs and Trade (DFAT 2012) website identifies the following as the nation's values:

- respect for the freedom and dignity of the individual;
- equality of men and women;
- freedom of religion;
- commitment to the rule of law;
- parliamentary democracy;
- a spirit of egalitarianism that embraces mutual respect, tolerance, fair play and compassion for those in need and pursuit of the public good; and
- equality of opportunity for individuals, regardless of their race, religion or ethnic background.

Australia is an egalitarian society; however this does not necessarily translate into everyone having equal wealth or property, or being treated the same. The early roots of Australian culture have elements of racism as demonstrated in the treatment the Indigenous inhabitants of the country at the hands of the British colonists, and by the treatment of migrants from Asia, particularly China, during colonial days (Lake 2013). The White Australia policy further reinforced segregation and xenophobia. In current day Australia, overt displays of racism and sexism are to be found in the media and modelled by public figures. Some of the more notable examples include the behaviour of politicians such as the newly elected leader of the Palmer United Party, Clive Palmer's damaging comments referring to his Chinese business partners and government as "Chinese mongrels" (Shanahan 2014). Other notable examples from politics include the election of Pauline Hansen in the mid 1990s to the Federal Parliament on the basis of criticism of multiculturalism, migration and assistance to Indigenous Australians (Agius 2014). Australians, however, do not tend to model their behaviour on leaders such as these, and there is a push back from an outspoken public in response to many of these debates.

Not confined to politics, social divisions have manifested themselves in racially motivated attacks on Indian students in Australia in 2009, which included two murders. At the time it was anticipated that around 120,000 Indian students were studying in Australia, many with the hope of remaining in the country after graduation to gain work experience (Millar and Doherty 2009). A further example is the race fuelled 2005 Cronulla riots in Sydney between Arab/Lebanese–Australian youths and the members of the public and the riot police (ABC Four Corners – Riot and Revenge 2013). Many of the racially motivated differences which are found in Australian society can be traced back to historical differences, including between the countries to which Australians can trace their ancestry.

Australians are generally law-abiding people; however, there is no absolute given or expected standard of behaviour towards those in positions of power. Respect for authority is limited, especially if there is an air of arrogance surrounding the people in power. This may be due to the egalitarian nature of the society and potentially to the convict ancestry.

In a multicultural society such as Australia it is easy to see why misunderstandings or conflict can easily arise due to different value systems, as behaviours expected and accepted in one culture may not be so in another. An example provided by a student of the second author of this chapter comes to mind: An international Japanese student was sharing a house with an Australian girl. The Japanese student always dutifully put the rubbish out on a weekly basis for collection by the truck. After some time, she thought that this should be a shared task and that it was her roommate's turn to contribute. So the Japanese student worked up the courage and decided to let her roommate know that it was her turn to put the rubbish out. She said the following to her roommate: "Look, the rubbish is full." The roommate looked at her and the rubbish, and calmly said, "Oh yes, you better put it out." The Japanese student was furious and embarrassed at the same time. In her high context cultural communication she had said the rubbish was full and therefore implied that the roommate should be putting the rubbish out. The low context Australian roommate, however, had only heard the spoken word and responded accordingly, in turn causing offence.

The Australian workplace culture and context

The Australian workplace is complex and at times contradictory. Informality is common, and it is often the case that people at all levels in an organisation address each other by given rather than family names or titles. Interviews and meetings are often friendly and conversational, with handshakes and nods as greetings and welcomes, and laughter and chatter being part of the atmosphere. Despite this lack of formality, meetings tend to commence on time, and be structured, even in smaller workplaces, in keeping with the monochronic time orientation. Communication styles in Australian workplaces tend to reflect the more direct approach, although managers tend to use collaborative rather than directive communication to get the job done. Humour in the workplace is expected, and sarcasm is common, as is self-deprecation. As with public life, Australians tend to frown on self-promotion, and in keeping with the tendency to 'cut down tall poppies' (Gannon and Pillai 2013) successful people can often find themselves the target of both sarcastic wit and disrespectful derision and humour. Generally a low power distance culture, Australians expect their leaders to 'earn' respect, rather than just have it granted by virtue of their role or position.

More traditional workplaces have tended to have a union presence, with a 'bosses' and 'workers' divide being present. This was inherited from the British adversarial approach and led to a strong trade union presence for much of the twentieth century (McPhail *et al.* 2015). Industrial relations and bargaining have been based on a pluralist approach, with ambit claims for wage increases and working conditions being agreed by negotiation by the union on behalf of the workers, or set by arbitration in industrial courts. The industrial relations landscape has changed in recent times with the move towards a more service-based economy and relatively prosperous times being associated with a decline in union membership. Industrial/employment laws have moved towards vesting power in individuals (Bray *et al.* 2014).

Workplace employment patterns have moved from what has traditionally been a 37.5 hour, 9–5 week to flexible working patterns, greater casualisation of the workplace, increased online/remote working and specialised working patterns such as fly-in fly-out in the mining and resources sector. Legislative frameworks associated with work have also evolved to sanction actions such as sexual harassment and certain categories of discrimination. Tolerance of workplace abuse, incivility and bullying has declined in certain sectors, at times through intervention (e.g. DARTF 2014), although workplace attitudes are still intolerant of difference and exclusive of the 'other' in many instances.

Workplace abuse, incivility and bullying in Australia

In 2010, The Australian Productivity Commission estimated that workplace bullying was costing between six billion and 36 billion dollars annually, but this estimate was based on international studies up to ten years old rather than Australian data (Productivity Commission 2010, p. 287). This report, along with lobbying and protests associated with a prominent workplace bullying case of a young cafe worker taking her own life, however, provided sufficient impetus for a Parliamentary inquiry at the national government level to investigate the phenomenon. The final report of the Inquiry into workplace bullying made a series of 23 recommendations ranging from legislative and regulatory frameworks, including sanctions, to preventative measures and development of supportive workplace cultures (HRSCEE 2012, pp. xix–xxiv). A central theme of the final report was the role of Australian workplace cultures in workplace bullying. The Inquiry found that workplace bullying thrives in cultures where individuals are in fear of speaking out about negative workplace behaviours (p. 107). More recently, Dollard *et al.* (2012), using a narrow definition of 'bullying' as part of a project examining psychosocial work climates in Australian workplaces, identified bullying as being at about 6.8 per cent, "substantially higher than international rates" (p. 8), and cited alarming levels of harassment including being yelled at, sworn at and humiliation. This data highlights the definitional issues associated with abuse, incivility and bullying.

There is still considerable debate in Australia over the definitions and concepts associated with workplace bullying. Generally legislation has tended to adopt definitions with three central characteristics: repeated occurrences; unreasonableness; and risk to health and safety (Chan-Mok *et al.* 2014). Statutes or guidelines exist in all states and at the federal level. There are separate provisions related to discrimination and harassment under equal opportunity legislation (e.g. *Equal Opportunity Act (WA) 1984 as amended*), but incivility and abuse are not explicitly proscribed, and would need to fall under either the harassment or bullying definitions for individuals to be able to seek legal redress. Chan-Mok *et al.* (2014) have expressed concern that under the current legislation an action must be repeated before action can be taken to redress bullying under occupational health and safety laws (Chan-Mok *et al.* 2014). In addition, there has been a call for workplace bullying to be reconceptualised as a multidisciplinary work and employment relations issue in order to facilitate prevention (Hutchinson 2012).

Research findings

Research into workplace abuse, incivility and bullying in Australia has been sporadic, scattered and diverse. Early Australian work on workplace bullying can be traced back to the 1990s, with the influential report conducted for Worksafe Australia (McCarthy *et al.* 1995), which highlighted the paucity of Australian research and identified the need for change in Australian workplaces. The research at that time was part of a worldwide interest in bullying which had led to legislative change in Sweden and Norway. Like much of the early work in other parts of the world, early Australian work tended to be focused on occupational health and safety, particularly from a psychological perspective, and to be quantitative work attempting to determine the nature and prevalence of bullying in workplaces. Barron (1998) identified that there was an overlap between workplace bullying and workplace violence in the Australian discourse, and that there was a need for increased awareness, preventative strategies and a recognition that in addition to one-on-one bullying, Australian workplaces also needed to address systemic bullying.

While Australia is known as an individualist culture, the acceptance of an individual into workplaces has often involved becoming part of a group. Gannon and Pillai refer to the notion of mateship as being part of the in-group/out-group distinction. "Becoming a member of the in-group requires time, patience and appropriate behaviour" (Gannon and Pillai 2013, p. 594). Australian workplaces have often been known to include indoctrination, hazing and 'bastardisation' practices, which have recently received attention in both the media and in research. Research associated with building and construction apprentices, for example, has identified that they neither confront perpetrators, nor make any report of the behaviour (McCormack *et al.* 2013). A recent Australian Defence Forces inquiry identified an unacceptably high level of 'bastardisation' in the ranks and in officer training. The Defence Abuse Response Task Force was established to examine the culture in the defence forces and led to the establishment of new systems for the reporting and management of abuse and bullying incidents, as well as the potential for retrospective review for current and former defence force personnel (DARTF 2014).

Australian research has tended, like that of other parts of the world, to demonstrate that abuse, bullying, incivility and harassment are understood by workers to be negative work behaviours. With harassment falling under equal opportunity legislation and abuse, bullying, incivility and violence being considered occupational health and safety matters, there is some level of confusion about the degree to which employees can take action in the event that they feel that they are subject to such behaviours. The evidence from other parts of the world is that human resource management policies and procedures to prevent and address these behaviours require a change in workplace culture, and a level of trust to be effective (Harrington *et al.* 2012). In Australia, too, the evidence is that employees feel unable or unwilling to report incidents of bullying for fear that the situation will worsen (e.g. McCormack *et al.* 2013). In addition, there is a tendency for workers to be of the view that individuals should 'toughen up' rather than 'run to teacher/dobbing', a legacy from school days. It is also the case that low power distance Australians, who have limited respect for their leaders, are less likely to trust that leaders will take action. In addition, Hutchinson *et al.* (2006) found evidence that practices implemented by management can be used to maintain domination over employees and create or perpetuate a 'them and us' culture, thus undermining trust in management.

The notion that workplace culture contributes to workplace abuse, incivility and bullying is reinforced by research undertaken in different Australian industries. Australian researchers have investigated workplace abuse, incivility and bullying in: the public sector (Omari 2007), education (Riley *et al.* 2011), the legal profession (Omari and Paull 2013), nursing (Hutchinson *et al.* 2006), aged care (Timo *et al.* 2004), in the security industry (Beattie and Griffin 2014), among white collar workers (Boddy 2011), in volunteer settings (Paull and Omari 2015) and among health workers in corrections (Cashmore *et al.* 2012). The significant level of research on bullying in health illustrates the recognition that this is a problem to be addressed, particularly given the other stressors associated with nursing, but there does not appear to be evidence that bullying rates are higher in nursing and health than in other industries. The enculturation of workplace behaviours is a theme throughout the bullying in nursing literature (Demir and Rodwell 2012; Rodwell and Demir 2012; Rodwell *et al.* 2013).

Different perspectives have been the focus of some of the Australian research, with Omari (2007) investigating the perspective of the alleged perpetrator, Standen and Omari (2009) examining reciprocal bullying, and Branch *et al.* (2007a; 2007b) investigating upward bullying. Paull *et al.* (2012) considered the perspectives of bystanders, and have considered the role of perceptions in interpreting behaviours as bullying (Standen *et al.* 2014).

Australian research has indicated that workplace cultures have tended to tolerate incivility, bullying and harassment of individuals who are different (Omari *et al.* 2014). The work of Power *et al.* (2013) identified that Australia, as a country in the GLOBE Anglo cluster, was less tolerant of physically intimidating bullying and work-related bullying than Confucian Asian countries, identifying that this may reflect a greater concern for 'fairness'. Despite this, Omari (2007), in a study of the public sector, found that there was evidence that employees with English as a second language reported significantly higher rates of being bullied despite the tight regulatory public service environment and significant policies; diversity was a factor that attracted the behaviour. Indicators included: not buying into racist conversations, sexism, ageism, sexual harassment and being from a minority group, with some alleged victims identifying the behaviour as culturally motivated. Evidence from research in the legal profession indicated that race and gender were considered by self reporting targets to be the underlying reason for bullying behaviours (Omari and Paull 2013), while difference in the form of 'fattist' behaviour was identified by one respondent to a survey on bullying in volunteering (Paull and Omari 2015).

The exclusion of 'others' is illustrated by work by Willis (2012) who found that Australian workplaces tend not to be welcoming of lesbian, gay, bisexual, transgender, intersex or queer (LGBTIQ) workers. The evidence of the in-group or mates acceptance is identifiable in this work. Further, Shallcross *et al.* (2013) examined the escalation of workplace conflict to 'mobbing' (in this context meaning group bullying), leading to eventual exclusion from the workplace all together. Their findings reveal a growing collaboration between the organisation and the alleged perpetrators which led to the target being labelled as mentally ill and forced out of the organisation. This work is in keeping with the notion of like-minded individuals forming alliances and co-operating to isolate or exclude an individual, and with such alliances serving to protect some individuals from scrutiny or due process (Omari *et al.* 2013). Similarly, sanctioned targets or 'fair game' is consistent with this understanding (Omari *et al.* 2014). Gannon and Pillai (2013) identified the equality matching culture as being an important factor in Australian workplaces, but it seems that this is complicated by the Australian in-group mentality.

The picture painted by research into Australian workplaces leads to a view of a culture which is not welcoming of newcomers and of those who are different. This is not the experience of many Australians, including new Australians. One of the products of the nature of research as it currently stands is that the stories of those affected by such behaviours are beginning to be heard, and while they are in a minority, it is important to recognise that awareness-raising requires concerted inquiry into their experiences. An interesting perspective which adds to this understanding is that of Zábrodská *et al.* (2011), who used a story-based diffractive methodology to illustrate co-implicated forces of managerial practice, workplace context and individual and interpersonal dynamics to suggest a move away from categorising individuals as bullies and to ask how situations develop, in particular associated with difference. Certainly the confluence of the difference of an individual or 'other' with the in-group mentality seems to be a contributor to the perception of acceptance or otherwise of individuals in the Australian workplace.

Implications and future directions

Abuse, incivility and bullying research is complex, and to date the work being undertaken around Australia is disparate and somewhat unconnected. Changing attitudes associated with what is acceptable and what is not are seeing the introduction of anti-bullying legislation and policies into workplaces. Multiculturalism brings with it many challenges. A scan of recent research shows that work has been concentrated in a small number of locations and industries. Hutchinson (2012) has called for a more multidisciplinary focus, while others have identified that in Australian workplaces there needs to be a recognition that negative behaviours are more than a workplace occupational health and safety issue. Evidence of the impact on the bottom line may be needed, as well as the insights which can be gained from hearing the stories of those affected. Uncomfortable conversations may ensue about the Australian sense of humour, and about derision for political correctness. The behaviours, including those associated with humour, which are part of the mateship of the Australian identity need to be revisited in order to grant outsiders a better 'fair go'.

Note

1 A category of workers holding temporary skilled employment visas.

References

ABC Four Corners – Riot and Revenge, 2013. (video file). Available from: www. youtube.com/watch?v=KabOOwXUk-8 [Accessed 1 December 2014].

ABS – see Australian Bureau of Statistics

Agius, K., 2014. Pauline Hanson returns to lead One Nation, plans to contest Queensland election. *ABC News.* Available from: www.abc.net.au/news/2014–11-19/pauline-hanson-returns-to-one-nation-helm/5902080 [Accessed 24 November 2014].

Australian Bureau of Statistics, 2012. *Cultural diversity in Australia: Reflecting a nation – Stories from the 2011 Census 2012–2013.* Government of Australia. Available from: www.abs.gov.au/ausstats [Accessed 30 November 2014].

Australian Bureau of Statistics, 2014. *Aboriginal and Torres Straight Islander prisoners.* Government of Australia. Available from: www.abs.gov.au/ausstats/abs@.nsf/Lookup/4517.0main+features62013 [Accessed 27 November 2014].

Australian Bureau of Statistics, 2015. *Population clock.* Government of Australia. Available from: www.abs.gov.au/ausstats/abs%40.nsf/94713ad445ff1425ca2568 2000192af2/1647509ef7e25faaca2568a900154b63?OpenDocument [Accessed 20 July 2015].

Australian Government Department of Foreign Affairs and Trade, 2012. *About Australia.* Available from: www.dfat.gov.au/geo/australia/ [Accessed 14 January 2015].

Australian Government Productivity Commission, 2010. *Performance benchmarking of Australian business regulation: Occupational health and safety.* Available from: www.pc.gov.au/inquiries/completed/regulation-benchmarking/ohs/report [Accessed 14 January 2015].

Barron, O., 1998. The distinction between workplace bullying and workplace violence and the ramifications for OHS. *Journal of Occupational Health and Safety Australia and New Zealand,* 14 (6), 575–80.

Beattie, L., and Griffin, B., 2014. Accounting for within-person differences in how people respond to daily incivility at work. *Journal of Occupational and Organizational Psychology,* 87 (3), 625–44.

Boddy, C. R., 2011. Corporate psychopaths, bullying and unfair supervision in the workplace. *Journal of Business Ethics,* 100 (3), 367–79.

Branch, S., Ramsay, S., and Barker, M., 2007a. Contributing factors to workplace bullying by staff – An interview study. *Journal of Management & Organization,* 13, 264–81.

Branch, S., Ramsay, S., and Barker, M., 2007b. The bullied boss: A conceptual exploration of upwards bullying. In Glendon, A.I., Thompson, B.M., and Myers, B. (eds.) *Advances in organisational psychology.* Bowen Hills: Australian Academic Press, pp. 93–112.

Bray, M., Waring, P., Cooper, R., and MacNeil, J., 2014. *Employment relations: Theory and practice.* 3rd Ed. North Ryde: McGraw-Hill.

Cashmore, A.W., Indig, D., Hampton, S.E., Heney, D.G., and Jalaludin, B., 2012. Workplace abuse among correctional health professionals in New South Wales, Australia. *Australian Health Review: A Publication of the Australian Hospital Association,* 36 (2), 184–90.

Center for Creative Leadership, 2012. *Leader effectiveness and culture: The Globe study*. Available from: http://www.ccl.org/leadership/pdf/assessments/GlobeStudy.pdf [Accessed 1 December 2014].

Central Intelligence Agency (CIA), 2014. *The World Factbook 2013–14: Australia*. Washington, DC. Available from: www.cia.gov/library/publications/the-world-factbook/geos/as.html. [Accessed 17 November 2014].

Chan-Mok, J. O., Caponecchia, C., and Winder, C., 2014. The concept of workplace bullying: implications from Australian workplace health and safety law. *Psychiatry, Psychology and Law*, 21 (3), 442–56.

DARTF – see Defence Abuse Response Task Force

Defence Abuse Response Task Force, 2014. *Report on abuse in defence*. Available from: www.defenceabusetaskforce.gov.au/reports/Pages/default.aspx [Accessed 13 December 2014].

DFAT – see Australian Government Department of Foreign Affairs and Trade

Dollard, M., Bailey, T., McLinton, S., Richards, P., McTernan, W., Taylor, A., and Bond, S., 2012. *The Australian workplace barometer: Report on Psychosocial safety climate and worker health in Australia*. Available from: www.safeworkaustralia.gov.au/sites/SWA/about/Publications/Documents/748/The-Australian-Workplace-Barometer-report.pdf [Accessed 20 December 2014].

Fair Work Building and Construction, 2013. *FWO to tackle exploitation of workers on 457 visas*. Australian Government. Available from: www.fwbc.gov.au/fwo-tackle-exploitation-workers-457-visas [Accessed 13 December 2014].

Gannon, M. J., and Pillai, R., 2013. Australia. In *Understanding global cultures: Metaphorical journeys through 31 nationals, clusters of nations, continents, and diversity*. 5th ed. Thousand Oaks: Sage, pp. 586–95.

Hall, E. T., 1966. *The hidden dimension*. New York: Double Day Anchor Books.

Hare, J., 2014. All unis make top group of research volume, quality ranking, *The Australian*, 19 November. Available from: www.theaustralian.com.au/higher-education/all-unis-make-top-group-of-research-volume-quality-ranking/story-e6frgcjx-1227127406682 [Accessed 19 November 2014].

Harrington, S., Rayner, C., and Warren, S., 2012. Too hot to handle? Trust and human resource practitioners' implementation of anti-bullying policy. *Human Resource Management Journal*, 22 (4), 392–408.

Horne, D., 1964. *The lucky country*. Melbourne: Penguin.

House of Representatives, Standing Committee on Education and Employment, 2012. *Workplace bullying: We just want it to stop*. Report of the Inquiry into Workplace Bullying. Canberra: Parliament of Australia.

HRSCEE – see House of Representatives, Standing Committee on Education and Employment.

Hutchinson, J., 2012. Rethinking workplace bullying as an employment relations problem. *Journal of Industrial Relations*, 54 (5), 637–52.

Hutchinson, M., Vickers, M. H., Jackson, D., and Wilkes, L., 2006. "They stand you in a corner; you are not to speak": Nurses tell of abusive indoctrination in work teams dominated by bullies. *Contemporary Nurse*, 21 (2), 228–38.

Kell, P., Cameron, R., Joyce, D., and Wallace, M., 2014. International developments in skills migration: A case study of the opportunities, threats and dilemmas for Australia. In Harris, R., and Short T. (eds.) *Workforce development*. Singapore: Springer, pp. 37–55.

Lake, M., 2013. Colonial Australia and the Asia-Pacific region. In Bashford, A., and Macintyre, S. (eds.) *The Cambridge history of Australia*. Milan: Cambridge University Press, pp. 535–59.

McCarthy, P., Sheehan, M., and Kearns, D., 1995. *Managerial styles and their effects on employees' wellbeing in organisations undergoing restructuring*. Brisbane: School of Organisational Behaviour and Human Resource Management, Griffith University.

McCormack, D., Djurkovic, N., and Casimir, G., 2013. Workplace bullying: The experiences of building and construction apprentices. *Asia Pacific Journal of Human Resources*, 51 (4), 406–20.

McGowan, B., 2004. Reconsidering race: The Chinese experience on the goldfields of southern New South Wales. *Australian Historical Studies*, 36 (124), 312–31.

McPhail, R., Jerrard, M., and Southcombe, A., 2015. *Employment relations: An integrated approach*. South Melbourne: Cengage.

Millar, P., and Doherty, B., 2009. Indian anger boils over, *The Age*, 1 June. Available from: www.theage.com.au/national/indian-anger-boils-over-20090531-brrm. html [Accessed 1 December 2014].

OECD – see Organization for Economic Co-operation and Development

Omari, M., 2007. *Towards dignity and respect: An exploration of the nature, causes and consequences of workplace bullying*. Saarbrücken: VDM Verlag Dr. Müller.

Omari, M., and Paull, M., 2013. "Shut up and bill": Workplace bullying challenges for the legal profession. *International Journal of the Legal Profession*, 20 (2), 141–60.

Omari, M., Paull, M., and Crews, J., 2013. Protected species: Perspectives on organisational life. Proceedings of the *European Academy of Management Conference, EURAM*, Istanbul, Turkey.

Omari, M., Paull, M., D'Cruz, P., and Guneri-Cangarli, B., 2014. Fair game: The influence of cultural norms in creating sanctioned targets in the workplace. Proceedings of the *9th International Conference on Workplace Bullying & Harassment*, Milan, Italy.

Organization for Economic Co-operation and Development, 2014. *OECD Economic Surveys Australia December 2014 Overview*. Available at: www.oecd.org/australia/ [Accessed 27 March 2015].

Paull, M., and Omari, M., 2015. Dignity and respect: Important for volunteers too! *Journal of Equity, Diversity and Inclusion an International Journal*, 34 (3), 244–55.

Paull, M., Omari, M., and Standen, P., 2012. When is a bystander not a bystander? A typology of the roles of bystanders in workplace bullying. *Asia Pacific Journal of Human Resources*, 50 (3), 351–66.

Phillips, J., and Spinks, H., 2013. *Boat arrivals in Australia since 1976*. Canberra: Department of Parliamentary Services. Available from: www.aph.gov.au/About_Parliament/Parliamentary_Departments/Parliamentary_Library/pubs/BN/2012–2013/BoatArrivals [Accessed 23 Jan 2015].

Power, J.L., *et al.*, 2013. Acceptability of workplace bullying: A comparative study on six continents. *Journal of Business Research*, 66 (3), 374–80.

Riley, D., Duncan, D.J., and Edwards, J., 2011. Staff bullying in Australian schools. *Journal of Educational Administration*, 49 (1), 7–30.

Rodwell, J., and Demir, D., 2012. Psychological consequences of bullying for hospital and aged care nurses. *International Nursing Review*, 59 (4), 539–46.

Rodwell, J., Demir, D., and Steane, P., 2013. Psychological and organizational impact of bullying over and above negative affectivity: A survey of two nursing contexts. *International Journal of Nursing Practice,* 19 (3), 241–8.

Shallcross, L., Ramsay, S., and Barker, M., 2013. Severe workplace conflict: The experience of mobbing. *Negotiation and Conflict Management Research,* 6 (3), 191–213.

Shanahan, D., 2014. Chinese "mongrels" eruption reveals Clive Palmer's true colours, *The Australian,* August. Available from: www.theaustralian.com.au/opinion/columnists/chinese-mongrels-eruption-reveals-clive-palmers-true-colours/story-e6frg75f-12270337259422 [Accessed 27 November 2014].

Sivasubramaniam, D., and Goodman-Delahunty, J., 2014. Cultural variation in Australia: Ethnicity, host community residence, and power-distance values. *Cross-Cultural Communication,* 10 (4), 130–8.

Standen, P., and Omari, M., 2009. Psychological warfare: The destructive cycle of reciprocal bullying at work. *New Zealand Journal of Human Resource Management,* 9 (1), 4–13.

Standen, P., Paull, M., and Omari, M., 2014. Managing workplace bullying: Propositions from Heider's Balance Theory. *Journal of Management & Organization,* 20 (6), 733–48.

Steers, R. M., Nardon, L., and Sanchez-Runde, C. J., 2013, *Management across cultures: Developing global competencies.* 2nd ed. Cambridge: Cambridge University Press.

The Hofstede Center, n.d. *Australia.* Available from: http://geert-hofstede.com/australia.html [Accessed 17 November 2014].

Timo, N., Fulop, L., and Ruthjersen, A., 2004. Crisis? What crisis? Management practices and internal violence and workplace bullying in aged care in Australia. *Research and Practice in Human Resource Management,* 12 (2), 57–89.

Tourism Australia, 2014. *Australia's culture 2014.* Available from: www.australia.com/about/culture-history/culture.aspx [Accessed 17 November 2014].

Trompenaars, F., and Hampden-Turner, C., 2012. *Riding the waves of culture: Understanding diversity in global business.* 3rd ed. London: Nicholas Brearley Publishing.

Ward, R., 1958. *The Australian legend.* Oxford: Oxford University Press.

Willis, P., 2012. Witnesses on the periphery: Young lesbian, gay, bisexual and queer employees witnessing homophobic exchanges in Australian workplaces. *Human Relations,* 65 (12), 1589–610.

Zábrodská, K., Linnell, S., Laws, C., and Davies, B., 2011. Bullying as intra-active process in neoliberal universities. *Qualitative Inquiry,* 17 (8), 709–19.

14 Workplace abuse, incivility and bullying

The challenge of translational research

Megan Paull and Maryam Omari

Introduction

The term 'translational research' often refers to the translation of theoretical and conceptual understandings derived from research into applied settings in order to inform practice. This is fundamental, challenging and important. In the case of cross-cultural comparisons and research with multicultural perspectives, translational research might also refer to the complexities associated with translating language and cultural understandings. These challenges are never more evident than when a sensitive topic is the focus, such as in this book. This concluding chapter will review and identify key common themes which have been examined by the contributors, and consider both future research and the challenge of translation into practice.

Determining what is or is not workplace abuse, incivility and bullying

The definitions and terminology associated with the behaviours discussed in this book include not only different understandings of abuse, incivility and bullying, but also of workplace violence, victimisation, unkindness and of the term referred to as 'forcing' (see Bozionelos this volume). Research to date has served to create discussion and debate about what constitutes abuse, incivility, and bullying and related behaviours, but as yet there is limited consensus. Key to the understanding of what is or is not misbehaviour is the context in which it occurs, as well as the frameworks used to understand, measure, proscribe, ameliorate and remediate in each setting.

The measurement of workplace abuse, incivility and bullying is complicated by the lack of consensus on definitions, and on forms of measurement (see Paull and Girardi this volume). This therefore leads to difficulties in comparing rates or prevalence as well as levels of tolerance, both in workplaces and in countries and regions. Comparative studies which outline rates, prevalence or tolerance of abuse, incivility, bullying and related behaviours are obfuscated by differences in approaches to measurement as much as by disagreement or at least lack of agreement on terminology and definitions. Comparison of research undertaken in different countries is complicated by the fact that not only do different researchers operate in different paradigms (see Samnani this volume), employ different methods and instruments (see Paull and Girardi this volume) and employ different cultural lenses (see Omari and Sharma this volume), but that there are also different understandings about the meanings and translation of words. An example of this is the term 'mobbing'. Perusal of the chapters in this book illustrates the various translations and interpretations which have evolved around this term (e.g. Pilch and Turska re: mobbing in Polish; Zábrodská and Květon re: Czech version of mobbing – this volume).

The added layer of cultural norms, in times of change, and against a backdrop of increased globalisation and multicultural understandings, further confounds the field. As can be seen from the evidence presented in this book, increasing awareness of inappropriate behaviours necessitates revision of what is considered to be appropriate. All of the chapters present a view of changing community and social understandings of appropriate behaviour. Changing levels of tolerance of certain types of workplace behaviours are associated with changing societal norms, as well as a product of awareness-raising and education campaigns derived from research in the field.

The role of history

History plays a role in the development of workplaces and workplace behaviour. It also contributes to the cultural context for those workplaces, and for the interpersonal behaviours of individuals at work. Historical influences on workplace behaviour are evident in the way different cultural groups mix with and react to one another at work and in business, and in the legal frameworks established for management and control. This is evident in the establishment or otherwise of laws which proscribe bullying, and of the level of reliance of individuals on existing laws to assist them if they are subject to such behaviours.

Many of the chapters presented in this book have offered brief historical pictures of the evolution of workplace behaviours. It is evident that even when historical similarities are identified, such as white settlement in New Zealand (see Catley, Blackwood, Forsyth and Tappin this volume) and Australia (Paull and Omari this volume), or the changes associated with the post-communist era in Eastern European countries (Poland, Czech Republic), there are local nuances which influence the collective understanding of behaviour in the workplace. It is history, too, which influences the relationships between different groups in multicultural communities.

The rule of law

Changing social understanding and new thinking about workplace conduct also has an influence when it comes to legal frameworks governing behaviour, and to the attention paid to these frameworks. Repeatedly, authors referred to issues of power, inequality and old traditions (see D'Cruz this volume) about who had what influence, and to the adherence, or otherwise, to the rule of law.

What is also clear is that the introduction of laws requires clarity about what is or is not appropriate workplace behaviour, which is difficult to achieve when agreement on terminology has not been reached. In addition, it is necessary for the workforce to be willing to lodge complaints, management to be willing to take action and for appropriate sanctions to be applied, in order for confidence in the ability of the law to achieve change to be raised. The law alone, however, is insufficient to achieve change.

Laws proscribing workplace abuse, incivility, and bullying and related behaviours vary from country to country. It is evident that the introduction of laws at the national and workplace level is a time consuming process. Such introduction both heralds changing community attitudes about what is acceptable, and seeks to promote change amongst those who have not modified their behaviour. As with any policy or law which seeks to modify behaviour, stages of awareness-raising and education need to be reinforced by actions which apply the penalties set down. The chapters in this book speak of a long way to go in changing behaviour in some quarters.

Fitting in – the role of difference

It was apparent across many of the chapters, however, that even when individuals realise that the behaviour to which they are subjected, or which they witness, is inappropriate, there is a widespread reluctance to use the systems in place to take action. The reasons for this reluctance appear to stem from cultural norms and are related to the human need to fit in. Curiously, it is also the case that many of the chapters identified that it is those who are different, or who do not fit in, who are likely to be subject to abuse, incivility or bullying. It is this human need to fit in which prevents speaking up, even in support of a friend or colleague.

Difference and the 'outsider' was a common theme throughout the chapters. The cultural profiles of countries offered by the models of cultural dimensions discussed in this book, from the work of Hofstede and others, Trompenaars and others, Hall, and Schwartz (see Omari and Sharma this volume) suggest consistency across a nation. It is clear, however, that all of the countries in this book are not as monocultural as a profile or metaphor might suggest. Often the diversity of a country is lost when a singular descriptor or dimension is described in terms of its mean value or orientation. Workplaces too are not uniform, and there are no universal truths about the workplaces in each country. Organisations are shaped by national culture, and by the industry in which they operate. Workplaces develop cultures of their own, and one element of abuse, incivility and bullying behaviour is whether individuals know or understand *new* norms, and whether they see benefit in modifying their behaviour.

Cross-cultural perspectives

The chapters in this book largely represent country specific discussions of research on workplace abuse, incivility and bullying to examine the national factors including culture, history and workplace norms which influence such behaviours. Cross-cultural perspectives mainly refer to the tensions between groups within particular countries rather than making comparisons between countries. Nevertheless there is a sense of comparison in many of the country profile chapters, particularly about the nature, type and prevalence of behaviours in relative terms, and in relation to the cross-cultural comparison tools available by way of frameworks and metaphors. It is clear that researchers identify that cultural dimensions play a role in the manifestation, understanding, tolerance and reaction to abuse, incivility and bullying in the workplace, and in society generally (see, for example, Meyer and Mikulincer this volume). It is also clear that the authors have identified a need for further cross-cultural research.

The research to come

Over the last twenty years research into workplace abuse, incivility and bullying has burgeoned. As can be seen from the contributions to this book there are many complexities associated with this research, including the challenges of cultural understandings of human behaviour. In 2002, Rayner *et al.* identified that there was considerable pressure on researchers to contribute to the development of knowledge about workplace bullying:

> At first academics were asked to provide evidence of the extent of bullying, and to help with how it should be defined. Then academics moved on to constructing the argument relating to cost. Our focus has now moved on to the assessment of interventions and the provision of models of good practice.
>
> (Rayner *et al.* 2002, p. 185)

These pressures have not abated. It might be argued that the countries represented by the chapters in this book are all at different stages, with the unfolding of understanding across various countries coming with workplace changes associated with globalisation. Loh (this volume) argues that in Singapore there has been limited research to date on workplace incivility because of cultural norms about interpersonal behaviour which have not been questioned previously. Singapore is, however, at the centre of globalisation and facing pressures associated with this. Similarly, Turkey (Guneri-Cangarli this volume) has experienced the rapid economic growth of a newly opened up economy at the gateway between Asia and Europe, and is in need of more research to explain the relatively high recorded levels of bullying. Is this rate due to the recent increase in awareness rather than a conflict based workplace culture?

Country linked studies offer an important contribution to the overall level of knowledge about workplace abuse, incivility and bullying, in particular by offering a specific focus on the contextual factors which are involved. There is a need for researchers to be cognisant of their cultural context and to seek appropriate data and consider this in analysis. Research in countries in which there has been extensive work has not always included cultural dimensions. Wholesale importation of understandings about abuse, incivility and bullying from one culture to another will not produce quality research and local adaptation will be required. In addition, in those countries where work is just beginning, the lessons learned in culturally similar countries need to be explored, tested and investigated as part of the expansion and development of research. Continued expansion of research into more workplaces in more countries should be accompanied by efforts to further refine the findings to date. Research which undertakes comparison between culturally similar and culturally diverse countries will enable identification of those elements which are derived from the human condition more generally, and those which are a product of a particular workplace or culture.

Cross-cultural comparisons are slowly beginning to emerge, although the challenges of definition and measurement (see Paull and Girardi this volume) make this difficult. Early work, using some of the more well-known instruments (e.g. Power *et al.* 2013), has begun to identify cross-cultural elements which can in turn inform country linked investigations. Rayner *et al.* (2002, p. 186) caution, however, that while research is likely to move away from large quantitative data collection to more qualitative work, "bullying at work involves multiple layers and multiple analyses, so trends and general indications are probably the most realistic outcomes to expect." It might be argued that this applies equally to the spread of cross-cultural research from country linked studies to more comparative investigations, which will require the delicate hand of sensitivity to be applied.

Sensitivity will also need to be exercised in delving further into the experiences of all the stakeholders in abuse, incivility and bullying. This is not confined to the targets/victims, alleged perpetrators and bystanders/observers/witnesses, but includes those charged with responsibility for management, counselling, training, awareness-raising and establishment of rules and procedures. Further, as the source of bullying behaviours has also been identified as including the public, clients, customers, patients and other stakeholders such as suppliers, providers and funders, it is also necessary to extend research into these spheres. Including cultural contexts in the data collection and analysis processes for this expansion of the research horizon will increase the capacity of research to contribute to the amelioration of the behaviours in workplaces.

Translation into practice

As with all workplace research, the greatest value is in the translation into practice. In all of the countries discussed in this book, the evidence is that workplace standards are changing, and levels of acceptance of abuse, incivility and bullying are reducing as research increases. One of the reasons for this is the increased understanding of the consequences of abuse, incivility and bullying for indivduals and organisations, which is derived from quality research and careful dissemination.

The development of awareness, the implementation of policies and procedures and the means of managing incidents of abuse, incivility and bullying all benefit from research informed practices. Similarly, quality research will be derived from collaborative efforts between individuals, organisations and researchers (see Paull and Girardi this volume). Rayner *et al.* (2002) called for the continuation of collaboration as the bedrock of efforts to minimise workplace bullying.

Organisations too can contribute to this effort by evidence-based policy making and by leveraging the outcomes of research for the implementation of frameworks. Further, the review of implementation processes and outcomes and the establishment of evaluative mechanisms to test or reflect on successes and failures will contribute to the capacity for increased dignity and respect at work.

Conclusion

This book has contributed to the increasing knowledge and understanding about workplaces by elaborating on methodological and cultural dimensions of abuse, incivility, and bullying and related behaviours. In all, nine country specific chapters are presented, with contextual chapters setting the scene to aid understanding, and providing a backdrop. This final chapter has highlighted some of the common themes identified by the country chapter authors, and brought together the key challenges of translational research.

References

Power, J.L. *et al.*, 2013. Acceptability of workplace bullying: A comparative study on six continents. *Journal of Business Research,* 66 (3), 374–80.

Rayner, C., Hoel, H., and Cooper, C., 2002. *Workplace bullying: What we know, who is to blame and what can we do?* London: Taylor & Francis.

Index

For Product Safety Concerns and Information please contact our EU
representative GPSR@taylorandfrancis.com
Taylor & Francis Verlag GmbH, Kaufingerstraße 24, 80331 München, Germany

www.ingramcontent.com/pod-product-compliance
Ingram Content Group UK Ltd.
Pitfield, Milton Keynes, MK11 3LW, UK
UKHW020958180425
457613UK00019B/740